ECONOMICS OF HYDROPOWER

ECONOMICS OF HYDROPOWER

Bharat Jhunjhunwala

PUBLICATIONS

KALPAZ PUBLICATIONS
DELHI-110052

Economics of Hydropower

Rs. 750

ISBN: 978-81-7835-740-2

Published in 2009 in India by
Kalpaz Publications
C-30, Satyawati Nagar,
Delhi-110052
E-mail: kalpaz@hotmail.com
Phone : 9212729499

Lasertype Setting by: Quick Media, Delhi
Printed at : G. Print Process, Delhi

CONTENTS

Preface 7

Acknowledgements 9

Abbreviations 11

1. The Larger Picture 13
2. Do we Need so Much Power ? 39
3. Benefits of Hydropower : Case Study of Kotlibhel 1B 69
4. Costs of Hydropower : Case Study of Kotlibhel 1B 75
5. Economic Assessment of Hydropower : Case Study of Kotlibhel 1B 183
6. Reply to Hydropower Experts 187
7. Main Conclusions 207

Annexure 1 : Survey of Hydropower Dams at Chilla, Maneri and Tehri 209

Annexure 2 : Survey of Pilgrims at Dev Prayag, Rishikesh and Haridwar 255

Annexure 3 : Survey of Pilgrims at Temple of Dhari Devi 265

Annexure 4 : Survey of Temples of Tehri 273

Notes 278

References 283

Index 297

PREFACE

I was a supporter of big dams like Tehri and Narmada. I shared the nation's dream of Bhakra being the 'Modern Temple of India'. I believed that dams were beneficial for the people of the country hence loss to local people could not be a reason for holding them back. Local people should, of course, be adequately compensated. The amount of compensation is to be determined politically through the democratic process, howsoever disorderly that might be.

In 2007 January, public hearing was to be held for the Kotlibhel 1B hydropower project on River Alaknanda where I live. Himanshu Thakkar of *Dams, Rivers and People* put me in contact with Gandhian activist Vimal Bhai who, in turn, drew my attention to the various adverse effects of dams. As I pored over the Environment Impact Assessment of Kotlibhel 1B, it became clear to me that the benefits projected were unsubstantiated, even imaginary, while many costs were ignored. A proper assessment of benefits and costs led me to the conclusion that this project was harmful for the economy of the country. It was being implemented by the bureaucracies of Ministry of Power (MOP) and National Hydroelectric Power Corporation (NHPC) to further their petty gains while imposing huge costs on the country. Speedily, I was converted from a supporter to opponent of dams. This book is the result of this learning. I wish to place before the nation the true costs and benefits of hydropower so that we do not make the mistakes done by our ancestors of Indus valley Civilization which led to their obliteration.

Experts claim that Run-of-river hydropower projects do not disturb the flow of the river nor contribute to deterioration of quality of the waters. On this basis, large number of believing Hindus support making of ROR dams on the sacred Ganga River. This claim is pure rubbish. The quality of water deteriorates in ROR projects because:

- Deprivation of chemicals and oxygen during flow through canals, tunnels and reservoirs.
- Destruction of cellular memory gathered during flow in front of Badrinath Temple.
- Fermentation of organic matter in reservoirs leading to methane emissions.
- Trapping of sediments in the reservoirs makes the waters 'hungry' leading to erosion of our coasts.

Pilgrims surveyed at Dev Prayag, Rishikesh and Haridwar tell of the reduction in the spiritual powers of Ganga waters due to dams. I have estimated the loss to people of the country from deprivation of free flowing waters is about Rs 5,000 to Rs 8,000 crores per year—far in excess of the gains from hydropower. Thus, I plead with believers to oppose hydropower projects that fuel the senses and deprive the heart.

Bharat Jhunjhunwala

Lakshmoli
PO-Maletha, Kirti Nagar
Uttarakhand 249161
Phone : 94111-09777

ACKNOWLEDGEMENTS

This book is really a collective enterprise of wise scholars of different ideologies who are all committed to the welfare and growth of India.

Shri D K Agarwal pointed out that opposition to hydropower projects plays into the hands of Multinational Corporations. His comments encouraged me to look deeper into the political economy of hydropower as given in the first chapter.

Dr G D Agarwal pointed out the spiritual value of waters of the Ganga and encouraged me to dwell deeper in this aspect.

Shri Vimal Bhai and Himanshu Thakkar provided much information and were always available for consultation.

Shri A B Giri provided a counterpoint with responses from two hydropower experts. These comments forced me to study methane emissions in detail.

Shri Puran Singh Kathait gave moral support by repeatedly asserting that Tehri Dam would not have been built if such a study had been done.

Shri Shankar Sharma suggested I study the Power Survey published by CEA. This helped me grasp the false projections of demand that are the backbone of hydropower generation.

Shri P S Sharda, Advocate gave the initial framework in which to make the study.

Officers of NHPC provided much information under RTI Act, which, though less than expected, has been helpful in formulating my assessment.

A large number of friends and well-wishers have given comments on earlier version of this report. Many do not agree with my conclusions. Deep thanks are due to all of them nevertheless. They include Sarvasri Anand Swaroop Arya, P C Bhatnagar, U K Choudhary, Sripad Dharmadhikari, V P Dimri, B N Gildiyal, Sunit Girnari, Ramaswamy Iyer, L N Jhunjhunwala, Acharya Jitendra, Shailendra Kotiyal, Ashwani Kumar, Pradeep Kumar, Asghar Nawab, Som Pal, Chitroopa Palit, Girdhar Pandit, Pranav Pandya, Priya Patel, D S Rawat, Dunu Roy, Ramesh C Sharma, Shekhar Singh, Nityanand Swami, Swami Swayambodhanand, Rajesh Thadani, Himanshu Upadhyaya, Vishaish Uppal, Tarun Vijay and Vinod Vyasulu. This book would not be possible without their critical comments, questions and encouragement.

Naresh Chandra Puri honestly and dutifully did the four surveys. He has struggled through bad weather and a shoestring budget to do excellent work.

Last, I wish to thank my life partner Madhu for quietly forbearing with my preoccupation with this study.

ABBREVIATIONS

AT&C	Aggregate Technical & Commercial (Losses)
BOD	Biological Oxygen Demand
CAGR	Compound Annual Growth Rate
CAMPA	Compensatory Afforestation Management and Planning Authority
CAT	Catchment Area Treatment
CEA	Central Electricity Authority
CMD	Chairman and Managing Director
CO2	Carbon dioxide
COD	Chemical Oxygen Demand
CPCB	Central Pollution Control Board
CPDAC	Coastal Protection And Development Advisory Committee
CWC	Central Water Commission
DO	Dissolved Oxygen
DPR	Detailed Project Report
DPR-ES	Detailed Project Report—Executive Summary
DSM	Demand Side Management
EIA	Environment Impact Assessment
EMCP	Extended Malaria Control Programme
EMP	Environment Management Plan
FAO	Food and Agriculture Organization
FCA	Forest Conservation Act
GDP	Gross Domestic Product
GEF	Global Environment Facility
GHG	Green House Gases
GOI	Government of India
HEP	Hydroelectric Project

ICMR	Indian Council of Medical Research
IITR	Indian Institute of Technology, Roorkee
MkWH	Millian Kilowatt Hours
MOEF	Minister of Environment and Forests
MOP	Minister of Power
MOWR	Ministory of Water Resources
MPN	Maximum Probable Number
Mtoe	Million tons of oil equivalent
MU	Million Units
MW	Mega Watt
NBA	Narmda Bachao Andolan
NBSAP	National Biodiversity Strategy and Action Plan
NCCP	National Coastal Protection Project
NHPC	National Hydro Power Corporation
NPC	National Productivity Council
NPV	Net Present Value
PEUM	Partial End Use Method
PLF	Plant Load Factor
RIS	Reservoir Induced Seismicity
ROR	Run-of-river
RTI	Right to Information (Act)
SEB	State Electricity Board
TERI	Tata Energy Research Institute
THDC	Tehri Hydrolectric Development Corporation
TVA	Tennessee Valley Authority
UKPCB	Uttarakhand Pollution Control Board
UNCED	UN Conference on Environment and Development
UNDP	United Nations Development Program
UNEP	United Nations Environment Programme
WHO	World Health Organization
WWF	World Wildlife Fund

1

THE LARGER PICTURE

Run of River Dams

Government of Uttarakhand is building a cascade of dams on Alaknanda River. Out of a flow of 270 km from Badrinath to Kaudiyala, construction of hydropower projects are already planned on a distance of 190 km as given in Table below. The remaining flow is also to be tapped as soon as possible. These dams are 'Run-of-River' type. They do not store water in one season for use in another season.

A similar cascade Run-of-River (ROR) of dams is being made on Bhagirathi River which, additionally is straddled with the Tehri Dam, which is of storage type.

The Government believes that these dams will not obstruct the continuous flow of water of Alaknanda River. There will be no adverse effect of the dams on the quality of water. We need electricity for the economic growth of the country. These ROR dams are in the larger interests of the country since they provide electricity without causing damage to the river and environment. The limited adverse impacts on local people can be mitigated by providing them with adequate compensation. In this way, it is claimed, ROR dams are beneficial for all the stakeholders.

It is undisputed that the country needs electric power for economic growth and for uplifting the standard of living of our people. Children can study better with assured supply of electricity. Such consumption of electricity is empowering. This author supports increase in production and consumption of power. However, this should be done in a way

Table 1.1. Dams proposed on River Alaknanda

Name of Dam	*Type of Dam*	*Capacity in MW*	*Length of reservoir in km*	*Length of Tunnel or Canal in km*	*Length of River Affected due to tunnel diversion*	*Total Length of River Affected in km*
Badri Nath	Not Known	260	1*	10*	13*	14
Vishnu-Prayag	Run of River	400	1	11	14*	15
Vishnugad-Pipalkoti	Run of River	444	1	13	18*	19
Bowala Nandprayag	Run of River	132	1*	10*	13*	14
Karna Prayag	Run of River	Not known	1*	15*	18*	19
Utyasu	Not known	Not known	1*	15*	18*	19
Srinagar	Run of River	330	25	5	6	31
Kotlibhel 1B	Reservoir	320	27	0	1	28
Kotlibhel 2	Reservoir	520	30	0	1	31
Total	-	-	88	-	102	190

*Author's estimates.

that the final impact on the people is positive. It should not happen that the long term economic growth is hit due to ecological destruction and people are adversely affected due to loss of spiritual benefits while benefits from generation of power are captured by materialist people.

Hydropower can be generated during peak demand hours in mornings and evenings when requirement of electricity is more. This is called peak load. State Governments are reported to be buying power at Rs 5 to Rs 6 per unit during peak hours to meet the requirement. They are suffering huge losses in such purchases. The cascade of dams will help reduce this burden because dam companies shall provide 12 percent free power to the host state.

Indeed, peak power problem must be solved. Children should get electricity for study in the evenings. But hydropower is not the only solution. Other solutions are available for meeting this requirement. One win-win solution is to enhance the price of power during peak hours along with a parallel reduction in non-peak hours. This will reduce the demand for peak load power and reduce burden on the SEBs as well as consumers. The latter would use less peak power and more non-peak power. Such a power pricing policy is in operation in cities like London. This can be implemented in India. Consumers will operate geysers, air-conditioners and washing machines during non-peak hours. That would remove the need of building a cascade of ROR dams on our rivers for generating peak power.

The author concedes that local people can be forced to make a sacrifice in larger interests of the country. However, facts discovered by the author indicate that these dams are not in national interest. Rather they are harmful for the nation. These dams are mainly beneficial for the dam companies, who make profits, and employees of the host State Governments, who get larger salaries and other benefits. They are supported in this misadventure by the bureaucracies of Government of India—Ministries of Power and Environment and Forests in particular. These bureaucracies are imposing harmful projects upon the country for serving their petty interests. They are destroying the ecology, economy and culture of India, Uttarakhand, dam-affected people, Mother Ganga and centres of pilgrimage in order to serve their selfish ends.

The author has given his estimates of the true costs of one ROR dam—Kotlibhel 1B—in this book. Dam companies and bureaucracies will dismiss these figures saying these are without basis and inflated. This argument would be sustained if these impacts had been studied and alternate estimates of the alleged costs presented. Alas! That is not the case. The costs enumerated in this book are wholly ignored in the environmental- and economic clearances given to the projects.

The hydropower bureaucracies claim that local people are in favour of making these dams. In order to confirm this fact the author got the following surveys done:

- Survey of people living around dams built earlier at Chilla, Maneri Bhali and Tehri. These people confirm negative impacts mentioned in this book.
- Survey of pilgrims at Dev Prayag, Rishikesh and Haridwar confirms that the dams are leading to deterioration of quality and spiritual power of water of our sacred rivers.
- Survey of pilgrims at to-be-submerged temple of Dhari Devi confirms that rebuilding the same on pillars will lead to deterioration of spiritual power of Mother Dhari.
- Survey of temples in Tehri indicates that the rehabilitation leads to loss of soul of affected people.

Detailed finding of these surveys are given in Annexure. These surveys give teeth to the findings regarding costs of hydropower.

Dams are mainly of four types:

- Large reservoir based storage dams like Tehri.
- Barrage- and canal based ROR dams like Chilla.
- Barrage- and tunnel based ROR dams like Maneri Bhali.
- Small reservoir based ROR dams like Kotlibhel 1B proposed at Dev Prayag.

The benefits and costs of each of these dams are different. The author has estimated the costs and benefits of one hydropower project. Readers can redo the calculations for other projects.

NHPC has proposed to make three dams in three directions of Dev Prayag that are known as Kotlibhel projects. These are small reservoir-based ROR dams. A 25-30 km long reservoir will be made in each of these three dams. The length of these reservoirs will be similar to those at Tehri though the volume of stored water will be less. The three dams are the following:

- Kotlibhel 1A: At Muneth upstream of Dev Prayag on Bhagirathi.
- Kotlibhel 1B: At Dev Prayag upstream of Dev Prayag on Alaknanda.
- Kotlibhel 2: At Kaudiyala downstream of Dev Prayag on Ganga.[1]

Water will not be stored for long period in these reservoirs. Water inflowing in a day will be released the same day. Water will however be retained in the reservoir for few hours to generate power during peak hours. This will disturb the flow of water at the Confluence at Dev Prayag.

Requirement of Electricity for Economic Growth

We need cheap energy to remain competitive in the global markets. We cannot forget that British were able to enslave India because cloth was produced cheap in textile mills of Manchester in comparison to the weavers of

Champaran. We must not make that mistake again. However, the nature of present economy is qualitatively different from the past. Now most income is generated in the service sector where requirement of electrical energy is less. This becomes clear by comparing the services- and manufacturing sectors.

Table 1.2. Sectoral contribution to growth

Sl. No.	*Item*	*Manufacturing*	*Services*
1.	Share in consumption of electricity (Newswire 2006)	35.6%	8.1%
2.	Share in national income—GDP (MOF 2006)	24.1%	54.1%
3.	Consumption of electrical energy in one percent share of GDP	1.48%	0.15%

An increase of 1.48 percent in requirement of electrical energy is necessary with an increase of one percent in income from manufacturing. The increase is only 0.15 percent if the same one percent growth comes from services sector.[2]

The same situation prevails with respect to employment.

Table 1.3. GDP and employment by sectors

Sl. No.	*Item*	*Manufacturing*	*Services*
1.	Share in GDP, 1981	21.6%	36.6%
2.	Share in GDP, 2006	24.1%	54.1%
3.	Change of share in GDP	(+) 2.5%	(+) 17.5%
4.	Employment in organized sectors, 1981	47.9 lac	17.6 lac
5.	Employment in organized sectors, 2004	46.5 lac	26.8 lac
6.	Change in employment	(–) 1.4 lac	(+) 9.2 lac

Source: MOF 2006, Table 1.3 and 3.2

These figures tell us that the source of economic growth and employment in the last 20 years is the services sector.

The requirement of electrical energy in this sector is small at 0.15% per one percent of GDP as shown in the earlier table. Thus, the contribution of electrical energy to growth of income and employment is small. The destruction of environment and livelihood of ordinary people for production of electrical energy is not necessary for economic growth as made out to be.

A study titled "Electricity consumption and economic growth in India" by Sajal Ghosh of Indira Gandhi Institute of Development Research, Mumbai found absence of long-run relationship between economic growth and electricity consumption. The study concluded that there exists a unidirectional "causality running from economic growth to electricity consumption without any feedback effect." Implication is that economic growth leads to higher consumption of electricity but higher consumption of electricity doe *not* lead to economic growth. The study concludes, "Electricity conservation policies can be initiated without deteriorating economic side effects" (Ghosh 2007).

Another study, titled "Electricity Prices in India" by Pierre Audinet of International Energy Agency, Washington concludes: There has been a "sharp decrease of the ratio of electricity consumption growth to GDP growth in the 1990s. In other words, in the past decade, electricity consumption growth did not follow economic growth" (Audinet 2002).

This same phenomenon has been observed for China (Zhou, undated). In a study of four Southeast Asian countries, it was found that "a bi-directional causality (exists) between electricity consumption and economic growth in Malaysia and Singapore... However, unidirectional causality runs from economic growth to electricity consumption in Indonesia and Thailand without any feedback effect. Thus, electricity conservation policies can be initiated without deteriorating economic side effects in the two countries" (Yoo 2005). India's situation is similar to that of Indonesia and Thailand as noted above.

This decoupling of electricity consumption and economic growth is not limited to developing countries. It is also happening in developed countries. A study of the United States says, "Recent data from the U.S. Energy Information Administration show that electricity costs and the overall economy are not as closely linked as they once were. The energy consumption used to create the Gross Domestic Product in the U.S. has been nearly halved since 1970. Nor do statistics for U.S. states show a correlation between electricity prices on the one side and growth in State Gross Product or changes in unemployment rate on the other" (Watcher 2007).

The conclusion of these studies is that we need more electrical energy for 'consumption' and not for 'economic growth'. This is confirmed by the 17th Electric Power Survey made by Central Electricity Authority. The actual and projected consumption of electrical energy is given as follows.

Table 1.4. Sectoral composition of consumption of power

Sl. No.	*Consumption Category*	*Share— Actual 2003-04*	*Share Forecast 2011-12*	*Change in Share*
1.	Domestic	24.8%	29.2%	(+) 4.4%
2.	Services Sector (Commercial)	8.2%	8.7%	(+) 0.5%
3.	Agriculture (Irrigation)	24.0%	20.2%	(-) 3.8%
4.	Manufacturing (Industry)	35.2%	34.5%	(-) 0.7%
5.	Others	7.8%	7.4%	(-) 0.4%
	Total	100%	100%	0

Source: CEA (2007:1803).

It is clear that main increase in use of energy is coming from the domestic sector.[3] This relates to consumption. To repeat, increase in consumption is desirable. This is low priority, however. It might be defensible to destroy our environment and livelihood of the poor if that was necessary for economic growth because benefits of growth later percolate to the poor. The same environment must not be destroyed for increase in 'consumption' because it does not percolate to the poor in the same way.

Should we follow China or United States?

Supporters of hydropower invoke the spectre of global economic war. China, European Union, Russia and United States are vying with each other to produce and supply cheap goods. Argument is that India should use hydropower in order to produce cheap goods and face this competition.

We have different experiences before us on this question. China has made the huge Three Gorges Dam, which is larger than Tehri. On the other hand, the United States has decommissioned many dams and restored free flow of many rivers. We have to examine which experience is relevant for us.

China's history is replete with major changes in policies. The Communist Government had merged agricultural land into about 25,000 communes in the fifties. In many cases, even small private plots were abolished. At that time, this was heralded as a great advance. In his book *Chinese Road to Socialism*, pro-Communist author Wheelwright says, "There were solid achievements in irrigation works by the communes and more than 16.5 million mou of land were brought into irrigation. A 30-percent increase (in agricultural production) was probably achieved" (Wheelwright 1970).

Twenty years later, in late seventies, this policy was reversed and private plots were reintroduced. Strangely, a similar increase of production was again claimed! A 1994 report in *Newsweek* says, under Deng Xiaoping "breaking up of Mao's system of collective farms boosted peasant incomes by almost 12 percent a year from 1979 to 1984, lifting most farmers from near-subsistence level" (Wehrfritz 1994). The point is that the policy of collectivization of land was twice reversed and success was claimed in both cases.

In mid-fifties China had embarked upon an ambitious programme of small-scale industrialization. The most exciting feature was Mao's call to make iron in every backyard. Wheelwright tells us about "a small blast of 3.5 cubic metres, capable of producing 180 tons of steel per year and employing eighteen people in three shifts. This cost only 200 yuan and was constructed by twelve people over nine days." Similar small factories were put up to produce acid, soda, fertilizers, pesticides and coalmines.

This small industry movement could not sustain, however. Peasants found themselves overloaded with work. The quality of output of these small industries was poor and cost was high. In early sixties, it was replaced with the New Economic Policy of establishing large state enterprises. These state enterprises are now being closed down and hopes placed on foreign investment. The policy was thrice reversed.

In mid-sixties Mao unleashed the famous Cultural Revolution. University Professors were labelled as bourgeois and sent to do manual work and to learn from the people. In the eighties the same professors were reinstated with the country having lost valuable teaching for more than two decades.

China appears to have a history of strong quick actions followed by equally severe reversals. Thus, we should not be carried away by China's making of the Three Gorges Dam. China may reverse this policy as the ill-effects of this adventure become visible.

The American culture, in comparison, is more open and transparent. Public discussions take place about the benefits and costs of dams. It has been assessed that benefits from generation of electricity were less than the costs to environment, fisheries, tourism, etc. They have decommissioned many dams like Harry Purcel Dam of New Jersey and Bear Rock Dam of Pennsylvania.

We have opposite examples before us. China is making large dams while the United States is decommissioning them. We should not blindly follow either. Instead, we should make our own independent assessment of benefits and costs of dams in our circumstances. Therefore, making of Three Gorges Dam by China cannot be invoked in support of hydropower dams in India.

We also face competition from Russia and Arab countries. Argument is that we must use our river-power to face the oil-power of these countries. This argument is based on the premise that competition must be faced head-on with same weapons as the opponent. That is rarely the case. Alexander faced Porus' elephant power with horsepower. Mao Zedong faced conventional weapons of the Kuomintang with guerrilla tactics. The Viet Cong faced the American airpower with hand weapons. They did not make air power or engage in carpet-bombing as was done by America. Similarly, it is not necessary for us to rely on cheap energy to face the competition from these countries. We should use weapons in which we have special advantage.

We must focus on better use of our limited sources of energy instead of trying to consume ever-increasing quantities of the same. Less water in the tap means that first we must use it for worship and drinking; and then for bath and garden. Likewise, we must establish priority between different uses of electrical energy. Education and services sector should have the first claim; followed by manufacturing and last by domestic consumption. We sell the same food grains to APL- and BPL households at different prices. Similarly, we can price electrical energy differently for these users.

We will not be able to face competition from China, Russia and Arab countries by developing our hydropower because it will entail other economic costs in the long run and pull us down.

Primitive Accumulation

England and United States destroyed their environment in the past is order to advance economically. Argument is that they have become economically advanced and it is now possible for them to decommission dams. They would not be able to decommission dams today had they not destroyed their environment earlier. Cities like Chicago were intensely polluted thirty years ago. The air is clean today. First they developed the automobile and went for economic growth even though it entailed polluting the environment. Then, riding on economic growth, they developed green technologies and cleaned up the environment. Today Chicago has both cars and clean air. Had they refrained from initially polluting the air; and not produced 'dirty' automobiles; they would not have green cars running on the streets today. It is said that similarly we must accept loss of environment for some time. The environment can be revived later after we have attained economic growth.

This argument fails to notice that the damage inflicted by the developed countries on their own environment was small in comparison to that inflicted on the environment of colonies and developing countries. Developed countries are sending their used ships for breaking to Alang in Gujarat. These ships contain asbestos, lead and other poisonous materials. Similarly, the consumption of wood, copper, iron and other metals by the developed countries is made possible by denuding the forests of the developing countries like India and Zimbabwe. Thus, the revival of environment in developed countries is only partial. They have not revived the environment of other affected countries. They have only compensated for damage within their borders while that in other countries remains. We will have to similarly transfer environmental degradation to some other country if we emulate this strategy. This is contra India's heritage. Our mantra is 'Vasudev Kutumbakam'—the whole world is one family. Exploitative and tyrannical states do not survive for long as has happened with Ancient Greece and Rome, Britain and is happening to United States presently.

Yet short-term damage to livelihood and environment may be necessary in special circumstances. Family members do not demand new dresses when a new pair of bullocks is to be bought. However, this is acceptable only when the loss is strictly in the short term and transparently leads to economic gains in near future. Three precautions are needed in accepting even such short term loss of environment.

- Temporary damage to environment and reduction in incomes of the poor is acceptable for long term growth. Hydropower imposes long term costs on the economy hence cannot be adopted on ground of ignoring temporary impacts.
- In present circumstances there is no need to destroy the livelihoods of the poor and our environment for securing an increase in investment. The country has foreign exchange reserves of $300 billion. Other sources like improving the quality of government expenditures must be tapped first.
- We must be very careful in imposing costs upon the poor for attaining economic growth. One partakes poisonous mercury very carefully for curing a disease. Our ancestors failed to exercise such care with the result that the Indus Valley Civilization and Mauryan Empire collapsed. Our poor people supported foreign invaders and led to India's enslavement.

For these reasons, we should not blindly follow the policy adopted by the developed countries. Instead, we should learn not to repeat the mistakes done by them.

Free Trade

Perception is that hydropower is cheaper than other sources. Whether it is indeed so is a matter of separate study. For the moment, let us assume that hydropower is cheaper. It follows that it will be disastrous to deprive our industries of this cheap power. Say, China is destroying her environment in order to produce cheap electricity and thus cheap goods. In such situation, if we place true price on our environment and keep the price of power higher than that charged by China, then our environment will be saved but our industries will be killed. Argument is that we must acquiesce to destruction of our environment in order to survive in the short run. We can regenerate our environment later if we survive today. Our environment will decay anyways if our economy does not survive.

The argument is correct but a better alternative is available. The root of the problem lies in free trade. We can face competition from cheap imported goods in two ways:

- Supply cheap power to our industries and lower the domestic cost of production.
- Impose high import duties and increase the price of imported goods in the domestic economy. Appropriate subsidies can be provided to export-oriented industries out of revenues obtained from such import duties.

Our submission is that we must follow the latter alternative. We must give up free trade instead of embracing cheap power.

Protection of livelihoods of our poor and of our environment can be done by adopting protectionism against countries that pay low wages and destroy their environment. We are unnecessarily adopting free trade and then destroying our environment to face the consequences of this wrong decision.

Modernization

Making of hydropower dams brings new economic activities and culture into the hilly hinterlands. Roads are made, heavy earthmoving machineries are introduced and skilled managers and engineers are brought in. Argument is that we should not glorify the old culture of the hills and liberate the people by exposing them to these new currents.

We agree with the basic proposition that people of the hills should interact with other peoples. However, this should not become the camouflage for introducing the bad cultures of the plains just as the child is not taught to steal in order to interact with bad boys. Other ways of enhancing exchange with wider peoples should be adopted such as tourism, pilgrimage and trade in herbs and flowers. The hills are suited for development of services sectors such as health, education and religious rituals (karma kanda). Our priests can obtain orders for japa and havana and undertake them along the banks of the Ganga. It is possible to export these services living in the beautiful and peaceful environs of the hills. Hospitals can be established and health tourism can be developed. Patients will be cured speedily with grace of the Ganga River. Our suggestion is that new influences should be brought in a constructive way. We do not import pornography from United States. Similarly, we need not import destructive machinery in the hills.

Thermal and Nuclear Power

The main sources of electrical energy in the country are thermal, nuclear and hydro. Renewable energy is expensive and has a very small share. Oil is expensive.

Thermal power has the problem of displacement in mining; and large CO2 emissions. Nuclear power makes us dependent on imports of uranium and our sovereignty is compromised. Argument is that if hydropower is rejected on environmental grounds then the country will be left with no viable source of power.

Truly, a comprehensive assessment of various sources should be made. We should dispassionately adopt the cleanest of the available sources of energy. The Planning Commission has made a comparative assessment of costs of various sources of energy in its Integrated Energy Policy Report (Planning Commission 2006). It has concluded that hydropower is the cleanest source of energy (Line 2a in table below). The author submits that the Commission has ignored many costs associated with hydro. These have been internalized by the author at Line 2b.

Table 1.5. Supply Side, Local and Regional Environmental Impacts (After Table 13.2 of Planning Commission 2006)

Sl. No.	Impact/Option	As per Planning Commission (Except Row 2b)							Additional Points by Author	
		SO_2 NOx TSPs	*Solid Waste*	*Liquid effluent*	*Thermal impact on receiving waters*	*Flora, Fauna impacts*	*Forest loss*	*Involuntary Resettlement*	*Sediment, Earthquakes, landslides, health and accidents, aesthetic value of river*	*Total Impact Nos Y = Yes*
1.	Thermal Power (including Mining)	Y	Y	Y	Y	Y	Y	Y	N	7
2a.	Hydro-power (Planning Commission's estimates)	N	N	N	N	Y	Y	Y	N	3
2b.	Hydro-power (Author's estimates)	Y	Y	Y	Y	Y	Y	Y	Y	8
3.	Nuclear Power (including Mining)	N	Y	Y	Y	Y	Y	Y	N	6
4.	Petroleum (including Mining)	Y	N	Y	Y	Y	Y	Y	N	6
5.	Transmission and pipelines	N	N	N	N	Y	Y	Y	N	3

The author submits that Planning Commission has wrongly portrayed hydropower as clean—giving it the minimum negative score of 3 (Line 2a); while actually it has the maximum negative score of 8 when assessed in the light of findings given in this book (Line 2b). Accordingly hydro becomes the 'worst' form of energy instead of being 'best'.

Development and Change in Nature

Argument is that it is a solemn responsibility imposed upon man to intervene and bring about change in nature. Lord Krishna and Arjuna burnt the Khandava forest and made that land suitable for inhabitation my man. King Bhagirath brought the Ganga down from the Himalayas to quench the thirst of pitars. Similarly, man must make dams on the rivers and quench the thirst for water and electricity.

The author agrees that there is no case for retaining the river in her present pristine form. However, the change should be beneficial. The river must be changed so that the whole nature is happy. Many hapless animals and trees died in the burning of the Khandava Forest. However, this was followed by development of agriculture, irrigation, pastures and grazing on those lands. The level of consciousness in the wild Khandava Forest was, in the reckoning of those great men, lower that that which prevailed in the rural economy that followed. Such burning of forests is acceptable.

Our submission is that hydropower brings tears of anguish to nature instead of tears of happiness. Our coasts are deprived of sediments, water ferments in the reservoirs and mosquitoes breed on its rim. We must not develop hydropower because Mother Nature is made unhappy. This is not like the burning of the Khandava Forest.

Spiritual Powers of the Ganga

Leaders of the country believe that conversion of Ganga into a series of tunnels, canals and reservoirs will not lead to deterioration of her spiritual powers. One leader asked this writer whether Ganga had any spiritual power at all.

"If Ganga had power," he asked, "then why did she allow the country to be enslaved by the British? Why did the Ganga not protect herself? This proves that she is bereft of spiritual powers."

Indeed, it must be examined why we were enslaved. It appears that India's downfall was not due to absence of spiritual power but it was due to imbalance between spiritual and material powers.

The Isavasya Upanishad says, "Those who are only engrossed in the material world fall into deep darkness; and those who are only engrossed in the spiritual world fall into deeper darkness" (Isavasya 9). It seems our ancestors made the latter mistake. They were so engrossed in spiritual pursuits that they did not give attention to the material aspects. They were not able to maintain balance between material and spiritual.

Today we are making the reverse imbalance. Our ancestors ignored the material world and fell into darkness. We are ignoring the spiritual world and equally falling into darkness. The Indus Valley Civilization collapsed for this reason. These ancestors failed to give adequate attention to the spirit aspect. 'Spiritual' and ecology are synonymous. Love for other beings is spiritual. Love for other beings is ecology.

Our ancestors have given the following formula: 'Dharma-Artha-Kama-Moksha'. The material pleasures, Kama, should be partaken in a way that economy, Artha, is not hit. Money, Artha, should be earned in a way that the social good, Dharma, is not hit. Social activities, Dharma, should be pursued in a way that spiritual gain, Moksha, is not hit. In this way a progression is made between material-economic-social-spiritual pursuits. Problem is that we have turned this order on its head. Highest priority is given today to Kama—power is required to run air-conditioners in shopping malls in Delhi and Dehra Dun. Medium priority is given to Artha—we need power for economic growth.

Lowest priority is given to Dharma—incomes of the poor and Moksha—pursuit of spirituality. It is assumed that a person is happy if he is roaming in a shopping mall. His inner self is totally ignored in policymaking.

History tells that this model meets with failure. The decline of Ravana's Lanka, Kaurava's Indraprastha, Ancient Greece, Imperial Rome and Princely States of Rajasthan are proof that loss of inner self leads to decline of a civilization. This has been described by historian Arnold J Toynbee in *A Study of History*. He says that a civilization grows as long as the leaders pay attention to the welfare of the common man and obtain support of masses by their policies. Such leaders he calls 'Creative Minority'. On the other hand, civilizations decline when the leaders impose policies on unwilling masses. Such leaders he calls 'Dominant Minority'.

Toynbee says the breakdowns of civilizations takes place because the rulers instead of creatively leading the masses, try to dominate them. This leads to loss of social unity. The society gets split into dominant minority and proletariat. The proletariat, or the aam aadmi, does not feel part of the society. This leads to breakdown of the civilization (Toynbee 1939:1.660-66).

The lesson is that civilizations have collapsed when the people and Mother Nature have been bled. The decline of the Great British Empire and deepening crisis of the American economy in the present times tells us that the model of impoverishing the common man for providing air-conditioned shopping malls to the rich will not sustain. These material pleasures must be expanded in a way that powers of the Ganga, Dev Prayag and Mother Dhari grows along with.

It is more likely that Mother Ganga, Dev Prayag Confluence and Mother Dhari Devi are contributing to the economic welfare as well. The success of the country in IT sector comes, in part, from the Ganga. Survey of pilgrims tells us they are reaping immense benefits from bath in the Ganga.

In conclusion, the enslavement of the country by the British was not due to lack of powers of the Ganga. It was more because our leaders failed to give proper direction to her powers. Just as not using the gun lying in the house against the thief does not mean that the gun is of no use; so also for the spiritual powers of the Ganga.

Relief and Rehabilitation

Hydropower projects provide special benefits to those people whose land is submerged in the reservoir or acquired otherwise. Usually the price paid for this land is much higher than the prevailing market price—sometimes more than ten or twenty times. Such landowners gain immensely from the hydroelectric projects (HEPs). However, the number of such landowners is less compared to the large numbers whose land is not acquired, who do not gain financially and are harmed in various ways such as by spread of malaria.

A section of the society should not push the whole into misery for its limited gains. We know that many Indians cooperated with the British rulers to make personal gains. The sepoys who fired bullets on Freedom Fighters were mostly Indians. However, we do not honour these. Instead, we honour Shivaji and Laxmi Bai and Jhalkari Devi who sacrificed their lives for independence of the nation. Many soldiers of the army sell vital information to enemies to further their personal interests. Such pursuit of self-interest is rewarded with death.

National Leaders like Gandhi taught the people to fight the British. Similarly we must teach the landowners to oppose hydropower projects in larger interests of the local people and the country. It is despicable on the part of Government of India to get local people to support hydropower by co-opting them by paying huge compensations. The King, in this case, is teaching adharma to the local people.

Moreover, compensation does not appear to lead to improvement in the life of the displaced persons. Proof of this is available from survey of three dams of Uttarakhand—Chilla, Maneri Bhali and Tehri.

Table 1.6. The life of displaced people has improved or declined upon receiving compensation for land? (Details at Annexure 1)

Sl. No.	*Dam*	*Improved*	*Deteriorated*	*No Change*
1.	Chilla, n=2	1	1	—
2.	Maneri, n=5	2	1	2
3	Tehri, n=12	—	9	3
4.	Combined	3	11	5

This table tells that compensation has not led to improvement in standard of life of those getting compensation. A similar result is obtained from survey of displaced persons living along the villages on the rim of Tehri Reservoir.

Table 1.7. What is the impact of acquisition of land on standard of living? (Details at Annexure 4)

Sl. No.	*Location*	*Improved*	*Reduced*	*No Change*
1.	Tehri, n=11	—	6	5

Both these surveys indicate that those receiving compensation do not ultimately benefit just as Indians who supported British rulers did not ultimately prosper.

The reason for this negative result is that money received as compensation is utilized in making of a pucca house, marriage of daughters, buying of motor cycles and TV and other items of comfort. Rarely has the money been deployed in productive investments. In the result, the displaced persons loose a regular stream of income and are impoverished in the end. This is compounded by 'loss of soul'. Survey of displaced persons at Tehri indicates they are unhappy. They tell that they do not feel comfortable in new surroundings.

Table 1.8. Are you happy with land acquisition? (Details at Annexure 4)

Sl. No.	*Location*	*Improved*	*Reduced*	*No Change*
1.	Tehri, n=11	—	6	5

Such costs are not conclusive arguments against HEPs. However, they indicate that we must factor in these costs in the project design.

Narmada Judgment

Judgment in Narmada Bachao Andolan case is often invoked in support of hydropower. The author submits that principles enshrined in that judgment lead to opposite results in case of hydropower.

Consumption of Power does not Necessarily Raise Standard of Living

The Supreme Court held: "One of the indicators of living standard of people is per capita consumption of electricity... it is necessary that generation increases" (Jain 2001).

Generation of electricity is one of the indicators of standard of living. The purpose is to raise the overall standard of living, which is a holistic concept. If there are no other negative impacts then standard of living is raised by generation of electricity. However, if there are other negative impacts then mere increased availability of electricity does not lead to higher standard of living. In present case, many negative impacts are seen such as decline in water quality, landslides, extinction of Smooth-Coated Otter, etc. Thus, a holistic assessment of standard of living leads to the opposite result.

Comparison with Other Alternatives

The Supreme Court held that there is a "perennial shortage of power in India, and, therefore, it is necessary that the generation increases" (Jain 2001:45). The need for generation of more power is well accepted. The question is whether hydropower is the best solution to meet this need. It is shown in the previous section that other sources of energy are better.

Impacts on People Living far Away

The Supreme Court held: "A river is not only meant for the people close by but it should be for the benefit of those who can make use of it, being far away from it or near by... In a democracy, welfare of the people at large, and not merely of a small section of society, has to be the concern of a responsible Government" (Jain 2001).

The underlying principle is that impacts on people living far away have to be assessed. The impact on deterioration of quality of waters of the Ganga at Prayag and Kashi, impact on coastal areas due to soil erosion and loss of flood-recession agriculture due to deprivation of sediment should also be accounted for. The picture changes once these impacts are taken into account as directed by the Supreme Court. It then becomes clear that hydropower projects are harmful for the people at large. Hence there is no conflict of interest involved between 'large benefits to others' and 'small costs to local people' as in Narmada case. This is a loss-loss proposition.

Improvement of Ecology

The Supreme Court held: With "proper channelisation of developmental activities, ecology and environment can be improved." Further, "The Petitioner has not been able to point out a single instance where the construction of a Dam has, on the whole, had an adverse environmental impact... Thermal power projects use fossil fuels... which contribute towards environmental pollution" (Jain 2001:33, 45).

The directive of the Hon Court is that developmental activities should be undertaken in a way that they lead to improvement in ecology and environment. This is wholly accepted by the author. This study shows that hydropower projects have many adverse impacts. These include development of virulent strains of malaria, erosion of our coasts at a hastening pace, increase in crime due to less mental peace from effect of taking bath in the Ganga, increasing incidences of landslides along rims of reservoirs, etc. These negative impacts are not taken into account hence the project is presented as eco-friendly when actually it is not so.

The greenhouse gasses emitted from thermal and hydropower plants can be sequestered by planting of forests but the erosion of coastlands, deterioration in water quality of our rivers, higher incidence and virulence of malaria and other effects of hydropower cannot be mitigated. Hence hydropower is worse than thermal. My friends in Narmada Bachao Andolan agree that an economic assessment of environmental costs was not presented before the court with sufficient rigour. The Court was possibly led to support Sardar Sarovar Dam because these details were not presented before it. In any event, the underlying judgment requires that environmental pollution be reduced. We show that hydropower pollutes more than thermal hence this makes a case against hydropower.

Greenhouse Gases

The Supreme Court held that "hydel power's contribution in greenhouse gases is negligible and it can be termed ecology friendly" (Jain 2001:43).

Latest research which shows that per Kwh contribution of hydropower reservoirs to greenhouse gases is larger than thermal.

Application of Mind

The Supreme Court held: When a decision is taken by the Government after full application of mind, the Court is not to sit in appeal over such a decision (Jain 2001:13).

The clearances to Kotlibhel projects, like many others, have been given without full application of mind, hence are liable to be quashed. The EAC has also not applied its mind to the submissions made by the people during public hearings.

Cost-effectiveness

The Supreme Court held that "India has experience of over 40 years in the construction of dams. The experience does not show that construction of a large dam is not cost effective..." (Jain 2001:25).

Many consequences of dams have become known since the Narmada Judgement. The operative principle is that projects should be cost-effective. This study shows that hydropower is not cost-effective. It is notable that Ministry of Power has not got any study of benefits and costs of large hydropower projects.

There is no Alternative

The Supreme Court held that the provision of water from Narmada was the only solution for the people of Gujarat—there was no other solution; hence, the hardship to the local people should be incurred but mitigated (Jain 2001:13).

In the present case, many alternatives are available for generation of power—solar, wind, micro hydel, etc.—which are renewable sources that do not suffer from the adverse impacts of hydropower impugned projects.

Global Experience

The Supreme Court observed "World over, countries having rich water and river systems have effectively exploited these for hydel power generation" (Jain 2001:45).

The situation has dramatically changed since the Narmada Judgment. About 500 dams have been decommissioned in the United States because the ecological and social harm was adjudged to be much more that the economic benefits. Hence, there is a need for a dispassionate re-study of the global experience with dams.

Precautionary Principle

The Supreme Court observed that "The precautionary principle suggests that where there is an identifiable risk of serious and irreversible harm, including for example, extinction of species...it may be appropriate to place the burden of proof on the person or entity proposing the activity." On the other hand, "when the effect of the project is known then the principle of sustainable development would come into play" (Jain 2001:49).

There indeed exists an identifiable risk of serious nature in the Kotlibhel projects. These include extinction of the species of butterflies and Smooth Coated Otter, development of virulent strains of malaria, erosion of our coasts and increase in crime due to less mental peace from effect of taking bath in the Ganga. Hence, following the judgement of the Hon Supreme Court the precautionary principle becomes operative.

In conclusion, the Narmada Judgment leads to opposite result when applied to Kotlibhel projects.

2

DO WE NEED SO MUCH POWER?

The case for hydropower rests on the need to fulfil the large requirements of power for sustaining economic growth and raising standard of living of our people. These large requirements cannot be met from other sources hence we need to develop hydropower. In this section we show that this argument does not sustain for the following reasons:

- Excessive forecasts of requirement of power are made by Central Electricity Authority and Planning Commission. Actual requirement is much less.
- Power is in reality required more for consumption and pilferage and less for production and economic growth as made out to be.
- Consumption of power does not add to standard of living beyond a certain point. Unending increase in consumption, therefore, does not add to standard of living.
- Lesson from other countries indicate that a glut of power is indeed likely in India.
- It is possible to meet genuine requirements of power by alternative approaches.

Excessive Forecasts by CEA

Three Methods of Forecasting

There are, in the main, three methods of forecasting:

Partial End Use Method (PEUM), Trend and Econometric. Each method has its advantages and disadvantages which are discussed in detail by TERI in its paper "Demand Forecasting for Electricity".[4]

CEA has used Partial End Use Method (PEUM) in making the forecasts (CEA 2007:31). Essentially the method involves estimating the (1) number of users and multiplying the same with (2) amount of energy required per user. CEA has made unrealistic assumptions that appear to be in great variance with other methods. Unfortunately the base data and assumptions used by CEA are not given in the 17th Power Survey hence it is not possible for this author to examine the nuts and bolts of the same. That said, the following unrealistic basis is used by CEA in making these forecasts.

Domestic: The 17th Power Survey has assumed that 'power to all' will be a reality by 2012 as mentioned in Electricity Policy (CEA 2007:32). This policy is merely a target. It cannot be assumed that it will turn into reality. Thus number of consumers is much overestimated. The increase in per-consumer consumption may be overestimated. No data is available hence detail comment cannot be made.

Commercial: This has been clubbed with domestic in the survey. The number of commercial users and their forecast level of consumption are not disclosed.

Irrigation: Number of pump sets is estimated on basis of "programme of pump installation furnished by SEBs" (CEA 2007:33). There is likely to be a huge gap in the actual achievement. Secondly, the decreasing trend in Consumption (CEA 2007:34) has been overwritten and a "marginally increasing trend" is taken for forecasting. Factors such as "extensive irrigation practices, multiple cropping, depletion of ground water" are given as basis of making this change. But these were present in the past hence their impact is already built into the decreasing trend noticed. There was no occasion to convert decreasing trend into a marginally increasing trend on these considerations. Change in forecast consumption could only be justified due to removal of restrictions of supply hours. But the extent of this is not disclosed.

Industrial: The forecast is based on information furnished by industrial units (CEA 2007:34). There is likely to be a wide gap between such information and reality.

The forecasts made by PEUM method are not reliable because of these assumptions on the higher side.

Record of 16th Power Survey

The 16th Electric Power Survey was published in 2000. Similar excessive forecasts of electricity consumption were made then. This is clear by comparing the forecasts with the actual situation in 2003-04.

Table 2.1. Comparison of 16th Survey forecasts and 17th Survey actual, for 2003-04

Sl.No.	*Item*	*Forecast—16th Power Survey, Page 24*	*Actual—17th Power Survey, Page 193*	*Percent over- or under estimation of forecast*
1.	Total Consumption (Mkwh)	467,759	362,799	(+) 28.9%
2.	T&D Losses (Mkwh)	130,188	161,500	(–) 24.1%

CEA overestimated consumption by about one-fourth; and underestimated T&D losses by one-fourth.

The PEUM method was followed in 16th Power Survey. Similar assumptions were made then. Since these assumption led to over-forecasts in 16th Power Survey, there is every reason to believe that the same over-forecasts are built into the 17th Power Survey.

Table 2.2. Comparison of basis of PEUM Forecasts in 16th and 17th Power Surveys

Sl.No.	*Basis of forecasts in 165h Power Survey*	*Basis of forecast in 17th Power Survey*
1. Domestic and Commercial	Higher rate of electrification reckoned in certain States. Anticipated improvements in standard of living and effects of power cut in recent past considered in raising forecasts (CEA 2000:18).	Power to all' will be a reality by 2012 (CEA 2007:32).
2. Irrigation	Decided on basis of discussions held with SEBs (CEA 2000:19).	Number of pump sets is estimated on basis of "programme of pump installation furnished by SEBs" (CEA 2007:33). The decreasing trend observed in consumption has been overwritten and a 'marginally increasing trend" is taken for forecasting (CEA 2007:34).
3. Industrial	For HT industries with a demand of 1 MW and above projection has been made "on basis of information furnished by the industrial units" (CEA 2000:20).	The forecast is based on information furnished by industrial units (CEA 2007:34).

It is seen from above table that the basis adopted in the two Power Surveys are nearly identical. Hence the estimates in 17th Survey are likely to be on the higher side as they were in the past.

Trend Forecast Explained Away

It seems that CEA is determined to make high forecasts. This presents a difficulty because the trend forecasts indicate a much lower level. In order to wriggle out of this difficulty, CEA has manipulated the trends to make appear as if the PEUM forecasts are not in much variance with trend forecasts.

The trend forecasts are explained as follows by CEA: "The electricity consumption and generation in India grew by 6.87% and 7.47% respectively for the last thirty years and the corresponding GDP Growth has been 5.4%... Taking cue from the foregoing, the electrical energy consumption is assumed to increase at CAGR (Compound Annual Growth Rate) of 10% up to 2012 as worked out and 9% up to 2022. This growth of electricity consumption is expected to support an average GDP growth of 9-11% over the period forecast" (CEA 2007:52). This approach has the following problems.

Problem 1: Using 30-Year Averages for forecast

30-year growth rates are used by CEA to make trend forecast instead of 5-year growth rates. The 17th Power Survey gives the following data:

Table 2.3. Growth rates of electricity consumption

Sl. No.	*Time Period*	*Electricity Consumption CAGR%*	*Gross Generation CAGR%*	*GDP (93-94 prices) CAGR%*	*Elasticity Ratio Consumption/GDP*	*Elasticity Ratio Generation/GDP*
1.	30 Years: 2004-05 to 1974-75	6.87	7.47	5.40	1.27	1.38
2.	5 Years: 2004-05 to 1999-00	4.30	4.37	5.90	0.73	0.74

There is a steep decline in CAGR of electricity consumption from 6.87% in last 30-years to 4.30% in last 5-years. Obviously one should use the latter 5-year data for forecast, which is closer to the period in question. Yet, in making forecast, CEA relies on the older 30-Year CAGR and ignores recent 5-Year CAGR. The declining elasticity of electricity consumption is thus wholly ignored.

Problem 2: Ignoring Data for 2005-06

The 17th Power Survey was released in March 2007. Data of electricity consumption for 2005-06, ending in March 2006, was available to the CEA. Yet, CEA ignores the data for 2005-06. Reason is that there is a steep decline in growth of electricity consumption in this year hence this data is inconvenient. This is clear from Table below, which is same as Table above, with figures for 2005-06 added from Economic Survey published by the Finance Ministry.

Table 2.4. 30-, 5-year and 2005-06 growth rates of electricity consumption

Sl. No.	*Time Period*	*GDP Growth Rate*	*Elasticity Ratio Generation / GDP*
1.	30 Years: 2004-05 to 1974-75	5.40	1.38
2.	5 Years: 2004-05 to 1999-00	5.90	0.74
3.	2005-06	9.00	0.53

Source: Table 1.24 and 1.6, MOF 2006

CEA wants to create high forecasts hence has ignored the fact that Elasticity Ratio of Generation/GDP has declined in 2005-06 to 0.53 along with an increase in GDP growth rate.

The conclusion is that CEA has force-manipulated trend forecasts upward to make them conform to the over-forecasts made by PEUM method.[5]

Econometric Forecasts Ignored

The 17th Power Survey provides forecasts using econometric model. These forecasts are made with the assumption that share of services sector will remain constant at "around 55 percent" (CEA 2007:278), hence these forecast rule out of court the main contributor to reduced requirement of electricity. Furthermore, even these high forecasts are ignored in the main report as shown in Table 2.5 below.

Table 2.5. Econometric Forecasts in 17th Power Survey

Sl. No.	*Forecast in Main Report (Table 3.1)*	*(Reasonable) Forecast by econometric model Table V-A (Scenario 2: Per capita GDP growth 7%, price increase 2% and electricity intensity declines on trend basis)*	*(High) Forecast by econometric model Table V-A (Scenario 9: Per capita GDP growth 7.5% price remains at 2001-02 level and electricity intensity remains at the level of 2003-04)*
2005-06	388,175	407,555	520,117
2011-12	755,847	447,049	698,416
Percent Increase	+94.7%	+9.7%	+34.3%

The reasonable increase in consumption predicted by econometric study is only 9.7%. The highest forecast by econometric study is 34.3%. Yet CEA forecasts an increase of 94.7% in the main report. No discussion is provided in the report for ignoring these econometric findings.

Increase in Share of Service Sector

The reason of these 'low' forecasts is that nature of our economy is qualitatively different from the past. At present most income is generated in the service sector where requirement of electrical energy is less. This becomes clear by comparing the consumption of electricity in agriculture, services and manufacturing sectors as shown in Table 2.6.

Table 2.6. Sectoral composition of consumption of power

Sl. No.	*Consumption Category*	*Share in Consumption of Electricity— Actual 2003-04 (17th Power Survey Table 3.1 Page 183)*	*Share in GDP (Economic Survey 2006-07, Table 1.3, Page S-5)*	*Increase in Requirement of Electricity for Generating one percent GDP*
1.	Domestic	24.8%	-	-
2.	Services Sector (Commercial)	8.2%	52.9	0.15%
3.	Agriculture (Irrigation)	24.0%	23.9	1.00%
4.	Manufacturing (Industry)	35.2%	23.4	1.50%
5.	Others	7.8%	-	-
	Total	100%	100%	-

An increase of 1.50 percent in requirement of electrical energy is necessary with an increase of one percent in income from manufacturing. The increase is only 0.15 percent if the same one percent growth comes from services sector. Since most increase in GDP is coming from the services sector, the requirement of electricity for supporting GDP growth is less. The low requirement of electricity in services sector is confirmed by CEA as shown in Table 2.7 below.

Table 2.7. Sectoral electricity consumption (Details at endnote 6)

Sl. No.	*Sector*	*Change in Share of Electricity Consumption 2006-12*	*Change in Share in GDP, 2006-12*
1.	Services (Commercial)	+0.4	+4.5
2.	Agriculture (Irrigation)	–2.6	–5.6
3.	Manufacturing (Industry)	–1.0	+1.1

The share of service sector in our GDP is increasing. This sector consumes electricity only in small quantities. CEA projects the share of consumption of electricity by this sector will increase by a meagre 0.4% between 2005-06 and 2011-12. Therefore, we do not need much electricity for growth, which is coming mainly from this sector. However, CEA has assumed, while making econometric analysis, that "the share of services sector would remain constant" (CEA 2007:278). The sector contributing to lower consumption of electricity has been ruled out of court ab initio.

True Trend Forecasts of Power Requirement

The author has used data from CEA, Planning Commission and Finance Ministry to arrive at more realistic trend forecasts of requirement of electricity. CEA has given 30-year and 5-year growth rates in electricity consumption per GDP. We can estimate the consumption in 2007-2012 using these figures.

The figures for 1974-75 to 2004-05 can be assumed to equal that at mid-year of this period i.e. 1991. The figures for 1999-00 to 2004-05 can be assumed to equal that at mid-year of this period i.e. 2002½. Now we can extrapolate figures for 2006-07 to 2011-12 using the figures for these two years. This is done as follows :

Elasticity in 1991 (mid-year of 1974-75 to 2004-05)	= 1.38 (Given by CEA)
Elasticity in 2002½ (mid-year of 1999-00 to 2004-05)	= 0.74 (Given by CEA)
Change in elasticity per year (0.74/11.5 years)	= (–) 0.056
Forecast of elasticity for 2009½ (mid-year of 2006-7 to 2011-12) = 0.74 – 0.056 X 7	= 0.35
Growth rate of electricity consumption at 10% GDP growth	= 3.5%

Accordingly, the true growth rate for electricity is only 3.5%. We can use this to estimate demand.

Actual Capacity in 2005-06 (Economic Survey Table 1.24)	= 143,800 MW
Rate of Increase 2005-06 to 2011-12	= 3.5% (Forecast by Author as per CEA data above)
Capacity in 2006-07	= 148,833 MW
Capacity Required in 2011-12	= 176,767 MW
Increase in Capacity Required 2006-07 to 2011-12	= 27,934 MW

The true increase required is only 27,934 MW against 60,000 MW projected by CEA if its own data is used properly.

True Forecasts using Planning Commission Data

Similarly, figures given by Planning Commission in Integrated Energy Policy Report can be used to forecast elasticity.

Elasticity in 1992½ (mid- 1980-81 to 2003-04)	= 1.30
Elasticity in 1997½ (mid- 1990-91 to 2003-04)	= 1.06
Change in elasticity per year	= (–) 0.048
Forecast for 2008½ (mid- 2004-05 to 2011-12)	= 1.06 – 0.048 × 11 = 0.53

Accordingly, the elasticity for this period is forecast at 0.53 instead of 0.95 assumed by the Planning Commission. This translates into a growth rate of 4.2 percent per year at a GDP growth rate of 8 percent (0.53 × 8 = 4.24). The true forecast of electricity requirement is given below.

Actual Capacity in 2005-06	= 143,800 MW (Economic Survey Table 1.24)
Rate of Increase 2005-06 to 2011-12	= 4.2% (Forecast by Author as per Planning Commission data above)
Capacity in 2006-07	= 150,702 MW
Capacity Required in 2011-12	= 184,063 MW
Increase in Capacity Required 2006-07 to 2011-12	= 34,223 MW

The true increase required is only 34,223 MW against 60,000 MW projected by Planning Commission if its own data is used properly.

True Forecasts Using Finance Ministry Data

We have calculated 5-year average growth rates of electricity generation from data given in *Economic Survey 2006-07* published by the Ministry of Finance and extrapolated it in table below.

Table 2.8. Simple forecast of 5-Year growth rates

Sl. No.	*Period*	*GDP Growth Rate (Economic Survey, Table 1.6)*	*Electricity Generated (Economic Survey, Table 1.24B)*
1.	1996-97 to 2001-02 (Actual)	5.9%	5.8%
2.	2001-02 to 2005-06 (Actual)	6.9%	4.8%
3.	2005-06 to 2010-12 (Forecast by Author)	8.0%	4.0%

The Author's assessment is that power consumption and generation in the next five years will increase at 4.0% assuming 8% GDP growth rate. The true increase required in generating capacity is calculated as follows:

Actual Capacity in 2005-06	=	143,800 MW (Economic Survey Table 1.24)
Rate of Increase 2005-06 to 2011-12	=	4.8% (As per Planning Commission data above)
Capacity in 2006-07	=	150,702 MW
Capacity Required in 2011-12	=	183,352 MW (Increase @ 4.0%)
Increase in Capacity Required 2006-07 to 2011-12	=	32,650 MW

The true increase required is only 32,650 MW against 60,000 to 80,000 MW projected by MOP and Planning Commission.

True Forecast as Given in CEA's Econometric Study

CEA has provided forecast of All India Electricity Consumption at Aggregate Level (CEA 2007: Annexure V, Table V-A). Twelve different scenarios have been given. The Author considers Scenario 2 to be the most likely case for the following reasons:

- Per Capita GDP Growth Rate = 7%. This is the middle-level of the three levels examined by CEA.
- Electricity Price to grow at 2%. The alternate scenario is for electricity price to remain at 2001-02 level, which is not acceptable in view of the liberalization of the power sector.
- Electricity intensity to decline on trend basis. The alternate scenario is for electricity intensity to remain at levels of 2003-04. This latter alternative is not acceptable because declining trend should be part of econometric analysis. There is no reason to ignore declining trend.

The predicted consumption of electricity in above scenario and pro-rata implication for increase in capacity is given below:

Consumption forecast in 2006-07	= 413,189 GWh (Annexure V, Table V-A, Scenario 2)
Consumption forecast in 2011-12	= 447,049 GWh (Annexure V, Table V-A, Scenario 2)
Increase 2006-07 to 2011-12	= 8.2% (Forecast by CEA)
Capacity required in 2006-07	= 150,702 MW (From section above)
Capacity required in 2011-12	= 163,059 MW (Add 8.2% to line above)
Increase in Capacity Required 2006-07 to 2011-12	= 12,357 MW

Four Forecasts Compared

The four forecasts for increase in capacity required 2006-07 to 2011-12 according to the author are as follows:

Based on CEA data = 27,934 MW
Based on Planning Commission data = 34,223 MW
Based on Finance Ministry dat = 32,650 MW
Based on CEA's econometric study = 12,357 MW

It is clear that the forecast of 60,000 to 80,000 MW made by CEA and Planning Commission are at wide variance with these various trend forecasts. The author feels the trend forecast according to CEA's econometric study is most realistic because it incorporates effect of reducing electricity intensity.

Peak Load Requirement is Similarly Overstated

The case for harnessing rivers for generation of electricity arises from the projected need for peak load electricity. The demand for peak load power grows approximately in same ratio. The forecast of increase in Electricity Energy Requirement and Peak Electric Load made by CEA are given below:

Table 2.9. Long Term Forecast of Power Requirement (After Table 2.3 of 17th Power Survey)

Sl. No.	*Period*	*Increase in Electrical Energy Requirement*	*Increase in Peak Electric Load*
1.	2011-12 to 2016-17	43.71%	42.89%
2.	2016-17 to 2021-22	37.52%	36.68%

It is seen that forecast of Electricity Energy Requirement and Peak Electric Load move in tandem. Hence, the excessive forecasts for requirement of electrical energy given above are equally applicable to peak load requirement and to the need for hydropower.

We do not need the huge amounts of electricity forecast by CEA and hence the case for exploiting rivers for hydropower must also be reconsidered.

Electricity Required for Consumption, not Production

CEA and Planning Commission make it appear that increase in electricity generation is necessary to support present high rates of economic growth. Electricity is presented as mobil oil of economy than as hair oil. CEA says: "The electrical energy consumption has been assumed to increase...at 10% up to 2012...This *growth of electricity consumption is expected to support an average GDP growth* of 9-11% over the period forecast" (CEA 2007:52, italics provided).

Similarly Planning Commission states: "We projected total primary commercial energy requirement on the basis of elasticity w.r.t. GDP, which gives percent change in *commercial energy requirement for one percent change in GDP*" (PC 2006:18, italics provided). Increase in generation of electricity is presented as necessary for securing higher economic growth.

Data given by CEA indicate that productive demand is much less.

Table 2.10. Sector-wise electricity requirement (Details at end note 8)

Sl. No.	*Sector*	*Annual Rate of growth, Percent (2003-04 to 2011-12)*
1.	Domestic	7.4
2.	Productive (Commercial + Irrigation + Industry)	2.7
3.	Others	6.6
	Total	4.3

It is seen that the rate of growth of consumption for productive purposes is only 2.7 percent. The rate of growth of electricity required for consumption and raising the standards of living by the people is 7.4 percent. While entirely laudable, this places increased generation of electricity on an entirely different footing. Electricity is required more for running geysers and air-conditioners and less for running computers for making software. Generation of electricity for economic growth provides large trickle-down or secondary benefits while that for consumption does not.

CEA fails to recognize this, and passes off increased need for electricity for consumption as necessary for economic growth. The true increase in capacity required for productive sectors is calculated below:

Actual Capacity in 2005-06	=	143,800 MW (Economic Survey Table 1.24)
Share of Productive Sectors	=	96,892 MW (67.38% as per end note 8, col 2)
Rate of Increase in 2005-06	=	2.7% (Table above)
Capacity required for productive sectors in 2006-07	=	99,508 MW
Rate of Increase 2006-07 to 2011-12	=	2.7% (Table above)
Capacity Required in 2011-12	=	113,687 MW
Increase in Capacity Required, Productive Sectors 2006-07 to 2011-12	=	14,179 MW

The requirement of electricity for 'supporting GDP', i.e. for use by productive sectors of the economy is only 14,000 MW against 60,000 to 80,000 projected by MOP.

We have referred previously to various studies indicating that economic growth and electricity consumption have decoupled. The implication is that demand for electricity is coming from consumption. Higher income is leading to higher demand for electricity just as it leads to more consumption of liquor or cigarettes. CEA ignores these studies and forecasts requirements of electricity for consumption as if it was necessary for sustaining economic growth, which is not the case.

Electricity does not add to standard of living beyond a plateau

It is universally accepted that higher consumption of electricity goes hand in hand with higher income. However income is not the best indicator of human welfare. Human Development Index is a better indicator. Expectedly, we find a positive relationship between HDI and per capita energy consumption. However, the relationship runs aground as the level of energy consumption rises. Initial increases in energy consumption have a positive impact on HDI; but later increases do not have such an impact.

A study titled "Electricity Supply and Demand Side Management Options" prepared for the World Commission on Dams by Anton Eberhard of University of Cape Town, South Africa and others says: "During this century, the most important way in which countries have increased energy availability for their economies has been to invest in electricity supply... Figure shows the relationship between per capita energy consumption (commercial and traditional energy) and the Human Development Index (HDI) for 100 developed and developing countries. The graph suggests that for countries with low levels of energy services, even small inputs of energy are associated with significant welfare improvements. *At higher energy consumption levels, further increases do not seem to impact greatly on human development.* The decreasing marginal benefits of energy supply on human development parallels GDP-energy decoupling that has taken place in various countries during the 20th century" (Eberhard 2000, italics provided).

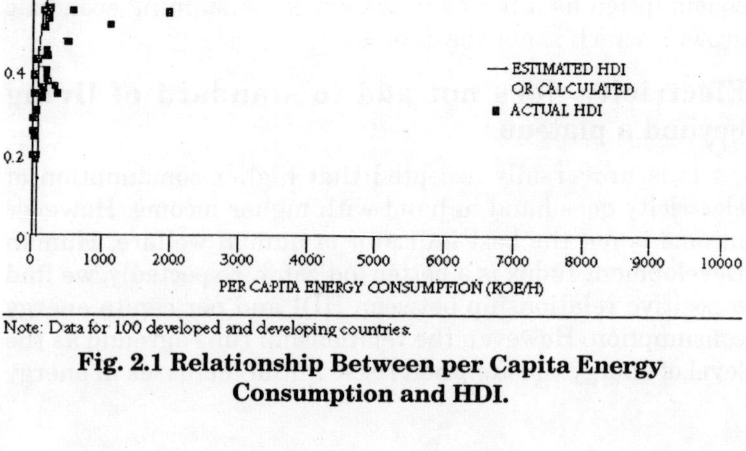

Note: Data for 100 developed and developing countries.

Fig. 2.1 Relationship Between per Capita Energy Consumption and HDI.

This indicates that higher consumption of electricity cannot be assumed to lead to higher welfare. It is more likely that higher consumption of electricity will lead to minimal increase in welfare or HDI.

Overproduction of power

Sectoral Composition and Decline in Demand in USA

According to the US Energy Information Administration (Caruso 2008), the growth rate of consumption of electricity in the U.S. is declining:

1960s	7.3 percent
1970s	4.2 percent
1980s	2.6 percent
1990s	2.3 percent
2000s	1.7 percent (forecast)

The energy situation in USA turned from shortage into glut in mere two years from 2001 to 2003. Rebecca Smith, Staff Reporter of The Wall Street Journal wrote in 2003: "A surplus of electric power across much of the nation has turned into a glut that isn't expected to ease until 2005 or 2006. The energy surfeit has slashed wholesale power prices and put the thumbscrews on companies that embarked on costly power plant projects in recent years. Indeed, if all the power plants proposed or under construction were to be completed, some regions would have twice as much excess capacity in a couple of years as is necessary to meet reliability standards ... Industry experts say it will be several years before today's surpluses are worked down. The situation underscores how quickly energy markets can pivot. Two years ago, California was suffering electricity blackouts and supplies were tightening in the Northeast, Texas and other regions. This sparked a construction boom in generating capacity in 2001 and 2002, just as the economy slowed and demand growth slackened" (Smith 2003).

Peaking power plants built in the U.S. are in trouble today. These plants were built to produce electricity from natural gas but the demand did not materialize. The Electricity Forum says: "Energy companies from Maryland to California got in line to build peakers in Illinois soon after utility deregulation legislation passed in 1997. Between 1999 and 2002, 9,339 megawatts of peaker plant capacity came online, according to the Illinois Environmental Protection Agency. Permits for another 4,529 megawatts have been granted. Total generating capacity is about 46,000 megawatts, 19,000 of which is owned by the major utilities. 'We have got power coming out of our ears,' said Susan Zingle of the Lake County Conservation Alliance, one of the environmental groups concerned about the rapid increase in peaker plants" (Electricity Forum 2007).

This glut of power in the US is parallel with increase in share of services in the economy.

Table 2.11. Sectoral share in GDP, United States

Sl No	*Sector*	*1990*	*2005*
1.	Agriculture	2	1
2.	Industry	28	22
3.	Services	70	77

Source: World Bank (2007: Table 4.2).

This experience indicates that the forecast demand for energy may not actually materialize. We must not make overinvestment in power based on inflated forecasts that do not take into account low levels of consumption of electricity in the services sector.

Producing Hydro for Sale

Developing countries are often tapping hydro not for meeting domestic needs but for export. Sudan is building hydro plants to export power to Kenya. Congo is doing the same to export power to Europe (Doya 2008).

Patrick McCully writes in *Silenced Rivers* that most bureaucracies make excessive projections:

> "Electricity demand forecasts consistently overestimate future needs for electricity. In more than 100 national demand forecasts used by the World Bank, actual demand seven years after the forecasts were made was on the average one-fifth lower than that had been projected. The deviation between projected and actual increased with the number of years from the date of forecast.
>
> "The economic justification of Yacyreta Dam used assumption that Argentinean electricity demand will grow at a rate of 8-10 percent during the 1980s. In fact, demand grew by an annual average of just over 2 percent so that when the first turbines of the $11.5 billion mega project came on-line in 1994, the country already had a sizable surplus of generating capacity.
>
> "Between 1970 and the mid-1908s, the World Bank and Inter-American Development Bank together lent Colombia a total of $3.8 billion for 12 large hydro dams and their associated infrastructure. Yet, by 1986, when these dams had mostly been completed, electricity demand in Colombia was one-third lower than forecast when the dams were planned, and the excess generating capacity was estimated to have cost Colombia more than $400 million" (McCully 1998 : 152)

The Author's assessment that the country is being pushed into excessive generation of electricity far more than the demand, therefore, is not imaginary and has precedents. Of course the situation of glut changes with time. For example, there is no surplus power in Argentina today as mentioned by McCully above. Presently Argentina is facing and energy shortage (Latin Focus 2008). However, there is glut of peaking power in USA. The main point is that we should not destroy our rivers today for demand for power that may not materialize tomorrow.

Alternatives to hydropower

Savings from Demand Side Management[9]

As indicated by the Planning Commission, Ministry of Power and many other agencies, the Aggregate Technical & Commercial (AT&C) losses in the power sector are about 30% against the international best practice of less than 10%. In this regard Ministry of Power has set itself a target of bringing the AT&C losses to below 15% in the short term. Such a reduction alone can result in reducing the effective demand on the power system of about 25%, which will be about 20,000 MW if we consider the fact that about 80,000 MW peak demand was met in year 2006-07.

As per the Planning Commission's Integrated Energy Policy, measures like higher efficiency in electrical energy usage, effective Demand Side Management (DSM), and energy conservation can yield a saving of about 20% of the peak requirement.[10] This works out to about 16,000 MW.

The techno-economically feasible benefits from renovation & modernization of existing power plants are considerable. Improving the Plant Load Factor (PLF) of thermal power plants from the national average of about 60% to about 80% can result in additional power availability of about 16,000 MW. Similarly, renovation & modernization of existing hydro–electric power plants can provide about 1,500 MW.

It is safe to assume that the additional net benefits and savings feasible from the better utilization of existing electricity assets itself will be in excess of 50,000 MW, which is about 4 times the peak deficit recorded during the previous year. This benefit can come at a much lower cost as compared to setting up new generating capacity. There will be no need to submerge agricultural or forest lands. There will be no displacement of human beings. The impact on the environment, including the flora and fauna, will be negligible. In the backdrop of global warming concerns the environmental benefits of these measures will be huge. The total GHG emissions (due to burning of fossil fuels in thermal power stations and due to fermentation of submerged bio-mass in hydropower dams) will be reduced by a considerable extent.

There are many technical benefits too. Because of the reduced losses, the voltage profile in different parts of the power supply grid will be optimum brining huge benefits to the end users. Because of the reduced need for additional generating stations, transmission & distribution lines and sub-stations the complexity of the power system also comes down, thereby increasing the reliability and availability of power.

Hydro and Energy Security

Question before us is whether it is in national good to harness rivers for generation of electricity.

The role of hydro in meeting the energy requirement of the country is small. The Planning Commission has developed alternate scenarios of our sources of energy. In all scenarios, coal remains dominant with oil following at the second position. The role of hydropower is very small—only 13 out of about 1800 Mtoe (Million tons of oil equivalent) required is likely to be provided by Hydro in the most likely coal-dominant scenario. Special efforts to develop hydropower sources will push this to 35 Mtoe or 1.9 percent of our energy requirements.

The savings from Demand Side Management (DSM) are estimated at 142 Mtoe, which is obviously much more than the maximum contribution of hydro".[11]

The total demand is reduced by 142 Mtoe from DSM. The Planning Commission, in its wisdom, has allocated all the savings from DSM to natural gas and coal (table below). We suggest that the savings are allocated to hydro. The consequent small increase of 3% in use of coal is sufficient to reduce hydro generation by 63% and liberate our rivers.

Table 2.12. Allocating savings from DSM (Details at end note 11)

Sl. No.	*Source*	*Projected Distribution of Sources of Energy by Planning Commission (Forced Nuclear+ Hydro+ Gas)*	*Project Distribution of Sources of Energy by Planning Commission (Forced Nuclear+ Hydro+ Gas + DSM)*	*Savings from DSM, as allocated by Planning Commission*	*Savings from DSM, as per alternate allocation by Author*
1.	Crude oil	486	486	-	-
2.	Natural gas	197	174	23	23
3.	Coal	835	715	120	85
4.	Hydro	35	35	-	35
5.	Nuclear	98	98	-	-
6.	Renewables	2	2	-	-
7.	Non-Commercial	185	185	-	-
	Total	1837	1695	142	142

It is clear from above that contribution of hydro to energy security of the country will be small. This is recognized by the Planning Commission: "Hydro potential is significant, but small compared to our needs and its contribution in terms of energy is likely to remain small."

Savings from DSM will be far in excess of the generation of hydro. Thus, the alternative to hydro is to implement DSM sincerely.

Contribution of Hydro to Peak Load Energy

Hydro electricity has the advantage that it can be produced during peak hours and shut off during non-peak hours. Coal-based thermal plants are suitable for base load only. The boilers, once fired, have to be kept going. Thus, Planning Commission notes: "Though its contribution to energy requirement is limited, hydro electricity's flexibility and suitability to meet peak demand makes it valuable ...

(We must) ensure that hydro is maximally used for meeting peak loads ... Power planning in the future should be based on the concept of an optimal mix of thermal/nuclear and hydro stations in which the hydro stations should take the peak and the thermal stations provide the base load."

It is accepted by this author that hydropower has this critical advantage. However, this is nullified for three reasons.

Hydro Unsuitable 1: ROR not for Peak Load

The ability to provide peak power lies mainly with storage dams. ROR dams are not suitable for this because water cannot be stored during non-peak hours to be used for generation during peak hours. Only storage schemes can store water and discharge during peak hours. Thus, the Planning Commission says, "Run of the river schemes, typically, have much lower capacity for delivering peak power compared to storage schemes... Of the 50,000 MW planned, 31,000 MW shall come from run of the river schemes... However... peaking capacity is minimal." Thus, ROR schemes cannot be justified for peak load requirements.

It may be mentioned here that the Central Electricity Authority is misrepresenting many storage-and-peaking projects as run-of-river projects. In a reply to the author under RTI Act, the CEA has said that there are two definitions of ROR:

(1) Run-of-River Scheme: Uses flow of the stream as it occurs.

(2) Run-of-River Scheme with Pondage: With sufficient pondage for meeting daily or weekly variation of power demand.

The ROR-Pondage Scheme involves storage of water during certain time of the day for use at other times. These are truly 'storage' projects and not ROR. This is the case with Srinagar Scheme upstream of Kotlibhel 1B. However, CEA is ingeniously passing of these storage schemes as ROR by reclassifying storage as ROR with Pondage.

Hydro Unsuitable 2: Storage has Environment Problems

Storage dams provide peak power and help in irrigation and flood control. However, they have greater environmental and R&R problems. Thus Planning Commission states: "The development of... storage schemes are critical for India as our per capita water storage is the lowest among other comparable countries. Creating such storages is critical to India's water security, flood control and drought control. The environmental concerns and the problem of resettlement and rehabilitation of project affected people can and must be satisfactorily handled." These benefits and costs of storage dams are to be studied separately. This is mentioned here to point out that 'hydropower' cannot be justified on this ground.

Hydro Unsuitable 3: Peak Load Pricing

The case for hydropower rests, in part, on its ability to provide peaking power. Assumption is that a given peaking requirement is to be met in order to improve standard of living of people.

However, greater enhancement in standard of living can be obtained by introducing dual pricing for peak and non-peak consumption. This will be beneficial for the consumer as well as the producer. A notional calculation is given at Table 2.13.

The Planning Commission errs in not exploring this win-win solution and instead advocating development of hydropower to meet peak demand.

Costs Admitted

The Planning Commission (2006) admits following costs of Hydropower :

- Displacement of traditional communities from their ancestral domains "inflicts a high social cost including change in the resource base of traditional culture and a loss of livelihood."
- Loss of pristine natural forests and its associated unique biodiversity may occur due to submergence.

- "Methane emissions, a major greenhouse gas, may also be emitted in large quantities if insufficient care is taken to remove vegetative matter susceptible to anaerobic microbial processes from the submerged area." (Additionally, it may be noted that that there is continuous large inflow of vegetative matter in reservoirs —Author).
- Submergence of large areas may increase the risk of seismic events.
- Failure of dam structures can be catastrophic.
- Hydro "leads to spread of water borne diseases such as Schistosomiasis."

Yet, surprisingly, the Planning Commission concludes, "Development of hydropower as a clean power source has to be given due priority. Full development of hydro potential while technically feasible, will require timely resolution of issues of water rights, resettlement of project affected people and environmental concerns. These issues can be and must be resolved satisfactorily." Needless to say, this is a false assessment made by ignoring the various costs admitted above; and needs to be revised.

True Costs of Hydro—Case of Kotlibhel 1B

The Planning Commission has recognized certain costs of hydropower and ignored others. These have been assessed by the author for Kotlibhel 1B project at Table 2.14. It is seen that total costs are Rs 705.3 crores against benefits of Rs 155.5 crores. Out of this, costs of Rs 512.5 crores per year are ignored by the Commission. The details of these estimates are provided in the next section of this book. These are extracted and reproduced here to show how greatly the Planning Commission errs in declaring hydropower as clean by ignoring various costs.

Admittedly, these estimates are dependent on many assumptions made by the author. The reader is welcome to make alternative assumptions and arrive at his own

Table 2.13. Benefits form dual pricing for consumer and producer

Sl. No.	*Item*	*Non-peak consumption*	*Peak consumption*	*Total*	*Explanation*
1.	Present rate of supply	Rs 2 per Kwh	Rs 2 per Kwh	-	
2.	Present electricity consumption (notional)	180 Kwh	60 Kwh	240 Kwh	This a notional consumption assumed to explain the point.
3.	Present total cost to the consumer (Row 1 × Row 2)	Rs 360	Rs 120	Rs 480	
4.	Present rate of purchase by SEB	Rs 1 per Kwh	Rs 4 per Kwh	-	Assumed by author
5.	Present cost to the provider (Row 4 x Row 2)	Rs 180	Rs 480	Rs 660	Supplier is incurring a loss of Rs 180. Buying power at Rs 660 and selling at Rs 480.
6.	Revised rate of supply (Suggested rates by author, instead of those prevailing presently as at Row 1)	Rs 1.5 per Kwh	Rs 4 per Kwh	-	Reduce non-peak rates along with increase in peak rates

Sl. No.	Item	Non-peak consumption	Peak consumption	Total	Explanation
7.	Revised electricity consumption (Forecast by author)	210 Kwh	30 Kwh	240 Kwh	Consumer will increase non-peak- and reduce peak consumption
8.	Revised total cost to the consumer (Row 6 × Row 7)	Rs 315	Rs 120	Rs 435	Gain to consumer is Rs 45 with same level of total electricity consumption
9.	Revised rate of purchase (Forecast by author)	Rs 1 per Kwh	Rs 3 per Kwh	-	Price of peak power will decline from Rs 4 to Rs 3 per Kwh with iess demand.
10.	Revised total cost to the provider (Row 9 × Row 7)	Rs 210	Rs 90	Rs 300	Gain to supplier is Rs 360 with same level of total electricity supplied

Table 2.14. Benefits and costs of Kotlibhel 1B (All figures in Rs crore/year)

Sl No	*Item*	*Benefit Estimated by Author*	*Costs Estimated by Author*	*Costs Recognized by Planning Commission*	*Costs Ignored by Planning Commission*
1.	Benefits from generation of power	103.8	-	-	-
2.	12% Free power to State	50.2	-	-	-
3.	Employment	1.5	-	-	-
4.	Sediment	-	99.1	N	99.1
5.	Quality of water	-	98.4	N	98.4
6.	Methane emissions	-	31.7	Y	-
7.	Forests	-	55.3	Y	-
8.	Earthquakes	-	8.4	Y	-
9.	Landslides	-	23.0	N	23.0
10.	Malaria and health	-	21.4	Y	-
11.	Biodiversity	-	11.7	Y	-
12.	Otters	-	20.0	N	20.0
13.	Road accidents	-	7.1	N	7.1
14.	Decline in temperatures	-	7.0	N	7.0
15.	Sand	-	5.8	N	5.8

Sl No	*Item*	*Benefit Estimated by Author*	*Costs Estimated by Author*	*Costs Recognized by Planning Commission*	*Costs Ignored by Planning Commission*
16.	River Rafting	-	8.0	N	8.0
17.	Bridges	-	3.3	N	3.3
18.	Aesthetic value of free-flowing water	-	65.0	N	65.0
19.	Loss of soul and miscellaneous costs	-	5.0	N	5.0
20.	Sub Total: Cost of Kotlibhel 1B HEP	-	470.2	-	341.7
21.	Add 50% due to cascade effect	-	235.1	N	170.8
		155.5	705.3	-	512.5

assessment of benefits and costs. The author's basic objection is that all the costs enumerated above are totally ignored in Environment Impact Assessment of the Kotlibhel 1B project. There is a deliberate attempt to misrepresent the project as beneficial while actually it is a loss proposition.

Implications of CEA Forecasts

It is clear that CEA and Planning Commission are making large over-forecasts of requirement of electricity. Further, electricity required for consumption is presented as required for GDP growth. Higher generation of electricity provides more leg room for increase in T&D losses by the power bureaucracy. Possible reduction in demand from Demand Side Management is wholly ignored. In the result, the country is being pushed at breakneck speed into harnessing nuclear and hydropower for providing more ostentatious consumption for the rich and more opportunities for incurring T&D losses to the power bureaucracy. The country is willing to surrender its economic sovereignty to foreign powers; and willing to destroy our ecology by forced development of hydropower because CEA and Planning Commission have wrongly made us believe that we need this huge amount of power for sustaining economic growth.

3

BENEFITS OF HYDROPOWER: CASE STUDY OF KOTLIBHEL 1B

We have shown in the previous section that Planning Commission portrays hydropower as clean, cost-effective and least disruptive of environment. This author's study, however, shows that this statement is made by ignoring many costs. The true costs of hydropower are enormous. In this chapter we give our assessment of the costs and benefits of one ROR hydropower project namely Kotlibhel 1B proposed by NHPC on Alaknanda River at Dev Prayag.

The benefits from generation of electricity, from free supply of power to the State Government and from generation of employment are discussed first. This is followed by discussion of costs and benefits of one ROR in the next chapter.

Electrical Power

Main benefit from hydropower is that of electricity generation. NHPC has made the project assuming cost of production of Rs 2.37[12] and sale price of Rs 2.80 per unit.

The difference in the cost of production and price of sale is the profit obtained by the NHPC. This is called "producer's surplus" in economics. This is part of benefits that accrue to the country from the project.

Additional benefits accrue to consumers who get power at this price. The quantum of this benefit can be assessed through the marginal product of power. Assume the country is presently using 1 trillion units. It can be assessed how much the next one unit of power will add to the income of the country. Say, the amount added to national income is

Rs 5. This is marginal product. Say, further, the cost of producing this one unit of power is Rs 3. In that case, the benefit to the consumer or consumer's surplus is estimated at Rs 2. The consumer gets a unit of electricity at Rs 3 while the value of that unit for him is Rs 5. This is the net gain to the country via the consumer.

However, let us say, power is available aplenty from other sources at a price of Rs 4. The consumer will buy power from this other source as long as he produces Rs 4.10 worth of goods from one unit. In this way, he will continue to buy power until the value produced from an additional unit is equal to the price. This means that the consumer's marginal product does not exceed the price at which power is freely available.

The total benefit from hydropower is the sum of profit obtained by the producer plus the consumer surplus generated by the consumer. A notional calculation of the total benefit on above basis is given below.

Table 3.1. Notional calculation of benefits from hydropower

Sl. No.	*Item*	*Cost, per unit*	*Sale price or marginal product, per unit*	*Net Benefit, per unit*
1.	Benefit obtained by producer ('producer's surplus')	2.37	2.80	0.43
2.	Benefit obtained by the consumer ('consumer's surplus')	2.80	4.00	1.20
3.	Total benefit to the nation	2.37	4.00	1.63

It is clear from above table that total benefit does not change with the price of sale. Total benefit to the nation is the difference between the cost of production by the producer and the marginal product obtained by the consumer. The cost of production is known from the DPR-ES of NHPC. Question is how to estimate the marginal product?

The problem is made complicated because of limited supply of power. The price of power is determined administratively. Excess demand is managed by power cuts rather than by increasing the sale price.

Let us say the marginal product of power is Rs 10. The consumer will continue to buy power till the price increases to Rs 10. But the price of power is administratively fixed at, say, Rs 2 per unit. Thus market mechanism only tells us that marginal product is greater than Rs 2 per unit but fails to give an estimate of the same. In these circumstances, we are left with no alternative but to make our own estimate of the marginal product of power. We assess this at Rs 3.30 per unit on the following basis:

- NTPC Vidyut Vyapar tells us the sale price of peak power was Rs 2.65 against average price of Rs 2.05 in 2004 (NTPC 2004). The difference between price of peak power and average price is Rs 0.60 per unit
- The average sale price of peak power in 2004 by NTPC Vidyut Vyapar was Rs 2.65 per unit. This is a good proxy of marginal product. This works out to Rs 2.87 per unit at 2006 prices. Against this, we have assumed Rs 3.30 per unit. The sale price of Rs 5 to Rs 6 for peak power, as reported from anecdotal sources, is probably the price for short-term demand in special circumstances.
- The sale price of base power is Rs 2. The maximum sale price of peak power is Rs 5 to Rs 6. The true price is likely to be somewhere in the middle.
- NHPC appears to have assumed a price of Rs 2.00 for base power and Rs 4.00 for peak power leading to average of Rs 2.80 as mentioned in DPR-ES (please see end note 13).

On the considerations a value of Rs 3.30 per unit for marginal product seems appropriate. The reader is welcome to make alternate estimate of the marginal product and, thus, social benefits of power.

The Kotlibhel projects are located downstream of peaking stations—Tehri on Bhagirathi and Srinagar on Alaknanda. The water discharged from Srinagar HEP will flow as a huge wave during peaking hours into the reservoir of Kotlibhel 1B which will, therefore, produce more electricity during the peak hours. Kotlibhel 1B is approved as pure ROR project. It will discharge as much water it receives at any time of the day so as to maintain a constant level of water in the reservoir. However, it will receive most water only during peaking hours hence will also produce power and discharge water only during peaking hours. Thus the Kotlibhel 1B project, when seen in conjunction with Srinagar project, de facto becomes a peaking station. The same situation continues downstream. Kotlibhel 2 will de facto become a peaking station because upstream Kotlibhel 1B will discharge most water during peaking hours. In this way, Kotlibhel projects are smuggled-in as ROR schemes while they actually provide peak power.

The benefits from Kotlibhel 1B are calculated in table 3.2 based on marginal product of Rs 3.30 per unit.

Table 3.2. Benefits of electricity generated from Kotlibhel 1B

Sl. No.	*Item*	*Amount*	*Basis*
1.	Total sale of electric power	111.6 crore units	Please see end note 13. This excludes free power to state, benefits from which are calculated separa-tely in the next section.
2.	Cost of production	Rs 2.37 per unit	DPR-ES
3.	Marginal product	Rs 3.30 per unit	Author's estimate.
4.	Social Benefit per unit	Rs 0.93 per unit	Line 3 – Line 2.
4.	Social Benefit, total	Rs 103.8 crore per year	111.6 Crore units × Rs 0.93 per unit.

It may be noted that the price at which power is sold by NHPC makes no difference to this calculation. Increase in sale price raises the benefits to NHPC and reduces the benefits to consumer. Reduction in sale price does the opposite. The total remains unchanged in either case.

Free Power to Host State

NHPC is to supply 12 percent free power to the host state. The benefits to Uttarakhand from this are estimated in Table 3.3.

Table 3.3. Benefits of free power to the State

Sl No	*Item*	*Value*	*Basis*
1.	Free peak power to state	15.2 crore units	12% of 126.8 crore units total generation
2.	Marginal product or total benefit	Rs 3.30 per unit	Cost is assumed as zero since this is supplied free.
3.	Total benefit to state	Rs 50.2 crore per year	

Employment

Number of employees in the three Kotlibhel projects as at October 2007 was 215 according to information provided by NHPC under RTI Act. We assume this will increase to 450 persons in the operation stage. Of this one-third or 150 persons will be in Kotlibhel 1B. The benefits from creation of employment are calculated below.

Table 3.4. Benefits from creation of employment

Sl. No.	*Item*	*Value*	*Basis*
1.	Additional salaries paid by NHPC to its employees	Rs 0.97 lac per employee	The average salary of employees is Rs 1.33 lac per year according to Balance Sheet of NHPC. We assume Rs 36,000 per year would be earned by these employees in absence of employment with NHPC. The incremental income is Rs 0.97 lacs per person.
2.	Benefits from employment	Rs 1.5 crore per year	150 employees × Rs 0.97 lacs per year = Rs 1.455 crore per year

This is the direct benefit from employment generation. Further benefits are obtained from secondary employment in taxis, shops, etc. These have not been calculated because similar secondary costs also occur from loss of sediments, etc. These secondary benefits and costs are both ignored in our calculation.

4

COSTS OF HYDROPOWER : CASE STUDY OF KOTLIBHEL 1B

In this chapter we have estimated the costs of producing hydropower from Kotlibhel 1B project. Some costs are included in the project design. These include the cost of land acquistion, relief and rehabilitation, compensatory afforestation, etc. These costs are not enumerated here because these are paid for in the price of Rs. 2.37 per unit estimated by NHPC. In this section we estimate only those costs that are not included in the project design. These are 'hidden' costs that are not included in the project design. These are costs that are surreptitiously imposed upon the society by the project. These costs are calculated here for Kotlibhel 1B. Every hydropower project is unique. These calculations have to be suitably modified for other projects. However, the framework given below can be used to make calculations for other projects.

Sediment

The Issue

Dams trap sediment in the reservoirs. ROR dams with barrages make small reservoirs to de-silt the water so that particles of sand do not damage the turbines. Larger projects like Kotlibhel 1B make huge reservoirs that settle sediment and prevent its flow downstream. This deprives the downstream areas of silt.

The silt deposited by the rivers is responsible for the making of the Ganges plains: "A recent study carried out by Rajiv Sinha, of Geoscience group, IIT Kanpur has brought to light amazing quantity of sediment load carried by the Ganga River in its present hydrodynamic regime. Gangetic Rivers erode bulk of the sediments from upstream areas in the Himalayas and deposit part of it in the alluvial plains and a significant part in the Bay of Bengal" (Joshi 2006a).

R. J. Wasson of Centre for Resource and Environmental Studies, Australian National University, Canberra, Australia has estimated sediment balance of the Ganges river as given at table 4.1. (Wasson 2003).

Table 4.1. Sediment Balance of the Ganga (million tons/year)

Source		*Use (million tons / year)*	
High Himalayas	635	Ganges flood plains	65
Low Himalayas	159	Bangladesh flood plains	361
		Bay of Bengal via Hoogly	328
		Bay of Bengal via Bangladesh	40
Total	794	Total	794

The construction of dams on Himalayan Rivers arrests the flow of this sediment to the downstream areas. This sediment flows into the Bay of Bengal up to the equator. The flow of sediment is critical in maintaining the coastline of the country. The sea has a tendency to erode our coasts. This tendency is counteracted by deposition of silt by the rivers. Construction of dams on the rivers, therefore, leads to the erosion of our coasts.

Consequence of Trapping of Sediment in Reservoirs

Girish Gopinath and others of Department of Marine Geology and Geophysics, Cochin University of Science and Technology, Cochin have studied the Sagar Island in West Bengal (Gopinath 2005). They give the area eroded and accreted as follows:

Table 4.2. Erosion of coast at Ganga Sagar

Sl. No.	*Years*	*Area Eroded (km2)*	*Area Accreted (km2)*	*Net Area Eroded per year (km2)*
1.	1967-96 (30 years)	29.8	6.03	0.79
2.	1996-99 (3 years)	16.9	0.48	5.47

It is seen that the net rate of erosion has increased about seven times in 1996-99 compared to the previous 30 years. Dams have made a huge contribution to this.

Hema Malini and Nageswara Rao have estimated a net loss of 1836 ha of land during the past three decades along Godavari delta shoreline. They attributed this to the reduced sediment supply from an annual average of 145 million tons in 1971-79 to 87 million tons in 1980-89 and 56 million tons in 1990-98 due to construction of a number of dams in the period (Rao, undated).

The Geological Survey of Japan tells us: "It is estimated that about 30% of the global sediments previously discharged to the oceans are now trapped in reservoirs behind dams. Because of the construction of the Aswan and Aswan High dams, the Nile River mouth area has experienced serious erosion, retreating more than 4 km during the last hundred years. Over the last 30 years, dam construction and increased water consumption have caused a dramatic decrease in the amount of sediment and water discharged from the Yellow River (Huanghe) in China, which previously was the second largest river in the world, after the Ganges–Brahmaputra, in terms of sediment discharge. During the 1980s, sediment discharge from the Yellow River dropped to 70% that during the 1960s–1970s and to 30% during the 1990s. Moreover, since the Xiaolangzi Dam began operation in 1999, discharge has become less than 10% that during the 1960s–1970s, resulting in serious coastal erosion" (Goodbred 2005).

The building of dams on the Ganga will similarly deprive our coastal areas of the sediment and lead to their erosion.

The Government of India has established Coastal Protection And Development Advisory Committee (CPDAC) that had prepared a Rs 1,600-crore National Coastal Protection Project (NCPP) in 1998 (Sudhi 1998). The need for such expenditures arises because we do not allow the rivers to do their work.

This author has studied the last four minutes of CPDAC (4th to 7th) available on the net. This author is unable to find any discussion of impact of dams in the minutes of CPDAC. It seems erosion of coasts is a Kamadhenu for CPDAC—more monies are sought to 'prevent' erosion of the coast while maintaining an eerie silence on the erosion created by dams. The main points covered in the minutes of the 7th meeting, for example, are as follows:

- To sort out inconsistencies in coastal lengths from various sources.
- To organise a coordinated programme of collection, compilation, evaluation and publication of data relating to various natural phenomenon and coastal processes, which affect the coastline.
- To organise general investigation, studies and research with the help of central and state engineering research institutions.
- To lay down principles in construction techniques of coastal protection measures for the guidance of state authorities.
- To review the performance of the works carried out by the States and evolve improved design techniques based on such experience from time to time.
- National cyclone mitigation project.

There is no effort to stamp out the problem of erosion at the root—i.e. by stopping construction of dams.

It is not easy to reverse this impact of deprivation of sediment. The cost of decommissioning of a dam becomes very high because of the silt that is accumulated (WCD 2000a:92).

Sediment-hungry Waters Downstream

Trapping of sediment in reservoirs makes the water 'clean', which, also means that it has higher capacity to absorb sediment downstream. These sediment-free waters undertake a cutting action on the riverbed downstream. Patrick McCully, in his study of dams titled *Silenced Rivers,* tells us "Clear water below a dam is said to be 'hungry': it will seek to recapture its sediment load by eroding the bed and banks of the river... Over time, all the easily erodable material on the riverbed below the dam will eventually be removed, and the bed will become 'armoured' with rocks... Riverbeds are typically eroded by several meters within a decade of first closing of dams. Within nine years of closure of Hoover Dam, hungry waters had washed away more than 110 million cubic meters of material from the first 145 kilometres of riverbed below the dam, lowering it in places by more than 4 meters. The deepening of the Colorado has undermined bridge foundations and rendered useless numerous intakes for the supply of municipal and irrigation waters" (1998).

These environmental impacts are wholly neglected in EIAs. In particular, the stretch between Kaudiyala and Rishikesh which is left for river rafting by NHPC may get affected by such cutting and impose huge costs on tourists and local people alike.

ROR Projects are as Harmful as Storage Projects

Hydropower experts assert that ROR dams are benign towards sediment in comparison to storage dams like Tehri. Sediment is flushed at regular intervals hence permanent deprivation does not take place. This is not convincing. Trapping of sediment for say, 15 days, and then flushing it in one go, creates a 'wave' of sediment flow. It is certain to change the carrying capacity of sediment by rivers. Just as butter taken out of milk, when reintroduced into the same milk, does not create the same taste and texture, similarly, flushing of sediment does not recreate the earlier natural balance.

Flushing of HEP reservoirs may lead to some of the arrested sediments being discharged. However, this may not be carried to the coast because it will come in intense spurts. Further, the ability of the coast to absorb such spurts of sediments is also to be examined. The coastline may be able to absorb slow deposition like layers of paper but not sudden discharges like those by muddy streams.

Proof of deprivation of sediment in ROR dams is available from survey of three HEPs in Uttarakhand.

Table 4.3. Is there more or less sediment in the water downstream of dam? (Details in Annexure 1)

Sl. No.	*Item*	*Net, HEP-wise Impact (Number of respondents affirming/number of total respondents)*
1.	Chilla	Reduced 1/9 = (-) 11%
2.	Maneri	Reduced 1/4 = (-) 25%
3.	Tehri	Reduced 1/6 = (-) 17%
4.	Combined	(-) 18%

People living near the three dams confirmed availability of less sand. Reduced availability means that sediment is trapped in reservoir.

Ignoring Consequences

EIA of Srinagar HEP says, "The annual silt load in the dam is 7.62 Mm3, and in due course of time (9.184 years) the dead storage will be silted up. However, as the spillway gates will be frequently operated, the accumulated silt behind the gates will be flushed out" (WAPCOS 2001:72). The silting up of the dead storage implies that sediment will be deprived to downstream areas. Flushing will only remove silt 'behind the gates' leaving silt on tail end as it is.

EIA of Kotlibhel 1B dismisses this problem with the following statement: "Since Kotlibhel 1B HEP is going to be located downstream of Srinagar Hydropower Scheme hence the sedimentation in the reservoir is not going to be a serious problem as the quantum of sediments flowing to the reservoir will be the sediments coming out of the Srinagar HEP and the sediments generated over 371 sq km, which is the intermediate catchment between both projects" (HNBU 2006a). Read this in conjunction with the statement in EIA of Srinagar HEP that the entire dead storage will get silted up in 10 years. Thereafter, the silt will flow into reservoir of Kotlibhel 1B and Kotlibhel 2 and they too will get silted up probably in 10 years each. The downstream areas will be deprived of sediment for about 30 years wholly; and the flow will continue to remain disturbed thereafter.

EIA of Kotlibhel 2, after listing the various ROR HEPs proposed above Kaudiyala concludes: "The sediment load will decrease considerably once all the above stated projects are commissioned and made operational" (ICFRE: 69).

These statements leave no doubt that these ROR projects will deprive downstream areas of sediment.

Cost of Sediment

The Author has estimated the loss of our coastal areas due to deprivation of sediments from three studies given in Table below.

Table 4.4. Estimates of cost of coastal erosion due to deprivation of sediment

Estimate 1: From Sagar Islands in Ganga Delta
Erosion of Sagar Coastline = 5.47 km2/year (Gopinath 2005). This is on a coast length of 12 km (Paul 1987).
Erosion of Indian coastline = 227 km2/year (on pro-rata basis for 500 km coastal length likely to be affected by the Ganga).
Reduce 75% for lesser erosion of mainland coast in comparison to an island = 57 km2 or 5700 ha/year.
Reduce 50% for lesser eıosion along distant areas of 500 km coastal length. Erosion will be less in distant areas = 2850 ha/year.

Estimate 2: From Godavari River

Erosion of Godavari Coastline = 1836 ha in 30 years (Rao, undated) or 61.2 ha/year.

Erosion of Ganga coastline = 612 ha/year (assuming rate of silt deposition from Ganga is 10 times that of Godavari).

Estimate 3: From Egypt coastline

Erosion of Egypt Coastline = 4 km in 100 years (Goodbred 2005).

Erosion of Egypt coastline during last 50 years = 3 km (assuming more erosion in the last 50 years due to Aswan Dam made in the fifties); or 60 metres/year.

Erosion of Indian coastline = 60 meters/year (assuming same rate of erosion after construction of HEPs).

Area eroded = 500 km coastline × 60 meters/year = 30 km2/year or 3000 ha/year.

Less 50 % for the long coastline. Distant areas will be affected less than the moths of the delta. Area eroded = 1500 ha/year.

The average of the three estimates above is 1654 ha/year. However, we take the lower estimate on basis of erosion of Ganga Sagar Islands at 547 ha/year. Accordingly, the cost due to Kotlibhel 1B HEP is calculated below.

Table 4.5. Cost of erosion of coasts due to Kotlibhel 1B

Sl. No.	*Item*	*Amount (Rs crore per year)*	*Basis*
1.	Annual erosion of Sagar Islands	5.47 km2 or 547 Ha/year	(Gopinath 2005)
2.	Estimated pro-rata erosion of India's coasts	22,791 Ha/year	Loss of 547 ha/year is taking place on a coast length of 12 km (Paul 1987). It is estimated that sediment reaches up the equator (Wasson 2003). We assume that 500 km of India's coast will be deprived of sediment loss from the Ganga. The erosion is estimated in this proportion: 547×500/12.

3.	Lesser erosion in distant areas	11,395 Ha/ year	Assume only 50% of above because less erosion of distant areas will take place.
4.	Contribution of Tehri HEP	1,139 Ha/ year	Assume 10% of this is contribution of Tehri Dam.
5.	Contribution of Kotlibhel 1B	113 Ha/year	Assume 10% of Tehri. The entire sediment flowing from Alaknanda will be trapped in the three reservoir-type ROR HEPs Srinagar, Kotlibhel 1A and 2. These may be considered to contribute 33% each to the same. However, we take a lesser figure to avoid unnecessary criticism.
6.	Value of Contribution of Kotlibhel 1B	Rs 71 crore/ year	Value of land acquired for HEPs in this area is Rs 1 crore per Ha. We take a price of Rs. 63 lacs per Ha this being in coastal area.

This author feels this is a huge underestimate. The country spent thousands of crores to recover few square kilometres lands from Pakistan during Kargil War. The cost of land lost will be much more than the commercial price. In any case, the Dam Companies are welcome to make alternative estimates and place before the country for scrutiny. This author's main objection is that Dam Companies, together with EIA Agencies, have chosen to ignore these huge costs. Having failed to discharge their solemn duty they cannot turn around and attack these estimates as unreal without producing alternative estimates on a scientific basis.

Depriving Flood-recession Agriculture of Nutrients

Another downstream impact of arresting of sediments is that flood-recession agriculture is deprived of nutrients.

Large areas of the country are flooded every year. The rivers bring nutrients and deposit it on the farmlands. Farmers cultivate these lands after the water recedes. The deposition of nutrients contained in silt will be less upon arrest of the same in HEP reservoirs. An estimate of this cost is made below.

Table 4.6. Estimate of cost to flood-recession agriculture from Kotlibhel 1B.

Sl. No.	*Item*	*Amount*	*Basis*
1.	Area under flood-recession agriculture	615,216 Ha	The area under flood-recession agriculture in Indus River plains is 1,230,552 ha ((FAO 2007). In absence of data for India we assume one-half the figure for the Ganges plains
2.	Value of production from this land	1,238,086 tonnes	According to Economic Survey published by Ministry of Finance, the production in Rabi in 2005-6 was 98.6 million tons from 49.0 million ha land or 2.01 tonnes/ha.
3.	Production lost due to nutrient deprivation from low-sediment floods	61,904 tonnes	Being 5% of the production—Author's best estimate.
4.	Contribution of Kotlibhel 1B	3,095 tonnes	Assume 5% contribution of total.
5.	Value of loss due to Kotlibhel 1B	Rs 3.1 crore/year	At rate of Rs 10,000 per tonne for grains.

Cost of Deterioration of Relations with Bangladesh

Deprivation of sediment will have a huge negative impact on Bangladesh. The silt load balance mentioned at the beginning of this chapter tells us that 401 million tons out of total 794 million tons sediment of the Ganga goes to Bangladesh every year. The ROR HEPs being made on Ganga will deprive Bangladesh of this life-saving material.

This is likely to lead to deterioration of mutual relations. Let us remember that India had to bend to Bangladesh's demands on Farakka Barrage on similar grounds (Prakash 1997). That investment has consequently become a near waste. It is likely that Bangladesh will create objections to these dams in due course and these may have to be decommissioned.

This deprivation of sediment to Bangladesh will lead to faster erosion of its coastal areas. This can create havoc in conjunction with rise in sea water levels due to global warming. In consequence, it is possible that there will be a huge influx of people wishing to escape drowning into India. This will impose a huge cost on us.

Deprivation of sediment to Bangladesh is against the principle of *Vasudev Kutumbakam*—whole world is one family. It is against the Constitutional mandate that we must strive to maintain friendly relations with our neighbours.

It is difficult to place a monetary value on these impacts. However, the author's least estimate is Rs 500 crores per year. Of this 5% or Rs 25 crores may be imputed to Kotlibhel 1B.

Benefits from Reduced need of Barrages like Farakka

Some benefits may accrue from arresting of sediment in HEP reservoirs. This would lead to less need for constructing structures like Farakka Barrage to flush the Hoogly of the sediment. Such costs will be saved. This saving is estimated at table 4.7.

Table 4.7. Benefit from reduced need of downstream flushing

Sl. No.	*Item*	*Amount*	*Basis*
1.	Cost of Farakka Barrage	Rs 156.49 crore	(Prakash 1997)
2.	Annualized capital cost	Rs 15.6 crore per year	Annual cost assumed 10% of capital cost at 10% interest rate.
3.	Maintenance cost	Rs 1 crore per year	Author's best estimate.
4.	Total cost	Rs 16.6 crore per year	
5.	Saving due to all HEPs	Rs 12.5 crore per year	Say 75% of the cost is recovered from silt centre.
6.	Saving due to Kotlibhel 1B HEP	Rs 0.6 crores per year	5% of all HEPs.

Benefits from Less Cost of Filtering Potable Water

The cost of clarifying river water for potable use will be less if sediment is arrested upstream. The benefit is estimated at Table 4.8.

Table 4.8. Benefits from lower cost of potable water

Sl. No.	*Item*	*Amount*	*Basis*
1.	Population affected	20 crore persons	Approximate riverine population of Ganges Basin.
2.	Urban population enjoying piped water supply	6.7 crore persons	Say, 33% of total riverine population.
3.	Urban population enjoying water supply from Ganges system	3.4 crore persons	Say, 50% draw water from Ganga River.
4.	Total cost of water supply to Municipal authorities	Rs 266 crores	Rs 121 per capita. Guwahati incurred cost of Rs 10.8 crores for supplying water to 8.9 lac persons (JNNURM 2006)
5.	Total saving due to less sediment	Rs 5.3 crores	Say, 2% saving.
6.	Saving due to Kotlibhel 1B HEP	Rs 0.5 crores per year	Say, 10% of total savings.

Other negative impacts will take place on fish catches. Fishes will be deprived of nutrients. However this is ignored in absence of data.

GOI is not Concerned

The Government of India is blissfully unconcerned with the erosion of the nation's coasts. The Central Water Commission has given the following replies to this author in response to query under RTI Act.

Table 4.9. Response of Central Water Commission on Erosion of Coasts

Sl. No.	*Question*	*Response (Dated 8.4.2008)*
1.	List of studies, minutes or reports (along with number of pages) available with CWC or CPDAC regarding the impact of dams on our coasts.	No such studies, minutes or reports are available with CPDAC regarding the impact of dams on our coasts.
2.	Copies of all project proposal or report of all projects relating to erosion of coasts at Gangasagar.	No project proposal or reports relating to erosion of coasts at Gangasagar have been received in this office.
3.	Has CWC or CPDAC drawn attention of Ministry of Power on the adverse effects of hydropower dams on our coasts? Please provide copies of letters, minutes, reports, etc.	CPDAC has not interacted with Ministry of Power in respect of effects of hydropower dams on our coasts.
4.	Is CPDAC aware that dams are holding sediment and leading to erosion of our coasts? Is CWC aware that dams are holding sediment and leading to erosion of our coasts?	Generally, retention of sediments by dams may not be significant factor contributing to erosion of coast.

Cost of Sediment

The total cost imposed by Kotlibhel 1B upon the nation because of sediment is estimated at Table 4.10 :

Table 4.10. Total cost of sediment lost

Sl. No.	*Item*	*Amount (Rs. crore per year)*
1.	Erosion of coastlands	71
2.	Loss to flood-recession Agriculture	3.1
3.	Cost of maintaining friendly relations with Bangladesh	25
4.	Benefit from less cost of making barrages like Farakka	(-) 0.6
5.	Benefit from less cost of clarifying potable water	(-) 0.5
	Total	Rs 98 crore/year

Quality of water

The Issue

Dam Companies argue that ROR HEPs do not store water for long periods or obstruct flow of the river and are, therefore, benign. It is argued in this section that such is not the case. ROR HEPs decisively alter the nature of river and negatively impact the quality of its waters for the following reasons:

- The river is altered into a reservoir.
- Water is deprived of oxygen.
- Water is deprived of chemicals.
- Water is sullied due to creation of greenhouse gasses in reservoirs.
- Cellular memory of water is hit.

A Reservoir does not Make a River

A river is defined as follows:

- Web Dictionary: "a large natural stream of water" (Webdictionary 2008).
- Free Dictionary: "A natural collection of waters, arising from springs or fountains, which flow in a

bed or canal of considerable width and length, towards the sea" (TheFreeDictionary 2008).

- Wikipedia: "A river is a natural waterway that transits water through a landscape from higher to lower elevations called divides" (Wikipedia 2008).
- Encyclopedia of Earth: "Rivers are natural watercourses, flowing over the surface in extended hollow formations (i.e., channels)" (Herbert 2007)

The characteristics of a river noticed from above definitions are not secured in reservoir-based HEPs. These definitions as applied to Kotlibhel 2 HEP are given below. This HEP proposes to convert the Confluence of Bhagirathi and Alaknanda at Dev Prayag into the tail end of a reservoir. The level of water in this reservoir is to be maintained at present average monthly levels.

Table 4.11. Definition of 'River' applied to Kotlibhel 2 Reservoir.

Sl. No.	*Definition*	*Applied to Kotlibhel 2 Reservoir*
1.	River is a stream of water	The tail end of Kotlibhel 2 Reservoir is a 'reservoir'. It is not a stream.
2.	River flows in a bed.	The flow at Dev Prayag will be in a lake, not in a riverbed. The water will be held by backpressure from dam, not by sides of the riverbed.
3.	A river transits water from higher to lower elevations.	There will be no transition from higher to lower elevation. The water will have constant elevation.
4.	Rivers flow in channels.	There will be no channel. It will be a reservoir.

It is submitted that the nature of Confluence is fundamentally altered by the Project. Mere maintenance of constant level does not retain its character; rather it destroys its character. A River in our culture is a free flowing living deity or person. This author had an occasion to stay at Dev Prayag for a week in the winter of 1995 before the Tehri Dam was made. The level of water would rise and fall between morning and evening by about two feet. Perhaps this was due to greater melt flowing during day time. The author felt that the river was breathing. The level of water rose and fell just at it does in a human being's chest. The river will be deprived of such breathing. It is as if a human being is put into an iron cask which does not allow any movement in the chest.

Why River is Better than Reservoir

Two hydropower experts have, while commenting on earlier version of this report, said that a lake is more valuable than river.

Comment 1: "Why is not a lake more valuable as it can be used for recreation, fisheries, perhaps even some irrigation?"

Comment 2: "The established trend is that water usable by tourists (in a lake) fetches better tourism value than non-usable running water. Compare Nainital with Karna Prayag: had it not been for religious reasons, no tourist would visit and spend time and money at Karna Prayag."

This is a serious objection. This author's response is as follows:

River has higher prana than reservoir: Every matter in this universe is form of energy. Man's role is to raise a matter from lower to higher form of energy or *prana*. When a root takes material from soil and converts it into grains and then grains are eaten by a scientist, the level of prana embodied in the soil rises. This is 'development'. On the other hand, when a wooden sculpture of Jesus is burnt as fuel wood then there is decline in level of prana. A river has higher level of prana than reservoir. Every particle of water in the river is dancing, singing and mingling while it is stagnant in a reservoir as if a person is put into jail.

Natural lakes do not reduce prana: Water flows down from a natural lake in the open. The total elevation from which the water flows freely is not reduced. It is only held back for a while. The water flowing from Nainital Lake again absorbs the chemicals and oxygen, irrigates plants and provides habitat for butterflies as it flows down from the lake. The prana of water is not reduced. Not so in a HEP reservoir. The down flow is through tunnel etc. where the prana is extracted and converted into energy. Hence, the two are qualitatively different.

Man should interact with nature purposefully: Nature, in her wisdom, creates many things such as malaria and fungus that appear undesirable to man. Man interacts and modifies nature by his activities like any other plant or animal. Wisdom lies in interacting in a manner that leads to development of prana. Man does not propagate malaria despite the fact that is found in nature. Similarly, existence of natural reservoirs does not mean that we must convert rivers into reservoirs.

Pleasure versus good: Tourists at Nainital benefit from the lake. Pilgrims at Karna Prayag benefit from the river. We have to decide which is higher. Watching the movie and studying for exams are both good for the student but the mother asks him to forego movie and study for exams. Similarly, the gains from pilgrimage are higher than from tourism. Pilgrimage caters to the higher inner needs while tourism caters to the lower sensual needs.

Ryan (undated), explains the meaning of pilgrimage: "Much of Christian pilgrimage has been an attempt to follow, in a literal sense, the 'footsteps' of Christ, retracing his walks and seeing the sites and the landscapes that he himself would have encountered. Many people feel that, in this way, they can make a closer and more meaningful connection with the texts of the Bible." Jesus' consciousness would have entered the places which he traversed. Following that route helps the pilgrim become one with Jesus' consciousness. Such travel involves many physical troubles though the pilgrim happily bears them in order to invigorate his inner self. Thus, we must give up physical pleasure of tourism and seek the spiritual benefits of pilgrimage.

The tourist consumes material things while the pilgrim abstains from them. The tourist wants a comfortable mattress while the pilgrim sleeps on the sand in the Kumbh mela. The tourist wants running hot water in his tiled bathroom while the pilgrim enjoys the cold waters of the Ganga. The tourist is extrovert and looks at the paintings and the markets, smells the scents and listens to music while the pilgrim is introvert and sits quietly listening to the discourse of the guru. The pilgrim journeys to experience a "source of awe," to answer an inner call, to give thanks, to express love of God, to draw near something sacred. The pilgrim enjoys abstinence. Pilgrimage requires that we maintain free flow in our rivers.

This author's plea is not to close all tourism. It is to develop tourism in barren deserts of the Thar. The low prana of the sand is uplifted at higher level with the trampling of tourists' feet and the vibrations of their singing film tunes. But the opposite takes place when we convert rivers into reservoirs. The higher prana of a free-flowing river is pushed down into a lower prana of a reservoir—no song, dance and mist. Between a river and reservoir, we should choose the former because it provides benefits at a higher level.

Alaknanda Waters are not Clean

The Central Pollution Control Board gives the parameters for the assessment of quality of water as given at Table 4.12. Of these 1-3 are the critical parameters according to CPCB (undated). Accordingly, the waters of Alaknanda River are not of Quality 'A' or 'B'. The waters of Alaknanda River fail these specificatuons. In the period November-April the BOD is higher than specified and during May-October coliforms are above the specified levels as shown Table 4.13. Therefore, waters of Alknanda River

Table 4.12. Primary Water Quality Criteria for Various Uses of Fresh Waters (CPCB undated).

Sl. No.	*Characteristics*	*A : Drinking water source*	*B : Outdoor bathing*	*C : Drinking water source with conventional treatment*	*D : Propagation of wildlife, fisheries*	*E : Irrigation, industrial cooling*
1.	Dissolved oxygen (DO), mg/l, Min	6	5	4	4	-
2.	Biochemical oxygen demand (BOD), mg/l, Max	2	2.5*	3	-	-
3.	Total Coliforms, MPN/100 ml, Max.	50	500	5,000	-	-
4.	pH Value	6.5-8.5	6.5-8.5	6-9	6.5-8.5	6.5-8.5
5.	Free ammonia (as N), mg/l Max	-	-	-	1.2	-
6.	Electrical Conductivity Micromhos.cm, Max	-	-	-	-	2,250
7.	Sodium adsorption Ratio, Max.	-	-	-	-	26
8.	Boron, mg/l, Max	-	-	-	-	2

* The CPCB mentions value of '3' for BOD for both for B and C quality waters. This is perhaps due to rounding off. Considering the progressive nature of pollution, we substitute 2.5 for 3.

Table 4.13. Alaknanda waters reckoned on CPCB parameters.

Sl No		*CPCB Parameters*			*Status of Alaknanda waters*			
		A: Drinking water source	*B: Out door bathing*	*C:Drinking water sources with conventional treatment*	*Spring Feb, Mar, Apr)*	*Summer (May, Jun, Jul)*	*Monsoon (Aug, Sep, Oct)*	*Winter (Nov, Dec, Jan)*
1.	Dissolved oxygen (DO), mg/l, Min	6	5	4	9.4	7.9	7.2	9.4
2.	Biochemical oxygen demand (BOD), mg/l, Max	2	2.5	3	3.0	2.2	2.2	3.4
3.	Total Coliforms organism MPN/100 ml, Max.	50	500	5,000	170-250	340-900	550-1500	-
	Fails 'A' and 'B' Quality Parameters on				BOD	Coliforms	Coliforms	BOD

Source: HNBU (2006b).

are already not fit for drinking or outdoor bathing. Creation of reservoirs will only lead to further deterioration in the same.

The impounding of river waters in a reservoir prevents rapid flow during which it absorbs oxygen from the air. This oxygen is necessary for cleaning the water. Micro organisms convert inflowing organic matter (C-H compounds) into CO2 and H2O if oxygen is available. This is measured as BOD (Biological Oxygen Demand) of water—i.e. how much oxygen is required to cleanup the biological material in the water.

The water of Alaknanda is already polluted and not fit for bathing. Creation of reservoir will cause further deterioration in the same. The building of a cascade of dams from Badrinath to Kaudiyala will not provide free flow to Alaknanda River to regenerate level of oxygen. The stretch after Kaudiyala has low gradient hence little oxygen may be absorbed. CPCB data indicate that the quality of Ganga waters progressively deteriorates as the river moves downstream. DO declines from 9.3 to 6.0, BOD increases from 1.4 to 2.0 and Coliforms increases from 20 to 15,500. (Table 4.14).

The reduction of DO and increase of BOD and Coliforms from the construction of upstream reservoirs, therefore, is likely to persist downstream. Bhagirathi may presently self-rectify its water after Tehri Dam because of the free mountainous flow from Tehri to Dev Prayag. This is not likely to happen after construction of a cascade of dams on Bhagirathi-Alaknanda-Ganga. In the result, the Ganga may stink after building of these dams.

The EIA of Kotlibhel 1B, after enumerating the composition of various inorganic chemicals in the water of Alaknanda River concludes: "The water in general is of good quality." In doing so, it ignores the fact that the water does not meet the standards for even 'B' quality as per CPCB norms. The fact that BOD and Coliforms levels are high is

Table 4.14. Water Quality of Rivers in Ganga Basin-2005 (CPCB 2005).

Location	*D.O. (Mg/L)*			*B.O.D. (Mg/L)*			*Total Coliforms (Mpn/100 Ml)*		
	Min	*Max*	*Mean*	*Min*	*Max*	*Mean*	*Min*	*Max*	*Mean*
Rishikesh	7.0	10.2	9.3	1.4	1.4	1.4	13	23	20
Kanpur	5.3	8.8	7.0	1.0	2.9	1.8	2300	21000	8713
Patina	7.5	9.4	8.1	2.0	2.1	2.0	1100	90000	23122
Diamond Harbour	4.7	6.9	6.0	0.9	3.2	2.0	7000	30000	15500

recognized in tables 5.4a and 5.5 of the EIA but no inference or plan of action is made thereon.

Chemical Quality of Ganga Waters

Waters of the Ganga River appear to have special chemical quality. In a study of Alaknanda River, Abhay Kumar Singh and Syed I. Hasnain of School of Environmental Sciences, Jawaharlal Nehru University say: "a relatively high contribution of (Ca+Mg) to the total captions (TZ+) and high (Ca+Mg)/(Na+K) ratio indicate that the carbonate weathering could be the primary source of the major ions to these waters" (Singh 1998). This observation tells us that rubbing with stones impart this quality to the waters of Ganga. HEP Projects deprive waters of this rubbing hence will certainly damage this property.

A study by NEERI indicates that Ganga may have small amount of beneficent radioactivity: The study titled "Self Purification Capacity of River Bhagirathi: Impact of Tehri Dam," says: "Quantification of U3O8, ThO2 and percent of K in sediment samples and comparison of these parameters with those present in other river sediment samples and freshwater lake sediment samples showed that Bhagirathi/ Ganga sediments were more radioactive than those collected from some of the aquatic bodies in Central India."

Prof G D Agarwal, former Member-Secretary of CPCB has kindly provided to this author two studies of Ganga waters. Devendra Swaroop Bhargava has shown that sewage settles three times as fast in Ganga waters than with those of the Yamuna. He has hypothesised that exocellular polymers and micro organisms present in Ganga act as coagulants (Bhargwa 1977). These polymers and micro organisms probably enter the waters as the river flows down the hill. The water will be deprived of these qualities after the flow occurs through canals, tunnels and reservoirs.

Another study by Kashi Prasad confirms that Coliforms die-off is more rapid in Ganga waters. More importantly, he says, this peculiar capability of the Ganga may be due to higher load of sediment: "Decreased Coliforms die-off observed in the filtered Bhairon Ghat water sample indicates that one of the factors responsible for rapid die-off is probably suspended solids" (Prasad 1977:39). Arresting of sediment in HEP Reservoirs will lead to deterioration of this quality of Ganga waters.

These studies leave no doubt that waters of Ganga have special qualities, which will be affected by HEP Reservoirs.

Study by National Productivity Council

NHPC has kindly provided to the author a study of water quality at power stations of NHPC done by National Productivity Council (NPC 1995). The study concludes: "*Under present conditions*, the water quality at the project site has not been affected adversely due to construction of dam and reservoir. The higher turbidity value and coliform concentration at different sites are mainly *attributed to rain fall* in the river catchment area" (italics provided).

This author has basic objection to the structure of the study. The quality of water has been tested at the tail-end of reservoir (inlet) and the spillway (outlet). The study concludes that "the water quality...has not been affected adversely due to construction of...reservoir." This means there is no deterioration of quality between the inlet and outlet. This author has shared the study with Dr G D Agarwal, Former Member-Secretary of Central Pollution Control Board who has said that data given in the study do indicate a small deterioration in the quality of water.

More importantly, our case is that the waters will be deprived of oxygen and chemicals being absorbed by it presently. In other words, the correct comparison was between pre- and post-construction of dams. This is not done in the study.

Say the water was absorbing MgCO3 during free flow of river water, which increased from, say, 5 mg/l to 7 mg/l in a particular stretch. This stretch of river is later converted into a reservoir or tunnel. The level of MgCO3 now remains unchanged at 5 mg/l both at inlet and outlet. There is no deterioration *under present conditions.* Can we conclude from this that "the water quality has not been affected adversely due to construction of dam?" No. The deterioration is visible only if we compare the quality of water pre- and post construction of dam. The method of examining the quality at inlet and outlet, both post construction of dam, is meaningless for the purpose of determining impact of dam on water quality.

Study by IIT Roorkee

The Indian Institute of Technology has tested the waters of Tehri Dam at five locations and reported that "River waters could be categorized as fit for drinking after removal of turbidity and chlorination or disinfection as per the guidelines specified in BIS:10500-1991" (Kumar 2007).[14]

This letter gives an impression that the waters are clean and no adverse impact of Tehri Dam is seen. However, a closer study of the report indicates otherwise.

The study does not capture the deterioration in water quality due to faulty design as shown at Table 4.15.

Loss of Cellular Memory

Another reason for decline of water is loss of cellular memory. It appears the waters of River Ganga have especial spiritual powers thus people from across the country come to this river to immerse the ashes of their dead. The secret of this quality may lie in cellular memory. Lord Mahaveer says that water can feel pain and pleasure though it cannot express or act upon it. It is possible that molecules of the waters of the Ganga imbibe certain memory as they flow beside the Brahma Kapali Shila and temple of Bhagwan Badri Vishal at Badrinath, temple of Mother Ganga at Gangotri and thousands of ashrams on the banks of these rivers where monks are doing penance continually. The water is purified at a very deep level just as a smile by the mother removes millions of tensions from the mind of the

Table 4.15. Assessment of IITR study

Sl. No.	*Possible adverse impact on quality of waters*	*What the IIT report says*	*Comment by Author*
1.	Dissolved Oxygen	River waters were rich in dissolved oxygen	5 samples were taken as follows: Upstream (2), Zero Bridge (1) and Dev Prayag (2). No sample was taken at the spillway of Tehri Reservoir or from the upper- and lower levels of the Reservoir. The DO levels upstream are not affected by Tehri Reservoir. DO levels at Dev Prayag are influenced by the free flow of 60-odd km. The finding at Zero Bridge, about 7 km downstream of spillway may indicate some deterioration. A comparative analysis with DO level at spillway was required. This was not done.
2.	BOD and methane emissions	River waters were found free from odour and colour. Low values of UV absorbance and total organic carbon indicate almost absence of any organic pollution.	The polluting organic matter is likely trapped in the reservoir but does not flow downstream with the water. Thus, there is no evidence of organic pollution downstream. It is fermenting within the reservoir and methane is forming. Methane

Sl. No.	*Possible adverse impact on quality of waters*	*What the IIT report says*	*Comment by Author*
			is being released into the atmosphere at the spillway. The water is regenerating DO in the 7 km flow to zero point. Thus, the pollution is present but it is not seen because organic matter, DO and methane within the reservoir are not measured.
3.	Total Coliforms	Turbidity and bacterial contamination of all the samples is not an unusual observation as surface waters generally contain turbidity and fecal Coliforms.	The last line indicates presence of fecal coliforms. Dr Pradeep Kumar has confirmed to the author on phone that the water fails CPCB parameters on this.
4.	Chemicals	No finding in the letter	Dr Pradeep Kumar has told this author that there is difference in chemical composition in the different samples.
5.	Radioactivity	No finding in the letter	-
6.	Cellular memory	No finding in the letter	-

child. This deep memory provides peace to the pilgrims when they take bath in these waters or carry the same in bottles to their home.

Cellular memory may be the secret of importance of Confluences at Dev Prayag etc. The thoughts of monks doing penance along the Bhagirathi are brought by that River to Dev Prayag. Similarly, thoughts of monks doing penance along the Alaknanda are brought by that River. The two streams of thought intermingle at the Confluence as if two sisters meet after many years. The minute memory is activated and energized and hence the special importance of taking bath at the Confluence.

Much discussion is taking place in Western countries about cellular memory. Scientists at University of Arizona studied the thought patterns of people receiving implants from other persons. I quote at length from Nexus Magazine:

"It is generally assumed that learning involves primarily the nervous system and secondarily the immune system. Hence, patients receiving peripheral organ transplants should not experience personality changes that parallel the personalities of donors they have never met. When personality changes have been observed following transplants, the kinds of explanations entertained include effects of the immunosuppressant drugs, psychosocial stress, and pre-existing psychopathology of the recipients.

"However, living systems theory explicitly posits that all living cells possess "memory"... Recurrent feedback loops exist in all atomic, molecular and cellular systems.

"The systemic memory mechanism has been applied to a variety of controversial and seemingly anomalous observations in complementary and alternative medicine, including homoeopathy. It also makes new predictions. One prediction is that sensitive recipients of transplanted organs can experience aspects of the donor's personal history stored in the transplanted tissues.

"In 1997, a book titled A Change of Heart was published that described the apparent personality changes experienced by Claire Sylvia. Sylvia received a heart and lung transplant at Yale–New Haven Hospital in 1988. She reported noticing that various attitudes, habits and tastes changed following her surgery. She had inexplicable cravings for foods she had previously disliked. For example, though she was a health-conscious dancer and choreographer, upon leaving the hospital she had an uncontrollable urge to go to a Kentucky Fried Chicken outlet and order chicken nuggets, a food she never ate. Sylvia found herself drawn toward cool colours and no longer dressed in the bright reds and oranges she used to prefer. She began behaving in an aggressive and impetuous manner that was uncharacteristic of her but turned out to be similar to the personality of her donor. Interestingly, uneaten Kentucky Fried Chicken nuggets were found in the jacket of the young man (her donor) when he was killed.

"When a 47-year-old white male foundry worker received the heart of a 17-year-old black male student, he presumed that the black youth would prefer 'rap' music. Hence, he dismissed the idea that his new radical change in preference for classical music could have come from the heart of the donor. However, unbeknownst to the recipient, the donor actually loved classical music, and died 'hugging his violin case' on the way to his violin class.

"If this observation is verified in future research, the implications for basic physiology as well as clinical medicine could be substantial" (Pearsall 2002).

Here is not the occasion to go deeper into this theory. It suffices to say this matches with the observation of Lord Mahaveer that water feels pleasure and pain. It also throws positive light on the practice of taking a bottle of Ganga waters home. The penance done by the monks along the Ganga is carried by the river waters and thence by the pilgrims to their home. This is explained by Swami Swayambodhanand who lives in the Himalayas (See Box).

Box 1: Swami Swayambodhanand on Quality of Waters of the Ganga

Indian tradition holds River Ganga as most sacred. It is the experiences of thousands of people that a bath in the flowing waters of River Ganga makes them feel fresh. The same experience is not obtained by taking bath from tap water. This effect of freshness is partly due to special properties of waters of River Ganga such as micronutrients, higher level of dissolved oxygen, high ionic content, etc.

The feeling of freshness is the same as reduced level of tension. The statement that 'Ganga is sacred' means that the feeling of guilt is removed by bathing in it; hence also the level of mental tension. The impact of such bath is equal to other efforts to reduce mental tension such as meditation.

Reduction of mental tension results in many benefits such as better human relationships, increased productivity, better health, higher level of intelligence, reduced rate of crime, etc. The benefits of meditation are obtained by the people through bath in the flowing waters of the Ganga.

It is difficult to quantify these economic benefits. However, quantitative studies in transcendental meditation (TM) undertaken by Maharshi Mahesh Yogi have been carried out by scientists like Robert Keith Wallace. These results have been published. Mr Wallace has shown through statistics that TM practitioners experience better health, improved social relationships, higher working capacity, better student performance and greater peace of mind. It was shown that even if one person in 100 practices TM the rate of crime in society declines. These benefits are secured by people of India through bath in the Ganga though they are not aware of this. The people will loose these benefits if a cascade of dams is built across the river.

The Government must be willing to make a trade-off between amount of power generated and maintenance of spiritual qualities of waters of the Ganga. This decision is entirely in the domain of the Government. Our objective is to point out the loss of benefits like better physical and psychological health, reduced crime rate, increased productivity etc. that will take place due to construction of dams.

This cellular memory will be weakened by impounding water in reservoirs or force-flowing it through tunnels. Evidence is available from survey of three dams in Uttarakhand.

Table 4.16. Do you ever worship on the banks of Ganga? What is the difference in Pooja before- and after making of dam? (Details at Annexure 1)

Sl. No.	*Item*	*Net Impact*
1.	Chilla	Reduced 4/20 = (-) 20%
2.	Maneri	Reduced 3/13 = (-) 23%
3.	Tehri	Reduced 25/32 = (-) 78%
4.	Average	(-) 40%

At Chilla, Gomati Devi of Village Khadri Khadak Map said, "There is less Pooja nowadays." Enumerator Naresh Puri explains: Due to less water, there is less worship of Ganga.

Table 4.17. Was the water of river fit for drinking previously? What is the condition now? (Details at Annexure 1)

Sl No	*Item*	*Net, HEP-wise Impact*
1.	Chilla	Reduced 10/20 = (-) 50%
2.	Maneri	Reduced 3/13 = (-) 23%
3.	Tehri	Reduced 28/32 = (-) 88%
4.	Combined	(-) 54%

One senior journalist told the author as follows after visiting the Ashram of Nityanand Swami near the head of Maneri Bhali Reservoir: "The water did not inspire. It had no prana." At Maneri Reservoir, Buddhi Lal of Maneri said, "We do Pooja on festivals. Previously there was more rush. Now there is less." Similar sentiments were expressed by Prem Singh Mahar, Village Netal; Dev Singh Gosain, Village Tiloth; and Chiranji Prasad Joshi, Village Gyansu—all around Maneri Bhali HEP. The significance lies in the fact that this HEP is otherwise reckoned less harmful. There is negative impact even in the 'better' of the three dams studied.

In order to remove any confusion, increase in worship at Village Jamak on Maneri Bhali Reservoir is reported.

Enumerator Naresh Puri explains that 85 people died in this village during 1991 earthquake. Since then, there appears to be more worship. This increase in worship should not be taken as an indicator of positive impact of reservoirs on quality of waters.

Nothing can Affect Qualities of the Ganga

A view is prevalent among the learned that the spiritual qualities of waters of Ganga cannot be affected by pollution etc. due to dams. One devout person strongly proclaimed, "Ganga has infinite capacity to purify. Put what you may into it, the Ganga cannot be sullied." Another learned professor said, "The spiritual- and material levels are different. Changes at material level do not affect the spiritual qualities." An important leader of BJP from Uttarakhand said, "I am against storage dam but in favour of ROR dams." The implication is that dams cannot be rejected on spiritual considerations even if they lead to deterioration in physical quality of waters.

It is true that 'spiritual' and 'material' levels are different just as colour and type of font are different. But they interact. Writing in light grey colour dampens the written text, for example. Such interaction is basis of eight-fold yoga of Patanjali. The cleanliness of food and body elevates the spiritual orientation. Similarly, the purity of river water enhances its spiritual impact. One does not undertake worship in the lavatory even though God is present there. Similarly, one must not sully the material quality of waters of our rivers even if it does not directly harm the spiritual qualities.

Level of Utilization of River Water

Human desires can be arranged in a hierarchy. Father of modern economics, Adam Smith, in his book *Theory of Moral Sentiments,* noted four types of desires in human beings:

1. Physical Pleasures: Necessities and conveniences of the body.
2. Wealth: Possession of external fortune.

3. Social Esteem: Safety of the society.
4. Self-knowledge: Sublime contemplation of the divine Being (1759:112-17).

These broadly conform to the Hindu fourfold classification of Kama (Conveniences of the body), Artha (External fortune), Dharma (Safety of the society) and Moksha (Contemplation of the divine). Objective of the society is to meet the higher needs. The Hindu formula is that lower needs should be fulfilled in a way that it does not hit at higher needs. Kama should be partaken such that Artha is not hit; Artha should be increased such that Dharma is not hit; and Dharma-Artha-Kama should all be given up for Moksha. The operating principle is that lower desires should follow higher desires.

Waters of the rivers can be used for the fulfilment of the four types of desires:

1. Physical Pleasures, Kama: River rafting.
2. Wealth, Artha: Irrigation and power.
3. Social Esteem, Dharma: Biodiversity and forests; Festivals on banks of rivers.
4. Self-knowledge, Moksha: Penance on the banks.

It would follow that river waters should be used for fulfilment of lower desires in a way that they do not hit at the higher desires. This formula can be used to assess whether river waters should be used for generation of hydropower.

Table 4.18. Use of river waters in ROR dams.

Sl. No.	*Purpose*	*Impact of ROR hydropower dam—Kotlibhel 1B*
1.	Physical Pleasures, Kama	(+) Will provide power for raising standard of living.
2.	Wealth, Artha	(+) Will provide power for running factories.
3.	Social Esteem, Dharma	(-) Reduces biodiversity and forests.
4.	Self-knowledge, Moksha	(-) Reduces spiritual powers.

The fact that Ganga is meeting the higher needs of people is attested from a survey of pilgrims.

Table 4.19. What is the benefit you have obtained from the blessings of River Ganga? (After Annexure 2 Table A-2.4)

Sl. No.	*Type of Benefit*	*Percent, Pilgrims*
1.	Kama: Health, Child	38%
2.	Artha: Business, Service, Exams	35%
3.	Dharma	Not asked
4.	Moksha: Mental Peace	77%

It is seen that Ganga's contribution to Moksha—mental peace—is stronger than Kama and Artha. This writer's objection is that ROR dams fulfil the lower desires—Kama (standard of living) and Artha (economic growth); while they hit at higher desires—Dharma (biodiversity) and Moksha (mental peace). This is unwise model of development and should be abstained from.

Costs Assessed by Pilgrims

The decline in quality of waters of River Ganga due to Tehri Dam is verified in a survey of pilgrims at Dev Prayag, Rishikesh and Haridwar.

Table 4.20. What is the impact of Tehri Dam on flow of waters of Ganga? (Percent of Pilgrims Responding in Affirmative, Details at Annexure 2)

Sl. No.	*Type of Pilgrim*	*Was Better Previously*	*Is Better Now*	*No Difference*	*Net, Percent Reporting Previously Better*
1.	Dev Prayag, n=41	88	12	-	76
2.	Rishikesh, n=87	47	15	38	32
3.	Haridwar, n=78	38	26	36	12

* At Dev Prayag, the question was phrased as follows: What will be the change in spiritual power of water after extraction of electricity?

The decline in quality of water is less as we move away from Tehri. This is likely because the water gets a chance to regenerate some qualities like Dissolved Oxygen. This regeneration will not happen after a cascade of dams is built and free flow of the river up to Kaudiyala is wholly denied.

An attempt was made by this author to make an assessment of harm perpetrated by dams on the pilgrims. This was done in two steps. First, pilgrims were asked to place a monetary value on the benefits obtained from taking bath in the Ganga. Next, they were asked by what percentage the benefit will increase from removal of Tehri Dam.

Table 4.21. How much value do you place on the benefit obtained? (Details at Annexure 2)

Sl. No.	*Level of Income*	*Dev Prayag, n=11*	*Rishikesh, n=6*	*Haridwar, n=9*	*Average, n=26*
1.	Average	29,427	59,041	66,177	51,548
2.	Median	1,000	26,500	10,000	12,500
3.	Number responding in priceless, invaluable, etc.	25	23	4	52

In response to this question a large number of pilgrims replied in terms of 'invaluable', 'lacs' or 'priceless'. These have been mentioned separately in the table. Only 26 pilgrims gave value of benefit in money terms. In comparison, 52 pilgrims said that the benefit derived was priceless etc. Now, 'priceless' would be higher than a fixed money value. In view of this, we take the higher average value of Rs 51,548 as the value of benefit derived by pilgrims, and not the lower median value.

Next, pilgrims were asked how much this benefit will increase if the Tehri Dam is removed. They were asked to give a percent value to the increase or decrease in the impact. These are given at Table 4.22 below.

Table 4.22. Impact of removal of Tehri Dam as assessed by Pilgrims (Details at Annexure 2).

Sl. No.	*Location*	*Numbers Reporting Increase*	*Percent Increase*	*Numbers Reporting Decrease*	*Percent Decrease*
1.	Dev Prayag	31	46.3	3	43.3
2.	Rishikesh	52	46.0	11	30.0
3.	Haridwar	42	29.5	17	42.7
4.	Combined	125	40.6	31	38.7

We can use these figures to make an estimate of effect of removal of Tehri Dam on pilgrims.

First, the weighted average is calculated:

Weighted Average of impact = (Numbers decrease × Percent decrease) – (Numbers increase × Percent increase)/ (Total number)

= – ((125 × 40.6) + (31 × 38.7))/(125 + 31) = – 24.8%

The benefit to pilgrims is increased by 24.8% upon decommissioning of Tehri Dam.

Present benefit per pilgrim is Rs 51,548 (Table 4.21 above)

Reduction in benefit per pilgrims: 24.8% or Rs 12,784.

This figure is used to assess the impact of Tehri Dam on the benefits obtained by pilgrims in Box.

Box 2: Impact of Tehri Dam on Pilgrims

The author estimates the number of pilgrims as follows: Dev Prayag 200, Rishikesh 1000, Haridwar 2500, other places before Haridwar 1,300, Total 5,000 per day.

Gain to pilgrims from decommissioning of Tehri Dam: 5,000 pilgrims × 365 days × Rs 12,784 = Rs 2333 crore per year.

A similar amount may be assessed for pilgrims downstream from Haridwar at Prayag, Kashi, Ganga Sagar, etc. The total loss to the pilgrims from Tehri may be assessed at double this amount at Rs 4,666 crores per year.

Further losses occur to family members who do not make these pilgrimages. Pilgrims take waters to their homes. The power of that water will also be reduced. Further losses occur to local people residing on the banks of Ganga and non-pilgrim travellers in the area.

The impact of Kotlibhel 1B can be reckoned on this basis. The differences between Tehri and Kotlibhel 1B are outlined below. The Tehri Dam is presently a stand-alone dam. There is free flow of water after discharge from Tehri to Rishikesh which enables regeneration of water presently. This will not be possible after a cascade of dams is built from Badrinath to Kaudiyala. Our objective in this exercise is to assess the applicability of estimates made by pilgrims in relation to Tehri; to Kotlibhel 1B project.

Table 4.23. Applicability of impact of Tehri to Kotlibhel 1B project

SI. No.	*Difference in the two dams*	*Impact of Kotlibhel 1B compared to Tehri*
1.	Storage versus ROR	(–) Tehri provides increased flow in lean summer months. Kotlibhel IB will not provide such increased flow hence impact will be relatively negative. (+) There will be no storage in Kotlibhel 1B hence there will be less fermentation.
2.	Distance from	(–) Dev Prayag is located about 50 km from Tehri. The negative impact of Tehri will be more near the spillway. Kotlibhel 1B is located 2 km from Dev Prayag hence impact of Kotlibhel 1B on deterioration of water quality at Dev Prayag will be more than that assessed by pilgrims for Tehri.
3.	Single dam (Tehri) versus Cascade of dams (Kotlibhel and others)	(–) Impact of Tehri assessed by pilgrims is attributable to a single dam. Water gets to regenerate after discharge from Tehri. The negative impact of cascade of dams will be more because no free flow of river will be left where the water may regenerate its sediment, chemical and oxygen content.

It is seen that impact of Kotlibhel 1B is likely to be more negative than Tehri.

The loss to pilgrims at Dev Prayag from Kotlibhel 1B is calculated on above basis. The loss from Tehri dam is assessed at Rs 4666 crores per year (Box 2 above). We assume the loss from cascade of dams from Badrinath to Kaudiyala to be of same magnitude. This loss occurs from dams built on the river length of 270 kilometres. The share of Kotlibhel 1B, which covers 27 km, is Rs 466 crores on pro-rata basis. We take one-half this amount—Rs 233 crores—to account for possible over-assessment.

Methane Emissions

HEP reservoirs have two types of inflow of organic matter.

- Vegetation in reservoir area ferments in the reservoir if not removed at the time of initial submergence.
- Continuous inflow of organic matter such as leaves, sticks, carcasses, etc. with inflowing water.

The organic matter at the time of initial submergence can be removed before inundation. However, continuous inflow of organic matter such as leaves, stems and domestic waste presents a perpetual problem. This organic matter settles at the reservoir bottom, decays and produces methane. In normal course, the methane rises slowly and is broken into CO2 and H2O as it rises. This leads to release of CO2 in the atmosphere, which, in comparison, contributes less to pollution of air and water. This does not happen when methane-laden water is sucked from the reservoir bottom by the turbines. After generation of electricity, the methane-laden water finds it way into the spillways where the methane is released directly into the atmosphere. This methane contributes to global warming.

The average methane gas released by three tropical storage HEPs was equivalent to 2,154 grams CO2 per Kwh (IRN 2006). This is more in comparison to 800 grams per

Kwh emission from thermal power plants. Thus, hydropower is not environmentally clean as assumed. Unfortunately, thermal power projects include costs of buying carbon credits to neutralize these gas emissions while emissions from HEPs are not accounted for.

The proceedings of a workshop on Greenhouse Gases held by the World Commission of Dams accepted the following sources of GHG emissions from reservoirs:

- Flooded biomass.
- Carbon in the soil and peat of the reservoir.
- Emergent biomass (e.g. dead trees).
- Dissolved Organic Carbon/Particulate Organic Carbon and organic debris from the catchment.
- Decomposition of macrophytes and algae following their death.

Of these contributors, only 'Emergent Biomass' can be managed by removal of trees etc. before submergence. The Planning Commission ignores these other sources of GHG emissions. The Integrated Energy Policy report says: "Methane emissions, a major greenhouse gas, may also be emitted in large quantities if insufficient care is taken to remove vegetative matter susceptible to anaerobic microbial processes from the submerged area." There is no recognition of other sources of GHG gases.

This is confirmed in survey of three dams. At least two respondents explicitly mentioned that they found foul smell in the water. One respondent at Chilla made this complaint indicating that deterioration of quality of water takes place in smaller ROR HEPs also.

Table 4.24. What is the change in smell of water downstream? (Details at Annexure 1)

Sl. No.	*Item*	*Net, HEP-wise Impact*
1.	Chilla	(-) 11/20 = 55%
2.	Maneri	(-) 2/13 = 15%
3.	Tehri	(-) 25/32 = 78%
4.	Combined	(-) 38/65 = 58%

A large number of respondents complained of less freshness in water. At Tehri, there is sharp decline in water quality. Enumerator Naresh Puri reported that strong foul smell is felt at Chilyanisaur. Many dead bodies are held up at the point of entry of water into the reservoir and the area stinks very much. It is difficult to stand there. THDC has reportedly given some money to the health department to spray insecticides. According to Enumerator Naresh Puri, the dead matter moves down slowly as the level of water in reservoir is reduced but it rises back up when the water level increases. It stays at the tail of the reservoir.

The foul smell of the reservoir affects people upstream at Villages Nagni Chhoti and Tilyada. The villages are on the tail end of the reservoir. Conclusion is that there is a strong negative impact on the quality of water. People are almost disgusted.

GOI is Unconcerned

GOI does not have standards for methane emissions. This is established by replies received by the author from the authorities produced in table below.

Table 4.25. Replies from GOI regarding methane emissions

Sl. No.	*Authority*	*Query under RTI*	*Reply received under RTI*
1.	Uttarakhand Pollution Control Board	What is UKPCB policy regarding maximum level of methane emissions permitted from a HEP?	There is no standard for HEP (RTI 7.9.2007).
2.	NHPC	The level of contribution of Kotlibhel 1B to Global Warming Emissions.	Global warming is a very gradual phenomenon having its repercussion spreading over hundreds of years and due to construction of the project a very small reservoir will be formed, therefore, the

Sl. No.	Authority	Query under RTI	Reply received under RTI
			level of contribution by Kotlibhel 1B in global warming may be insignificant (RTI 13.7.2007, Item 47).
3.	Ministry of Power, GOI	Has the MOP made any assessment of the relative contribution of HEPs and fossil fuel based power plants to global warming? Please provide details of the contributions by the two types of power plants. What is the expected emission of methane from the turbines, spillways and downstream flow of river under HEPs?	No such studies have been carried out by the Ministry (RTI 23.8.2007)

Lessons Learnt by World Planners

Hydro-Quebec is one of the largest producers of Hydroelectric Power in the world. Hydro-Quebec had hosted a "Workshop on Dam Reservoirs and Greenhouse Gases" on February 24 & 25, 2000, at Montreal, Canada (WCD 2000b) as a part consultations promoted by the World Commission of Dams. From studies undertaken on about 30 reservoirs, the following conclusions were drawn:

- Greenhouse gases are emitted from all dam reservoirs.
- The evaluation of net greenhouse gas emissions from reservoirs requires comparison to the emissions that existed prior to flooding.
- The rates of GHG emission measured so far justify consideration of these emissions in... evaluating

individual future reservoir sites, such as hydroelectric dams (most particularly in tropical regions).

- GHG emissions cannot be directly explained by the volume of submerged biomass nor its carbon content. The sources of the carbon in GHGs emitted from reservoirs include: (a) Flooded biomass; (b) Carbon in the soil and peat of the reservoir; (c) Emergent biomass (e.g. dead trees); (d) Dissolved Organic Carbon/Particulate Organic Carbon and organic debris from the catchment; (e) Decomposition of macrophytes and algae following their death.
- Emissions of methane and CO2 from water passing through the turbines spillway and downstream may also be a significant source.
- To assist comparisons between the global warming effects of different gases, the baseline gas is CO2. The impact of one unit of methane on global warming is equivalent to 21 units of CO2.

This author understands the amount of methane emissions is dependent upon the amount of inflow of organic matter that settles in the reservoir and ferments. We see that small amount of stale water in a flower vase emits large amounts of foul gasses because the amount of organic matter is large even though the amount of water is less. Methane emissions, therefore, are more related to the amount of organic matter and less to volume of water. Yet, the volume of water will also have a bearing because it will influence the amount of organic matter trapped. We adjust the level of methane emissions reported at 2154 grams per Kwh (IRN 2006) from three tropical HEPs in Table 4.26 below to account for these factors.

Table 4.26. Adjusting methane emissions from tropical large storage projects for Himalayan ROR reservoirs

Sl. No.	*Item*	*Adjustment Factor*	*Discussion*
1.	Sub-tropical location	Less	Colder temperatures in Lower Himalayas will lead to less emission.
2.	Higher flow	More	ROR reservoir will have high inflow of water hence inflow of organic matter will be large.
3.	Lower volume	Less	Surface area of KB1B is 4.5 km2 against 1014 km2 of the benchmark tropical reservoirs

Based on above comparison, this author estimates that GHG emissions from Kotlibhel 1B would be about one-half of that emitted by large storage dams. Accordingly the cost is worked out below.

Table 4.27. Cost of GHG emissions from Kotlibhel 1B

Sl. No.	*Item*	*Amount*	*Basis*
1.	Power generated	973.05 MU	DPR Page 1.8
2.	Total Carbon emissions	1,047,975 tons	Carbon emissions per unit of power = 2.154 kg × 50% adjustment factor
3.	Cost of carbon credits Kotlibhel 1B HEP	Rs 31.4 crore per year	Value @ $7.5 per ton (Business Standard 2007) × Rs 40 per dollar

Forests

The Issue

Following issues have to be considered in assessing the impact of HEPs on forests:

- Indirect services provided by forests.

- Proprietary value of submerged forest land.
- Disturbance to Fragile Himalayan Environment.

Indirect Services Provided by Forests

The Supreme Court had set up a Committee (Chair: Kanchan Chopra) to determine the value of services provided by forests that should be recovered from users of forestlands (Chopra 2006). The Committee has listed various services provided by the forests. Some of these have been internalized in the NPV (Net Present Value) calculations.[15] A comparison of the two lists indicates that some benefits have been excluded in NPV calculations. These costs are incurred by the society in addition to the payments made under NPV calculations.

The objective of this book is to bring into open for public scrutiny various costs that are passed on to the society by HEPs. For this purpose, the value of services excluded by Kanchan Chopra Committee is to be internalized. These are to be added to the NPV to arrive at the total cost relevant for assessment of HEPs.

A Working Paper of the Planning Commission examined the contribution of forests of Himachal Pradesh (Mathur 2003). Apart from direct consumption benefits, the study also accounted for direct non-consumption and indirect benefits. The study suggested that the indirect benefits far exceed the direct benefits of forests. Notably, even this study does not value the spiritual and inspirational contribution of forests. The Union of International Associations brings home this point: "The diversity and variations found in nature provide experiences and inspiration. This value is difficult to measure, but has great importance" (UIA undated-b). The Author lists these unaccounted values in the table 4.28 below. Value of these services is estimated at Table 4.29.

Table 4.28. Costs excluded in NPV calculations by Kanchan Chopra Committee

Sl. No.	*List of services provided by forests (Vide Para 2.2.2 of Kanchan Chopra report (Chopra 2006)*	*List of services internalized in NPV calculations by Kanchan Chopra report (Vide Table 1 of the report)*	*List of services that remain unaccounted in NPV calculations by Kanchan Chopra report*
1.	Provisioning goods such as wood, non-timber forest products, fuel, fodder, water and provision of services such as grazing, tourism, wildlife protection and life support	Timber, Fuel wood and fodder, Non-timber forest products (including grass), Eco-tourism	Grazing, wildlife protection
2.	Regulating Services: climate regulation, disease control, flood moderation, detoxification, carbon sequestration and health of soils and water regimes	Carbon storage value, Watershed services (soil conservation and hydrological)	Disease control, flood moderation, Detoxification.
3.	Non-material benefits obtained from ecosystems: spiritual, recreational, aesthetic, inspirational, educational, communal, and symbolic.	–	Spiritual, recreational, aesthetic, inspirational, educational, communal, symbolic.
4.	Supporting: Services necessary for the production of all other ecosystem services: Biodiversity, Nutrient cycling, Primary production.	–	Biodiversity, Nutrient cycling, Primary production.

Table 4.29. Value of services excluded in NPV calculations

Sl. No.	*Item*	*Cost*	*Basis*
1.	Indirect benefits not accounted in NPV	Rs 5.9 lacs per ha	NPV of direct benefits from forests is Rs 5.9 lacs per ha. This is average of lower and higher values of NPV of Rs 4.1 lacs and Rs 7.7 lacs per ha (Upadhyaya 2007). Indirect costs are estimated equal to direct costs on the basis of Verma (2000) statement that indirect benefits are greater than direct benefits
2.	Inspirational benefits	Rs 5.9 lacs per ha	Assume equal to indirect benefits on basis of UIA statement (undated-b)
3.	Total NPV cost	Rs 11.8 lacs per ha or Rs 58.3 crores	Total forestland to be submerged is 494 ha.
4.	Annual cost	Rs 5.8 crores per year	At 10% interest rate.

Disturbance to Fragile Himalayan Environment

The Kanchan Chopra Committee explicitly recommended that "No permission for non-forest use can be given to certain kinds of areas such as: Protected Areas, Sacred Groves, Fragile Ecosystems (e.g. mangroves)." The riverbed of many HEPs being built in mountainous regions is such a fragile ecosystem. This is established by following authorities:

- The Report of The Steering Committee on The Environment and Forests Sector for the Eleventh Five Year Plan, Government of India, Planning Commission, March 2007 mentions, "Provide conservation measures to *the fragile ecosystems* such as coastal areas (mangroves and coral reefs), *hills and mountains,* wetlands, shifting cultivation areas, biodiversity hotspots etc." (Planning Commission 2007, italics provided).

- The FAO Corporate Document Repository document *FRA 2005 - Pilot study for country reporting: India (Draft)...* says: "The Himalayan eco-system is a *fragile ecosystem* and its fragility increases with altitudes" (FAO 2005, italics provided).
- Dr Ramesh C. Sharma, Department of Environmental Sciences, H N B Garhwal University, Srinagar says in his paper 'Restoration of aquatic habitat and fish passage degraded by widening of Indian Highway 58 in Garhwal Himalaya': "Sustainable approaches to the construction and widening of roads and highways are essential to offset negative influences on aquatic habitat and fish passage in *the fragile ecosystem of the Himalayan Mountains* in northern India (Sharma 2006, italics provided).
- The Master plan for development of trekking routes in Uttarakhand prepared for the Department of Tourism, Government of Uttarakhand by Pannell Kerr Forster Consultants Pvt Ltd, New Delhi says: "The intrusive nature of tourism and the fact that trekking occurs in some of *the most fragile environments* on the planet necessitate the regulation of such activities" (Forster 2003, italics provided).

These documents establish that HEPs like Kotlibhel 1B are disturbing the fragile ecosystems of Himalayas in violation of Kanchan Chopra Committee norms. In absence of any study, the cost of disturbing fragile ecosystem is assessed by the author to be equal to the indirect costs, i.e. Rs 5.8 crore per year.

Proprietary Value of Submerged Forest Land

In the opening paragraphs of its report, the Kanchan Chopra Committee clarified that the NPV payment under

CAMPA "is for protection of the environment and not in relation to any proprietary rights."

This principle was clarified by Government of Orissa, Revenue and Disaster Management Department, Circular (GOO 2007), which states:

"2. NPV is being collected as per the directives of Hon'ble Supreme Court of India since 30.10.2002 to compensate for the loss of tangible as well as intangible benefits flowing from the forestland diverted for non-forest use.

"3. Thus, NPV does not include premium of the forestland. The State Government, being the owner of the land, can collect premium at rates decided by the Government in addition to NPV.

"5. It is, hereby, clarified that premium in respect of forestland used for different purposes may be collected from the user agencies in the manner as prescribed in this Department Circular referred to above in addition to NPV, cost of compensatory afforestation etc."

The economic valuation of HEPs has to account for the proprietary cost borne by the people of the state for the extinguishing of the forestland due to submergence. This cost is calculated below.

Table 4.30. Cost due to proprietary loss of submerged forest land

Sl. No.	*Item*	*Amount*	*Basis*
1.	Forest land to be submerged	495 ha	EMP Page 118
2.	Value of submerged forest land	Rs 495 crores	Srinagar HEP has paid land compensation at Rs 2 lacs per nali or Rs 1 crore per ha.
3.	Annual incidence of cost	Rs 49.5 crores per year	At 10% rate of interest.

Inefficiency via Compensatory Afforestation

The original circular of MOEF provided that projects would have to acquire new land for afforestation. This was later diluted to allow for compensatory forestation on degraded lands (Singh 2002:23). Degradation of forests occurs because the Forest Department fails to discharge its duty. Thus, double costs are imposed upon the people—first by failure of Forest Department to maintain forests in good condition; and again by people being deprived of forest produce in the name of protecting forests that are planted.

There is also a question of equity. CAMPA or compensatory afforestation may take place in area other than that affected. Thus, one people are deprived of forests while another gains. The rights of affected people should be protected.

This writer, based on his experience as consultant to NGOs working in the field of afforestation in Rajasthan, believes that the basic problem of degradation of forests is overgrazing and overexploitation by forest department and local people alike. Shri Jagat Singh 'Jangalee' of District Rudra Prayag has been able to create dense forests by simply protecting them from grazing. Thus, regeneration forests will only take place if grazing is prevented. However, local people have traditional rights to grazing and fuel wood from the forests. The solution, therefore, is to compensate local people for the loss of grazing and then protect the forests. However, such a strategy would provide benefits to local people; and not provide opportunity to give out contracts for making pits, buying plants, etc. to the forest department. Thus, forest departments repeatedly replant forests and local people graze them. Needless to say, the simple solution is to compensate local people to protect the forests.

Costs of Forests Submerged under Kotlibhel 1B

The costs imposed upon society due to submergence of forests by Kotlibhel 1B are calculated below.

Table 4.31. Costs due to submergence of forests by Kotlibhel 1B

Sl. No.	*Item*	*Amount Rs. crore per year*
1.	Indirect benefits excluded in NPV calculations	5.8
2.	Cost of disturbing fragile environments	5.8
3.	Proprietary value of forest land submerged 494 ha	49.5
	Total cost of Kotlibhel 1B HEP	61.1

Earthquakes

The Issue

HEPs have two relations with earthquakes: (1) The stability of the dam is threatened; and (2) HEPs may contribute to increased frequency of earthquakes. The latter is known as Reservoir Induced Seismicity.

Scientists have developed the capability to design dams that can withstand anticipated levels of seismic activity. However, EIAs are often silent on the cost imposed on the people due to Reservoir Induced Seismicity.

Global Experience of Impact of HEPs on Seismicity

Shekhar Singh of Indian Institute of Public Administration has given a list of 30 large dams that have induced earthquakes within a few years of their impoundment (2002:29).

Pradeep Talwani of Department of Geological Sciences, University of South Carolina gives a summary of knowledge on Reservoir Induced Seismicity (Talwani 1997). His findings are summarized below:

"Reservoir-induced seismicity (RIS) has been observed at over seventy locations worldwide. RIS is of two types—'initial' and 'protracted'. Initial RIS occurs upon initial impoundment of a reservoir and then settles down to pre-impoundment levels. Protracted RIS continues for many decades after impoundment. The ongoing seismicity at Koyna, India, three decades after impoundment; the observed seismicity at Lake Mead for over three decades, the current seismicity at Lake Jocassee and Monticello Reservoir South Carolina are examples of protracted RIS.

"RIS is associated with the reservoir and local site characteristics. There is a general absence of seismicity beneath the deepest part of the reservoir and widespread seismicity on the periphery, migrating outwards in one or more directions.

"RIS occurs because of an increase in pore pressure in closed pores which causes seismicity. The time for an increase in pore pressure due to diffusion depends on the depth of the reservoir, geometry, availability of faults/fractures, etc."

Harsh Gupta and Kusala Rajendran of Center of Earth Science Studies, Trivandrum write in a widely quoted paper on RIS in Himalayas: "There are now 60 well-documented cases of reservoir-induced seismicity and, with passage of time, more cases are being reported" (1986:205).

These studies indicate that creation of a reservoir increases the chances of an earthquake in the area. Whether, and to what extent, this is likely to happen in the Himalayas remains a matter of debate, however.

One section of scientists holds that increase in RIS is likely here. This viewpoint has been well documented by Vinod K Gaur in his book *Earthquake Hazard and Large Dams in the Himalaya* (1993). Other scholars contest these findings. The author has spoken by phone with many scholars including Prof Ashwani Kumar of IIT Roorkee, Mr Anand Swaroop Arya, Advisor to Government of India and Dr V P Dimri, Director, National Geophysical Research Institute. The issues raised by these scientists and this writer's response are given below:

Argument 1: *There is no evidence of RIS in the Himalayas. The geology of Central India is older than*

Himalayas. There is greater chance of RIS in older geologies. Hence, the experiences of Koyna and other dams of Central India do not apply to Himalayan Reservoirs.

Response: The newer geology of the Himalayas only reduces the probability of RIS. It does not eliminate that possibility. Further, this position is contra the higher level of natural seismicity observed in the area. Uttarakhand has seen eight major earthquakes in the last 100 years. If newer geology reduces RIS, then it should also reduce natural seismicity. It appears contradictory that the same geology may produce more natural earthquakes but lesser RIS. The underlying issue here is the depth to which load of reservoir affects the geological formations. The epicentre of earthquakes in Himalayas is about 15-20 km below surface. Indeed, there may be no RIS if the load of reservoir does not reach that depth. However, this is an unsolved riddle and does not cancel the average levels of RIS observed across the globe.

Argument 2: *Measurements at Tehri and other Himalayan Dams do not indicate higher levels of seismicity than surrounding areas.*

Response: Measurements at surface do not tell us about the happenings 15-20 km below surface. Surface measurements at Latur would probably not have predicted an impending earthquake. The geological pressures build over long time at sub-surface levels and erupt suddenly. The measurements on surface for 'long time' do not predict happenings at the time of eruption.

Argument 3: *There is greater danger in the Himalayas from natural seismicity than from manmade dams or other activities. There is no evidence that human activities have contributed to the earthquakes of Uttarkashi, 1992 and Chamoli 1999.*

Response: The fact that human activities have not contributed to earlier earthquakes does not establish they will not do so in future. Statistical theory tells us that probabilities interact in exponential manner. The probability of an accident increases exponentially if the gear and horn are both malfunctioning. Similarly, construction of dams is likely to increase the chances of RIS in conjunction with pre-existing high levels of natural seismicity.

Further, the higher chances of natural earthquakes do not cancel the lesser chance of RIS. Say, the chance of natural seismicity is 1:10 while that of RIS is 1:450. That does not mean that 1:450 chance of RIS is non-existent.

Argument 4: *Dam structures are adequately protected against possible earthquakes.*

Response: The dams may enhance RIS while maintaining their own stability just as a man standing on a rock can throw stone below.

Argument 5: *The idea that seepage can lead to RIS is not an accepted theory. The impact of seepage is likely to be minimal since water exists at deeper levels already.*

Response: The impact of seepage has not been studied hence we do not know its impact. The existence of pre-existing sub-surface water can be triggered in a different direction by new influx.

In conclusion, the author feels that the lack of RIS till date tells us little about the future. It is more likely that the already high natural seismicity will be enhanced by reservoirs. The proponents of dams have produced no evidence that seismicity is *reduced* in the Himalayas due to construction of dams. Hence, we should assume that it would increase in line with global averages.

It is reported that studies have been made about the probability of RIS in the United States as well as Northeast India. It was incumbent upon the EIA Agency to assess this probability. The author has calculated the cost of RIS due to Kotlibhel 1B using his own best estimates in absence of such study.

People's Perception

People residing near three dams in Uttarakhand were asked about the possible increase in earthquake due to construction of reservoirs.

Table 4.32. The probability of earthquake has increased or reduced due to construction of the dam? (Details at Annexure 1)

Sl. No.	*Item*	*Net, HEP-wise Impact*
1.	Chilla	Increased 1/19 = 5%
2.	Maneri	Increased 4/13 = 31%
3.	Tehri	Increased 0/32 = 0%
4.	Combined	Increased 12%.

People have assessed a 12 percent increase or 1:8 chance of RIS in the area. In comparison, we have taken a lower figure of 1:45 in calculations below.

Costs

The World Commission on Dams says that the world has about 45,000 large dams. Harsh Gupta and Kusala Rajendran tell us that 60 cases of RIS are already reported and more are being reported" (1986:205). Thus, we may assume that the true figure of RIS will be about 100. This works out to a ratio of 1:450 globally.

Uttarakhand falls in Zone IV of high seismic activity (HNBU 2006b:50). The area under Zone IV is approximately 1/50 of the total land mass of the country. The chance of RIS in this area would be more than the national average. The author estimates that there is a 10-times greater chance that RIS will take place in Uttarakhand in comparison to the global average. The chance of a RIS induced by Kotlibhel 1B is thus estimated at 1:45.

VK Joshi, who worked as a geologist with the Geological Survey of India for 36 years and retired as Director, Northern Region, at Lucknow gives figures for damages from two earthquakes in Uttarakhand (Joshi 2006b) as shown in Table 4.33.

Table 4.33. Cost of earthquake

Sl No	*Item*	*Uttarkashi 1991*	*Chamoli 1999*	*Average*	*Value per unit*	*Total cost (Rs Crore)*	*Basis*
1.	Deaths	768	106	437	19,01,288	83.1	Average income is Rs 29,235 per person or Rs 131,557 per family. This is discounted @ 10% for next 20 years.
2.	Injured	5066	NA	5066	1,90,128	96.3	Value is, say, 10% of death.
3.	Houses damaged	100,000	187,619	143,809	1,00,000	1438	Author's estimate
4.	Civil property	-	-	-	Lump sum	1438	Assume equal to loss of private property
5.	Loss of income, cost of trauma	-	-	143,809 families	Rs 50,000 per family	719	Author's estimate
	Total					3774	

The cost due to Kotlibhel 1B is assessed as follows based on above estimate.

Table 4.34. Cost of Earthquake—Contribution of Kotlibhel 1B

Sl No	*Item*	*Value*	*Basis*
1,	General probability of RIS	1:450	Gupta (1986)
2,	Probability of RIS in Zone IV of the Himalayas	1:45	There is likely to be a multiplier effect
3,	One-time cost due to Kotlibhel 1B	Rs 83.8 crore	The cost of an earthquake is estimated at 3774.6 crores above. This is reduced in 1:45 ratio.
4,	Annual incidence of cost due to Kotlibhel 1B	Rs 8.4 crore per year	Annual cost estimated at 10 percent.

Landslides

It is mentioned in the previous chapter that the Himalayas have recent geology hence the chances of earthquake are less. This same factor works in the opposite direction in relation to landslides. Recent geology implies that the hills have not yet stabilized and there is a greater chance of landslide. Some HEPs are tunnel based. Blasting is done in the mountains to make these tunnels. This destabilizes the hillsides leading to higher incidence of landslides and greater havoc during earthquakes. Village Jamak on the rim of Maneri Bhali barrage was deeply affected during the 1992 Uttarkashi earthquake. Reportedly, 85 persons died in this village. The hillside had been destabilized during blasting and the village virtually collapsed when stuck by a natural earthquake.

Other HEPs are reservoir based like Tehri or Kotlibhel. Water is stored in a reservoir in a valley. This water tends to rise up the hills through capillary action and weakens its stability. The hills begin to slip like the tyre of car in slush.

Harsh Bahuguna and D P Dangwal of Geological Survey of India have studied the stability of villages along the rim of Tehri Reservoir. They report that villages Barola, Kangsali, Raulakot, Nakot, Talla Uppu, Bhald, Badhan and Hadiari "are assessed as highly vulnerable and need immediate attention before next filling in the reservoir.s.. Slopes below Sod Uppu, Baldogi and Mundra Sera in Bhagirathi Valley are assessed as vulnerable" (2007). This author has visited some of these villages in April 2007 and found that many houses had developed cracks. Some houses had started to tilt as the lower slopes tended to slip. Earth had developed cracks at some places.

This author has spoken to scientists who hold less chance of RIS in the Himalayas. Even these scientists admit greater chance of damage from landslides. Especially, impounding leads to higher chance for water to rise by capillary action.

Admittedly, the situation in Kotlibhel Reservoir will be somewhat different from Tehri because the fluctuation in level of water will be very less. That may or may not reduce the probability of landslide, however. The impact may increase insofar as it is due to capillary action. It may be less insofar as it is due to fluctuation in water level. This requires greater study of slopes in other ROR HEPs in the Himalayas.

These landslides can be catastrophic. Harsh Gupta narrates the example Vajont Dam, Italy "when an estimated volume of 250 to 300 m3 mass of cretaceous strata broke off in one piece from Mount Toc and fell in the reservoir. The overflow water erased the town of Longarone and claimed over 2000 human lives" (1986).

Similarly, Patrick McCully tells us that deprivation of sediments has "led to cliff collapses which caused millions of dollars of damage to property and road during the 1980s" (1998:41). Increased cutting action can lead to higher incidence of landslides downstream.

People residing along the HEPs in Uttarakhand are aware of this danger as evinced from the replies given in Table below.

Table 4.35. Have houses in the village developed cracks or damage due to sinking of earth etc. after construction of dam? (Details at Annexutre 1)

Sl. No.	*Item*	*Net, HEP-wise Impact*
1.	Chilla	No impact = 0%
2.	Maneri	Yes 6/13 = 46%
3.	Tehri	Yes 15/32 = 47%
4.	Combined	Yes, 31%

It is notable that huge impact on landslides is assessed at Maneri Bhali, which is a much smaller reservoir than Kotlibhel.

It is difficult to estimate the cost imposed by the Kotlibhel project upon the people due to landslides. However, an attempt is made below.

Table 4.36. Cost of landslides due to Kotlibhel 1B

Sl. No.	*Item*	*Amount*	*Basis*
1.	Number of families living on the rim of Kotlibhel 1B Reservoir	1035 families	HNBU (2006c:151)
2.	Value of houses of families living on the rim of Kotlibhel 1B Reservoir	Rs 51.7 crores	Assume Rs 5 lacs per house.
3.	Value of houses of families living on the rim of Kotlibhel 1B Reservoir that is likely to be affected due to landslides	Rs 16.0 crores	According to survey quoted above there is a 31 percent chance of houses developing crack etc. due to dams.
4.	Cost of damage of houses on the rim of Kotlibhel 1B Reservoir	Rs 4.0 crores	Assume 25% cost of damage.

Sl. No.	*Item*	*Amount*	*Basis*
5.	Cost of damage of houses above the rim of Kotlibhel 1B Reservoir	Rs 2.0 crores	Assume loss at 50% of those residing on the rim.
6.	Value of land of families living on the rim of Kotlibhel 1B Reservoir	Rs 207.0 crores	Assume 10 nali per family. Valued at Rs 2 lacs per nali.
7.	Value of land of families living on the rim of Kotlibhel 1B Reservoir that is likely to be affected due to landslides	Rs 97.0 crores	According to survey at Tehri, 15/32 persons have reported damage to land within 3 years of making of reservoirs (Table 4.35). We assume impact in this ratio.
8.	Cost of damage to land on the rim of Kotlibhel 1B Reservoir	Rs 9.7 crores	Assume decline in value of affected land is 10 percent.
9.	Cost of damage of land above the rim of Kotlibhel 1B Reservoir	Rs 4.8 crores	Assume loss at 50% of that on the rim.
10.	Sub-Total	Rs 20.5 crores	Total of lines 4, 5, 8 and 9
11.	Add costs due to trauma	Rs 10.2 crores	Assume 50% of Line 10
	Total	Rs 30.7 crores	

Malaria and Health

The Issue

The creation of a reservoir, particularly one that has a near-constant level of water as in Kotlibhel HEP, provides ideal breeding ground for mosquitoes, who are carriers of diseases. Areas near reservoirs around the world are found to have higher incidence of malaria and other diseases such as, diarrhoea, zoonoses, bilharzia (Schistosomiasis), river blindness (Onchocerciasis) and elephantiasis (Filariasis).

Reservoirs also lead to the growth of toxic algal blooms (WHO 1999). Snails that are carrier of many diseases flourish along the reservoir rim (Jobin 2004). Shepards that wade into the slush along the rim are particularly at risk.

The malaria vector is becoming virulent. Number of deaths among the patients is increasing because the vector is becoming resistant to chloroquin and other drugs. This virulent strain then spreads to other populations. Every reservoir that provides breeding ground adds to this long-term cost.

Virulence and Resistance

The experience of Malaria control in India indicates that malaria is becoming both virulent and resistant.

Table 4.37. Increasing virulence of malaria in India

Year	*Cases*	*Deaths*
1984	2.18 million	247
2001	1.97 million	928

Source: Panda (2004).

The total number of cases has become stable around 2 million since 1984 while the number of deaths is increasing due to virulent strains of the disease. This is despite stronger drugs being used for curative treatment under EMCP launched in 1997. The authors conclude: "In EMCP programme, it is observed that funds were allocated, but result is not satisfactory... it is found that there lacks timely supervision of superiors. As a result, there was a lack in the radical treatment, in time... Earlier... malaria was controlled to a great extent... only due to a set of dedicated malaria control staff. Now that much of voluminous staff is not affordable, the growing population can be used in the community level... " (Panda 2004).

The conclusion is that curative treatment with stronger drugs under EMCP is leading to increased virulence instead of reduced disease. This may be due to improper implementation. However, that only underscores the higher contribution to spread of malaria by HEP reservoirs.

Malaria was successfully controlled in India from fifties until seventies by the use of DDT. The use of this chemical was, however, banned because it was found to be persistent ((Brown undated). Further, an ICMR report indicates that certain species were becoming resistant to DDT (Raghavendra 2002). Subsequently new insecticides—HCH, Malathion and deltamethrin—were used. However, the species continued to develop resistance. With the result, that the species culicifacies has become resistant as follows:

Table 4.38. Level of resistance to anti-malarial drugs in India

Name of insecticide	*Number of insecticides*	*Number of districts showing resistance*
DDT	1	286
DDT + HCH	2	233
DDT + HCH + Malathion	3	71
DDT + HCH + Malathion + Deltamethrin	4	2

Source: Raghavendra (2002).

The country faces two insurmountable problems. One, DDT, the most effective insecticide is persistent. Two, the species is becoming resistant to increasing number of drugs. ICMR warns that new molecules are not available for control of 4-resistant species and the focus must shift to "management tactics."

The best strategy is to prevent mosquitoes from breeding. Unfortunately, HEP reservoirs do exactly the opposite. They provide breeding grounds for mosquitoes by making available a constant level of slow-moving water for breeding.

Impact of Reservoirs on Malaria

There is large evidence that HEPs contribute significantly

to the burden of disease among those living near the reservoir:

"Schistosomiasis prevalence in Ghana erupted when the Lake Volta was constructed to provide a dammed lake for the Akosombo hydroelectric power station. The prevalence of this disease, which until then was only observed in certain areas, has now spread to many communities along the Lake Volta" (JICO 2005).

"The presence of aquatic weeds along the lake and within the tributaries has resulted in even greater devastation to local human health. The weeds provide the necessary habitat for black-fly, mosquitoes and snails, which are the vectors of water-borne illnesses such as bilharzias and malaria. Since the instalment of the dam, these diseases have increased remarkably" (Wikipedia 2007).

"The miles of *slow-moving* or stagnant water (of the High Aswan Dam) are ideal breeding-grounds for mosquitoes that carry malaria, and the snails that are reservoirs of the parasite that causes Bilharzia, or Schistosomiasis. Malaria used to be considered controllable by insecticides and medication, but new virulent strains are now appearing" (University of California, undated, italics provided). Attention is attracted to 'slow-moving' waters mentioned above. Dam companies assert that there is likely to be no increase in malaria because waters in ROR Reservoirs will not be stagnant. They ignore the fact that 'slow moving' waters contribute equally to higher incidence of disease.

"Engineers who design spillways for dams and other water projects can do a great deal to prevent outbreaks of a disease called River Blindness, common in hilly areas of Central America, Ecuador, Venezuela and northern Brazil. This parasitic infection is spread by small black flies which breed in white-water rapids of mountain streams, and also on dam spillways. The parasite is transmitted to people through the painful bite of the black fly. As the parasite develops in its human host, it lodges in the eye of the victim, eventually causing blindness. The disease is also known as Onchocerciasis (Jobin 2004).

An excellent study by Jennifer Keiser and others undertaken by Swiss Tropical Institute, University of South Carolina, Oxford University, World Health Organization and Princeton University has provided a summary of global experience of impact of reservoirs on malaria.[16] The findings are summarized in the table below.

Table 4.39. Impact of Reservoirs on Incidence of Malaria (after Keiser 2004).

Sl. No.	*Dam*	*Change in malaria, percent*	*Basis*
1.	Khon Kaen, Thailand	(-) 0.6	Incidence was 1.2 percent in 1968. It reduced to 0.6 percent in 1969. Insecticides were sprayed.
2.	Nanak Matta, Uttaranchal, India	(-) 1.8	Incidence of malaria in dam area was nil in ccmparison to 1.8 percent in the plains.
3.	Kanchanari, Thailand	(+) 9	Incidence was 16% in 1972. Increased to 25% in 1976.
4.	Bamedijjin, Cameroon	(+) 11	Incidence near dam was 36%. Away from dam 25%.
5.	Manatali, Mali	(+) 19	Incidence near dam was 47%. In plains 28%.
	Average	(+) 7.3	

We shall later use this figure to estimate the impact of Kotlibhel HEP. These are given here to indicate that the problem is both severe and widespread in HEP Reservoirs.

Difficulties in Operational Management

The typical strategy used for control of malaria is regular spraying of the reservoir surface with insecticides. This is ineffective as evident from persistence of 2 million cases in the country despite such spraying. The more effective method is to operate water systems in a way to kill mosquitoes:

In a paper titled "Dams and development co-operation," prepared for the German Development Agency GTZ, Prof. Dr. Volkmar Hartje, Berlin and Dr. Klaus Horstmann, Dortmund say that "Theoretically, problems associated with water-borne diseases can be addressed adequately to avoid project-induced increases of diseases. A thorough examination of the accompanying risks is possible. No major investments are required, apart from buildings and equipment, if any. *But the operation of the services is difficult to sustain; it requires due diligence in running the local services* and a regional health policy with adequate budgets and a focus on adequate distribution of health care benefits" (Hartje 1999, italics provided).

William Jobin, Director, Blue Nile Associates has detailed the relationship of water level in a dam and mosquito-borne disease in a paper titled "Prediction of health hazards in tropical reservoirs and evaluation of low-cost methods for disease prevention," presented at UNHYDRO 2004 at Beijing (Jobin 2004). Jobin tells us:

"One of the methods still in use for mosquito control by Tennessee Valley Authority engineers in the U.S. of America is repeated fluctuation of the reservoir water level during the breeding season of the mosquitoes. This operational technique causes the mosquito eggs to be stranded on the shoreline or flushed out into open water where fish can eat them. The fluctuation cycle used by the TVA dam operators is 1 foot vertically with a period of one week, and requires steady inflow and certain corresponding design features in the outlet structures. This fluctuation schedule is adequate for controlling malaria mosquitoes in most of the Americas, but must be adapted to the seasonal pattern of mosquito breeding and malaria transmission for other tropical regions."

Such controlled fluctuation is more difficult in a Run of River HEP like Kotlibhel 1B because the water level will remain constant except for variations determined by inflow from upstream HEPs. This will provide ideal breeding ground for mosquitoes.

Experience of Uttarakhand

Survey of three dams in Uttarakhand confirms an increase in mosquitoes in reservoirs.

Table 4.40. Are mosquitoes and insects seen near the reservoir? When? How many? (Details at Annexure 1)

Sl. No.	*Item*	*Net, HEP-wise Impact*
1.	Chilla	Increase 6/19 = 32%
2.	Maneri	No impact, (0)
3.	Tehri	Increase 23/32 = 72%
4.	Combined	Increase 35%

A negative impact of dam on people's health is also reported.

Table 4.41. What is the change in people's health before- and after construction of dam? (Details at Annexure 1)

Sl. No.	*Item*	*Net, HEP-wise Impact*
1.	Chilla	(0)
2.	Maneri	Negative 1/13 = 8%
3.	Tehri	Negative 2/32 = 6%
4.	Combined	Negative 5%

The low level of negative impact should not be taken lightly. It is possible that people do not associate decline in health to the construction of reservoir. Be that as it may, it suffices to note that some negative impact on people's health is reported.

The EMP of Kotlibhel 1B promises that insecticides will be sprayed to control malaria. However, people's experience in other dams indicates that dam companies do not actually spray insecticides as promised.

Table 4.42. Does the Dam Company spray insecticides for killing mosquitoes? (Details at Annexure 1)

Sl. No.	*Item*	*Net, HEP-wise Impact*
1.	Chilla	Not done 15/19 = 79%
2.	Maneri	Not done 12/13 = 92%
3.	Tehri	Not done 32/32 = 100%
4.	Combined	Not done 90%

HEPs Ignore Breeding of Mosquitoes

The EMP of Kotlibhel 1B states: "Since this is a run-of-river scheme; the fear of water stagnation is not expected. Continuous flow of water in the reservoir will resist breeding of mosquitoes" (HNBU 2006b:210).

This prophetic statement ignores that the reservoir will create many small coves, which will serve as ideal breeding ground for mosquitoes. The author knows from personal knowledge that a huge stagnant pool will be created at Kandoli in Village Lakshmoli measuring about 100 x 150 meters. This pool will be fed through a small mouth from the reservoir. There will be no flow in this pool. The author asked NHPC about this under RTI Act. The question and replies given by NHPC (dated 7.9.2007) are produced below:

Table 4.43. Replies given by NHPC to query regarding Malaria

Question	*Reply by NHPC*
What is the size of water pool at Kandoli under Kotlibhel 1B Project.	There shall be no localized pool exclusively at Kandoli.
What is the inflow of water in pool at Kandoli under Kotlibhel 1B Project.	There shall be no exclusive water inflow at Kandoli. The water inflow from upstream catchment and project shall be in the reservoir inclusive at Kandoli.

This shows that NHPC solves the problem by simply denying it.

Costs

WHO has estimated that mosquitoes from a reservoir directly affect an area up to 10 km. Further, they are carried as far as 50 km by the winds. The reservoir has a draw-down zone that may extend 5 km laterally around the perimeter of the dam. Longer migratory flights or long-range transport of insects by prevailing winds imply that if a project creates new insect breeding sites then sooner or later they will be colonised. The migratory distance for flies is given as follows: Anopheline mosquitoes: 50 km, Culicine mosquitoes: 50 km and Tsetse flies 4 km (WHO 1999).

The population that will be affected by the Kotlibhel 1B Reservoir will, therefore, extend 50 km on each side—as the bird flies. The Author has estimated the cost to local people from malaria and other diseases on this basis.

Table 4.44. Costs to people due to malaria from Kotlibhel 1B

Sl. No.	*Item*	*Amount*	*Basis*
1.	Increase in number of persons affected by Malaria along the rim of Kotlibhel 1B Reservoir	1797 persons	Number of people living along the rim is 4924 (HNBU 2206b: 151). Assume five times this number in area up to 10 km km = 24,620. An increase of incidence of malaria of 7.3 percent is expected (Table 4.39 above)
2.	Cost of disease on directly affected area	Rs 3.5 crore	We assume that there will be a 15% loss of income.[17] The average per capita income of the country is Rs 29,235 (MOF 2006). The family income may be estimated at 4.5 persons per family at Rs 131,557. The cost is thus 1797 persons x Rs 131557 × 0.15 = 2.6 crores.
3.	Cost of disease burden on surrounding area (in 50 km	Rs 7.1 crores	Assume number of persons residing in 50 km range to be 100 times = 492,400. Let us say the incidence of disease

	migratory range)		will increase by 0.73% in the larger area against 7.3 percent in adjoining area. Accordingly, about 3,594 new persons will be affected. Cost = 3594 persons × Rs 131557 × 0.15 = 8.1 crores.
4.	Other costs	Rs 10.6 crores	The society will incur additional costs from (1) virulence and resistance, which will affect the entire nation; (2) Reservoir-borne Diseases other than malaria; (3) Disease burden on livestock; (4) Loss from death of some patients. Assume these equal to direct costs estimated above (Line 2 + line 3).
5	Total	Rs 21.2 crores	

Before we close, it is pertinent to mention that some positive health impacts of HEP reservoirs are also known. For example, River Blindness has been eliminated in the Owen Falls area of Nile because construction of a reservoir has deprived the black flies of their breeding ground near rapids.[18] Such benefits may appear where an area is already infested with some disease. That is not the case at Kotlibhel 1B hence no positive impact is envisaged.

Biodiversity

The Issue

Biodiversity refers to the variety of living organisms. Union of International Associations, a non-profit clearing house for information on over 60,000 international organizations founded by Henri La Fontaine, Nobel Peace Prize laureate of 1913 tells us that according to the Convention on Biological Diversity the term 'biological diversity' includes diversity within species, between species and of ecosystems, from all environments including terrestrial, marine and other aquatic ecosystems (UIA, undated-b).

Biodiversity is an economic resource for future. The ability of living beings to adjust to changing climatic factors depends upon availability of diversity. It is possible that one variety of, say, black pepper, which provides huge economic returns today, is unable to withstand the rise in climatic temperatures. In absence of biodiversity, humankind will be deprived of pepper if the global temperature rises. However, other varieties of pepper may be able to withstand such increase in temperatures. These resistant varieties may not be profitable today. Thus, there exists a trade-off between present and future economic benefits. In order to ensure survival of temperature-resistant varieties of pepper, it is necessary to preserve biodiversity. Mankind must give up some present benefits from cultivation of profitable varieties to preserve other varieties. Preservation of biodiversity, therefore, involves giving up present economic benefits for securing future economic benefits. A UNDP study, thus notes, "Biodiversity is a futuristic economic resource" (Mathur, undated).

The arguments against giving too much consideration to biodiversity revolve around the economic cost of such preservation (UIA, undated-b). The arguments and our response are given below:

Argument: *If we try to save all biological diversity, we will not be able to maintain our present living standard.*

Response: Maintenance of present living standards should not come at the expense of future generations.

Argument: *Biodiversity is not an object to be conserved. It is an integral part of human existence, in which utilization is part of the celebration of life.*

Response: Indeed, man must 'utilize' nature, which is celebration. However, 'celebration' is indicative of happiness, which comes from a positive relation with other species. One does not 'celebrate' killing and eating of one's pet dog. Thus, celebration must be moderated by discrimination.

The negative impact of HEPs on biodiversity is not merely a speculation. A study of *Environmental impact of water resources projects* tells us that "Dams and barrages have had a major impact on dolphins. The Indus dolphin now exists only as a meta-population consisting of four or five artificially isolated sub populations" (Abbasi, undated).

Other known instances of loss of biodiversity include the Kasturi Deer, Eagle and Peacock. A program to preserve the Falcon is being undertaken in Kumaon presently. Therefore, loss of biodiversity is real. It is not idle speculation.

Such loss of biodiversity may be one cause of the spread of diseases like AIDS. The connection between the two has been a subject of many conferences (ABCG, undated).

The conclusion is that preservation of biodiversity is not an economic cost imposed by environmentalists on HEPs. Rather, it is a plea for a proper economic assessment of the impact for long term economic welfare of the human species.

Negative Impact of HEPs on Biodiversity

The World Commission on Dams which was supported, among others, by Ministry of Water Resources, GOI; International Hydropower Association (representing hydropower companies); Asian Development Bank and World Bank has enumerated following impacts of HEPs on biodiversity:

- The construction of a storage dam and subsequent inundation of the reservoir area effectively kills terrestrial plants and forests and displaced animals. As many species prefer valley bottoms, large-scale impounding may eliminate unique wildlife habitats and affect populations of endangered species (WCD 2000a:75).
- Over 60 percent of the projects studied indicated that "impeding passage of migratory fish species" was a significant impact of HEP projects (WCD 2000a:82).
- A study of threatened fish of Oklahoma suggested that the loss of free-flowing river habitat due to

reservoirs had led to 55% of the human-induced species loss, while a further 19% was caused by dams acting as barriers to fish migration (WCD 2000a:82).

People's Assessment of Impact of HEPs

An indication of impact of HEPs on biodiversity is obtained from survey of people living around three dams in Uttarakhand.

Table 4.45. Did any trees, plants, butterfly, insects, animals, birds or fish exist previously that have now become extinct? (Details at Annexure 1)

Sl. No.	*Item*	*HEP-wise Impact*
1.	Chilla	Less 4/19 = (-) 21%
2.	Maneri	Less 3/11 = (-) 38%
3.	Tehri	No change
4.	Combined	Less, 20%

There are also some reports of increase in biodiversity. Some say new species of fish were introduced and quantity of fish catch is more. Snakes have increased Near Old Tehri (Sangeeta, Narayan Singh and Narendra Rao, Village Tiwar, Tehri). Snakes have moved up wards near village habitation. Previously they were living below near the riverbed. No adverse impact on biodiversity is reported from Tehri. One possibility is that the time of 3-4 years is less for such impact to become visible.

Possible Benefits of HEPs

HEPs do not have a positive impact on the creation of biodiversity, which takes millions of years to generate. However, it can help in stabilization of some endangered species. The World Commission on Dams quotes a case study of Waitaki River of New Zealand. Building of a HEP has stabilized the flows and helped increase the population of Chinook salmon. In the same breath, however, it has deprived the endangered 'black stilt' bird by depriving it of it habitat that consisted of large exposed sandbars that were created by the previously unstable river (WCD 2000a:78).

T. V. Ramachandra and R. Rajinikanth of Centre for Ecological Sciences, Indian Institute of Science, Bangalore likewise say that one of the benefits of wetlands and lakes is the preservation of biodiversity (Ramachandra, undated). However, this does not apply to reservoirs created by HEPs because 'preservation' implies pre-existence of biodiversity in and around a lake. Since new reservoirs are created by HEPs, there is no pre-existent biodiversity that may be preserved by such creation of reservoirs.

Impacts of Loss of Biodiversity

Robert Costanza of the University of Maryland has calculated that the Earth provides a minimum of $16-54 trillion dollars worth of 'services' to humans per year in 1997. (1997). Further, there are non-economic benefits of biodiversity. The Union of International Associations lists the following (UIA, undated-b):

- Moral and ethical: All life has an intrinsic value. People have no right to exterminate species or local populations of a species.
- Biological: There is a complex interplay in nature whereby all species affect one another. Variations in genetic material between individuals of the same species ensure that the species is more capable of surviving in the long term.
- Aesthetic: The diversity and variations found in nature provide experiences and inspiration. This value is difficult to measure, but has great importance.

The United Nations Development Programme in its report *Conserving Forest Biodiversity: Threats, Solutions and Experiences* says that biodiversity is destroyed because benefits occur to the influential, rich and urban sections of society while costs are borne by the weak, poor and rural people (Boyle 2003). Ignoring the impact on biodiversity, therefore, hides a conflict of interest between the rich and poor.

The Union of International Associations says, "The main cause of species extinction is loss of habitat. In particular, more than half the world's species live in the tropical forests. Some calculations show that 140 species are made extinct every day in the tropics. It is estimated that by 2020, deforestation could wipe out between 5 and 15% of those species" (UIA, undated-b). HEPs lead to submergence or drying of riverbeds hence contribute to this extinction.

Preserving Habitats

There is increasing evidence that preservation of biodiversity cannot be done successfully in artificial environs such as 'biodiversity parks'. The best way to do this is to preserve natural habitats.

According to the *Convention on Biodiversity Conservation*, following actions are needed to preserve biodiversity (UIA, undated-a):

- Protect and encourage customary use of biological resources in accordance with traditional cultural practices that are compatible with conservation or sustainable use requirements.
- Support local populations to develop and implement remedial action in degraded areas where biological diversity has been reduced.

The *Global Biodiversity Strategy: A Policy-maker's Guide 1992* says, "The best way to maintain species is to maintain their habitats. (Another) component is restoring lost species to their former habitats" (Genesis 1992).

The *1st Workshop on National Biodiversity Strategies* held in 2000 at Beijing noted: "Many countries have requested Environmental Impact Assessment for big projects that may cause environment damages. Environmental management, auditing & evaluation are parts of EIA. However, very few of EIAs have included the biodiversity "impact assessment, which means biodiversity is not considered while these countries are conducting EIAs." The

Workshop concluded: "It is strongly suggested by the participants that the very key issue in EIA is conservation of biodiversity. EIA should be and primarily for biodiversity conservation and should be identified in national, regional level of legal framework" (Yan 2000).

The Government of India has formulated a National Biodiversity Strategy and Action Plan (NBSAP). It is a project of Ministry of Environment and Forests funded by the Global Environment Facility through United Nations Development Programme. The objectives of NBSAP include the "Integration of biodiversity concerns into relevant sectors" (NBSAP, undated). Thus, HEPs are required to incorporate biodiversity concerns in their project plans.

The relevance of these lessons for HEPs is as follows:

- Conservation of biodiversity requires maintaining natural habitats. This is not done in HEPs, which divert water flows into tunnels or submerge riverbeds and destroy natural habitats.
- Conservation requires that traditional users of bio resources should be protected and promoted. HEPs displace them.
- Proper assessment of biodiversity impacts requires specialized study. EIAs typically fail to do so.
- Valuation of biodiversity must be done for not only present but also taking into account the impact on future generations.

Inadequacy of EIAs

Biodiversity Planning Support Programme of UNDP (UIA, undated-b) has made a study of the Sankosh Multipurpose Project located on the Indo-Bhutan border. The Study says the following about the EIA:

Unsubstantiated prophetic statements: The EIA confused impacts by hypothesizing post-project scenarios through 'prophetic' statements with little regard to ecological concepts.

Few examples are as follows: (1) "Since the area falling in the submergence area is small and is the outer peripheral rim of the sanctuary, the impact of reduction of animal habitat is likely to be insignificant." (2) The shrinkage of the sanctuary by about 6.6% will have no adverse impact on wildlife. (3) "The movement of elephants across the canal can be restored by seven bridges." (4) "Tor tor, a migratory fish species may find it difficult to survive as their migratory route will be blocked. However, in the new ecological environment, fresh spout of species will be witnessed. The lacustrine environment is also likely to be rich in biodiversity and quite a few useful varieties of fish will evolve."

Simplistic approach to mitigation: The mitigation approach adopted was too simplistic. Mitigation measures have been suggested without any prior efforts of evaluating the technical, physical, financial and operational feasibility of the measures proposed.

In another case study of 200 MW Lower Subansiri HEP at Gerukamukh on the Assam-Arunachal border, the EIA "identifies 55 fish species, even though recent records of Lakhimpur-based biologist Lakhi Hazarika show 118 species, including some which are endemic to the Subansiri, and one entirely new to science."

The EIA of Kotlibhel 1B is flawed like that of Sankosh Multipurpose and Subansiri HEPs:

Unsubstantiated prophetic statements: "Since the project is a run-of-the-river scheme, significant change in microclimate is not expected. Creation of lake will (have) its submergence mostly along the gorge. The project is not likely to be a threat to butterflies. No significant affects are foreseen on mammals (HNBU 2006c:228).

Simplistic approach to mitigation: The EIA recognizes that one species of butterfly falls under Schedule I, Part IV of Indian Wildlife Protection Act and two species of Graphim fall in the Threatened Category of IUCN Red Data Book. These species are less likely to find replacement habitats.

The EIA recommends that more research should be done before extinction takes place (HNBU 2006b:132-133). However, the EMP makes no mention whatsoever of this study and does not propose any mitgative measures.

Fails to capture biodiversity impacts: The EIA does not study genetic variants within a species as suggested by experts (UIA, undated-b). The EIA agency has not conducted any focussed meetings with local people to assess the biodiversity prevailing in the area. It is likely that the extent of biodiversity is understated.

Dr G D Agarwal, former Member-Secretary of CPCB has studied the EIA of Kotlibhel 1B. His comments are given below at length:

"The methodology for field surveys are entirely adequate and I could not wish for anything more.

"EIAs are essentially done with the objective of obtaining environmental clearance for the project, *whatever and wherever it might be.* This is clearly stated at Para 1.7 of EIA: "The main objective of this study is to prepare the environment impact assessment report *for obtaining environmental clearance from regulatory agencies."* Consequently, any data or observation that would go against is either diluted or omitted. Thus, the data presented may not be all the data observed.

"Nevertheless, extensive and competent studies have been carried out *in the study area chosen.* I have not seen so good ecological data in any EIA before. I would heartily appreciate and congratulate the Garhwal University for this.

"The large number of species present in the study area shows that the area has a very high biodiversity and rich ecology. This point is not made out *clearly* and *strongly* in the report.

"Chapter 8, listing impacts expected from the project, appears to be committed to state 'None or only marginal adverse impact from the project will take place'. Primarily it relies on the fact that "there is no vulnerable/endangered species" and "there is no wildlife sanctuary/national park/ biosphere reserve." For saying just this, so much fieldwork was not required. *No impact assessment has been done.* It would be ridiculous to call it 'impact assessment'.

"Ecology of a flood-basin totally depends on flow and storage variabilities (quantity, velocity, depth, spread, frequency, duration, seasonality, etc.)

"An impact study cannot be done without data on current and post-project flow variabilities being available. The EIA report does not even mention flow variabilities. Therefore, it is meaningless.

"The weakest aspect of EIA is the selection of study area. What would be the influence zone of the project? For ecology it would be the entire valley downstream of the project."

Prof R C Sharma of Department of Environmental Sciences expressed the following sentiments in relation to an earlier version of this study:

"What is left out of the EIA is more important. Aesthetic, environmental and emotional costs are not evaluated.

"Downstream impacts are severe. There was a depletion of oxygen downstream within a week of closing of sluices of Tehri. Fishes suffocated. They went back and people fished them.

"We are overexploiting the water resource. Give water space to recover.

"ROR projects change the morphology of the river—discharge, width, bottom substrata, habitat of aquatic insects—is modified.

"Riparian vegetation grows in up- and down variation in water levels. This provides bushes and shelter to animals. We do not know whether and how much and when this will regenerate."

The EIA of Kotlibhel 2 follows this same pattern. The biological environment is enumerated in detail in 64 pages.

This is followed by the following observation under the heading *Impacts on Flora:*

"Neither any tree species, shrub, herb nor any climber or grass species is either vulnerable or endangered...There will be no *significant* loss to the habitat...There will certainly be loss of riverine vegetation during the project activity period which will be restored in the reservoir periphery in due course of time" (ICFRE: 203). These statements are made prophetically. They are not backed by studies or analysis. Same situation prevails regarding fauna. It is said that no damage is likely to occur despite the fact that the body of EIA enumerates threat to the masheer and butterflies. Thus, the very objective of EIA is negated. Instead of *Impact-* these studies become *Inventory Assessments.*

Costs of Kotlibhel 1B

It is difficult to place money value on loss of biodiversity due to Kotlibhel 1B project because (1) the extent of loss in terms of species is not known; and (2) the money value of that loss is difficult to calculate. We have tried to calculate below the costs due to this project despite these inherent difficulties.

Table 4.46. Cost of loss of biodiversity due to Kotlibhel 1B

Sl. No.	*Item*	*Amount*	*Basis*
1.	Value of total services provided by earth	Rs 47.1 crores per year per km2	Services of $35 trillion are provided by earth from 2,973,190 Sq km land area (CIA, undated).
2.	Value of services provided by land area submerged in Kotlibhel 1B	Rs 233.3 crores per year	Pro-rata for 495 ha or 4.95 km2
3.	Value of biodiversity services provided by land area submerged in Kotlibhel 1B	Rs 11.7 crores per year	Say biodiversity consists of 5% of total services provided.

The learned reader is welcome to make alternate estimates of this cost. These can then be discussed and scrutinized. It is unforgivable, however, for these to be entirely ignored as has been done in EIAs of these projects.

Otters

The Issue

The riverbed of Alaknanda River to be submerged under Kotlibhel 1B HEP is the habitat of Smooth-coated Otter—an endangered species. Wildlife Institute of India, Dehra Dun has given the status of Smooth-coated Otter in its publication *Status of Otter Conservation in India*. There are 13 species of otter distributed worldwide. Five species occur in Asia of which three species are found in India:

- Eurasian otter, Lutra
- Smooth-coated otter, Lutra perspicillata
- Oriental small-clawed otter, Aonyx cinerea

"All the three species of otters are protected in India under the Wildlife (Protection) Act, 1972 and are listed as endangered... In India, major threats to Otter populations are loss of wetland habitats, reduction in prey biomass, pollution and poaching. *Development projects such as dams and barrages*, and aquaculture activities took the major toll of wetlands" (NBA 2005, italics provided).

Threats to Smooth-coated Otter from Kotlibhel Reservoir

It is proposed to catch the otters from their natural habitat between Dev Prayag and Srinagar and resettle them in the area between Kirti Nagar and Srinagar, which will be declared as a 'restricted area'.

This author has spoken to Dr R C Sharma of Department of Environmental Sciences, H N B University, Srinagar and Shri Asghar Nawab of World Wildlife Fund, Delhi. Based on these discussions and study of material available on the internet, the author believes that Kotlibhel Reservoir is likely to exterminate the Smooth-coated Otter in this area. The proposed resettlement will fail for the following reasons.

Fragmentation of Populations

A deep 'V'-shaped reservoir will be formed instead of the present meandering flow of the river. Otters do not like deep waters. Their populations are likely to be fragmented on two sides of the river. This will happen also above Kirti Nagar where the depth of reservoir will be increased in comparison to the present.

Loss of Riparian Vegetation and Sand Beaches

Otters love riparian vegetation that grows along the riversides. This refers to vegetation that grows on the riversides that is inundated at some times and not at other times. The variation in level of water provides stimulus for the growth of peculiar vegetations that are liked by the otter. This riparian vegetation will undergo substantial change as the water level will vary only 2-3 metres intra-day and not 15 meters intra-season as presently. The Otter makes its feeding groves amidst riparian vegetation.

It is a fearful animal. It escapes and hides among these bushes. The nature of the vegetation will change and it may not provide such shelter in the new environs.

The Otter plays and rolls in the sand, which enhances the quality of its fur and enables it withstand the cold in the winters. The sand beaches are formed along the riverside during the flood times. This will not happen after dam is made and variation in water level is reduced to mere 2-3 metres. The otter will no longer be able to roll in the sand with attendant consequences.

Change in Nature of Feeding Species of Fish

The Wildlife Institute of India says "The damming of a river has been called as cataclysmic event. By changing the flow of water, sediment, nutrients, energy, and biota, dams interrupt and alter most of the rivers' important ecological process" (NBA 2005). These changes will impact the fish and thence otter.

The project appears to envisage introduction of new species of fish. The EMP says: "Stocking of fish seed in a reservoir is a step of prime importance for management practice in reservoirs" (HNBU 2006c:222). The EMP makes no study of the experience of artificial seeding of endemic species and also of the habitation conflict between endemic and new species to be introduced, if any. Thus, the availability of fish for the survival of endangered Otter is not ensured.

Aversion to Human Habitation

The Otter is known to shun proximity to human habitations:

- Otters avoid areas with high levels of anthropogenic disturbance (Shenoy 2006).
- Otters require undisturbed forest or dense scrub adjacent to the water ((ROPS, undated).
- Otters are elusive creatures, fearful of man (Bloynx, undated).

The difficulty is that the area between Kirti Nagar and Srinagar proposed to be reserved for their conservation is intensely populated by human beings on both banks hence is unsuitable for Otter conservation. The EMP overlooks this important point.

It is reported that Otters were found in large numbers along Bhilangana and Bhagirathi rivers that have since been converted into Tehri Reservoir. Local people used to catch them with local contraption called Kadaki. They have become extinct in that area. They could not adapt to the reservoir conditions in that area. The same is likely to happen in this area.

Can the Otter Readjust?

The above observations do not lead to a definite conclusion that Otter will become extinct in the area. It is possible that it may adapt to the new circumstances. Consider the following:

- Otter can survive on the rim of reservoir as in Periyar Tiger Reserve. They have learnt to feed on exotic species of fish.
- Otters can adapt to small human habitations. A den of otters was located on a tributary of Ramganga in Corbett Tiger Reserve close to a hamlet of six houses.

The task before us is to assess whether the negative factors mentioned above are so adverse that the otter will not be able to adjust. In other words we have to assess whether the otter will become extinct as in Bhagirathi-Bhilangana are or readjust as in Periyar Tiger Reserve.

The impact of dams on dolphins was assessed in an international workshop (Abbasi, undated). These impacts provide us with a takeoff point to examine the possible impacts on otter due to making of Kotlibhel Reservoir as shown in Table 4.47.

The conclusion from the above chart is clear: The impact is likely to be negative. Given the extinction of this species in Tehri area, there is a great chance that it may happen here. It was incumbent upon the EIA agency to study the following:

- Experience of adaptation of Otter in Periyar, Ramganga and other areas and applicability of the same to Kotlibhel.
- Reasons for extinction of otter in Bhagirathi-Bhilangana area of Tehri Reservoir.
- Suitability of the proposed area between Kirti Nagar and Srinagar for resettlement of Otter.
- The dispersal of Smooth-coated Otter in other areas of the country and whether the species is likely to survive in other areas if it becomes extinct in Kotlibhel area.

Table 4.47. Applicability of experience of Indus Dolphin to Smooth-coated Otter

Sl. No.	*Impact of dams on dolphins*	*Positive factors—Otter may survive*	*Negative factors —Otter may become extinct*	*Author's Conclusion*
1.	Fragmentation of populations into genetically isolated subpopulations.	May survive in fragmented populations.	Conversion of river into reservoir will fragment the population of otters into two parts by a deep river.	Negative. Smaller sub-populations more likely to become extinct. Survival of sub-population will be less than whole population.
2.	Reduction in prey due to blocked migratory routes, less diversity, smaller prey due to lowered nutrient availability, changes in prey caused by changes in flow rate, sediment transport, and estuarine salinity.	Otters may adapt to exotic species of fish.	Migratory routes of fish will be blocked and lead to change in prey.	Uncertain. Whether otter will adjust to new species of fish from artificial seeding of the reservoir is uncertain.

Sl. No.	*Impact of dams on dolphins*	*Positive factors—Otter may survive*	*Negative factors —Otter may become extinct*	*Author's Conclusion*
3.	Dispersal of dolphins between river systems is reduced.	Otter not known to habit upstream and downstream areas of Kothibhel 1B hence no impact may take place.	We do not know the precise area of its habitation. The EMP denies its existence downstream of Kirti Nagar but this author has seen them at Lakshmoli.	Negative. The upstream and downstream areas are similar and Otter may exist there. Anyways, dams will reduce the access of otter to these habitats.
4	Otters dislike human habitations[19]	Otters can survive near small human populations	Proposed area for resettlement is highly inhabited hence inappropriate.	Negative. Area proposed for their protection is totally unsuitable.
5	Deprivation of riparian vegetation and sand beaches on river-sides	Otters known to adapt to existence on rim at Periyar Sanctuary.	Adaptation possible but not certain. Conditions in Periyar Reserve, which is a reserve forest, are different from at Kirti Nagar, which is hugely inhabited.	Negative. Adjustment in Periyar Sanctuary does not involve conflict with human habitation.

In absence of these studies, this author feels that there is a very good chance that Smooth-coated Otter will become extinct in this area and this may contribute to wider extinction of that species.

Costs of Kotlibhel

Extinction of Smooth-coated Otter will impose a cost on future generations. The author has not been able to access a method for estimating the same. The author's best estimate for this one-time loss is Rs 200 crores. The annual cost is estimated at 10% to be Rs 20 crores per year.

Road accidents

The Issue

Road accidents are a recurring feature of the Garhwal Himalayas. Presently a vehicle falling down into the valley from the highway falls on dry land. Many persons travelling in the ill-fated vehicles survive because they can come out of the damaged vehicle. Creation of a reservoir along NH-58 will mean that such ill-fated vehicles will fall into the reservoir because the rim of the proposed reservoir is close to the highway. The chances of survival will be almost zero.

Costs

The number of accidents, deaths and injuries along NH-58 is available from a report published in the leading newspaper of the area—*Dainik Jagaran* dated October 22, 2007.

Table 4.48. Accidents on NH-58

Sl. No.	*Item*	*Jan-Sep 06*	*Jan-Sep-07*	*Average*
1.	Number of accidents	19	32	25
2.	Number of deaths	40	84	62
3.	Number of injured	105	154	129

The numbers of injured persons are likely to be converted into deaths upon making of reservoirs along NH-58. The consequent additional cost is estimated at table 4.49 below.

Table 4.49. Cost imposed upon travellers by Kotlibhel 1B due to accidents

Sl. No.	*Item*	*Amount*	*Basis*
1.	Persons injured in one year	172 numbers	Pro-rata for 12 months on basis of Dainik Jagaran Report at table 4.48.
2.	Persons injured in the 27 km stretch of highway along Kotlibhel 1B.	23 numbers	Total length from Badrinath to Rishikesh is 300 km. Of this traffic is more in the first 100 km. Of the 172 injured, we assume 87, 58 and 27 in the three 100-km stretches. Kotlibhel 1B reservoir will be made in 27 km of the first 100 km. Pro-rata 23 persons likely to be injured in this stretch every year.
3.	Loss to nation from death of the presently injured persons	Rs 4.4 crore per year	The per capita GNP of the country was Rs 29,235 in 2005-06. Assuming a family of 4.5 persons the income of the breadwinner is estimated at Rs 131,557 per year. This totals to Rs 19,01,288 discounted Net Present Value at discount rate of 5% as used by Kanchan Chopra Committee. For 23 persons this is assessed at Rs 4.4 crores per year.
4.	Loss to family members	Rs 2.2 crore per year	Cost of trauma etc. to family members is assumed to be one-half of the cost of death.
5.	Loss to vehicles etc.	Rs 0.5 crore per year	On average, 5 persons are injured per accident according to Dainik Jagaran report. Thus, pro-rata 5 vehicles will be submerged in the reservoir on 23 injured persons. These are valued at Rs 10 lacs each.
6.	Total loss	Rs 7.2 crore per year	

Decline in Temperature

The Issue

The temperature of the area declines with the building of a reservoir. This will have an impact upon crop yields, living costs and health. Health impacts are accounted within the cost of disease in previous section. Here we deal with crop yields and living costs.

Impact of HEP

Two studies provide some indication of the impact of reservoir on the local temperature. Russell M. Preece and Hugh A. Jones of NSW Department of Land and Water Conservation, Parramatta, Australia tell us that "Keepit Dam... one of several deep-release structures in the basin, (is) causing ecologically significant temperature modification over a large length of river... Modifications to... the river's annual temperature cycle were quantified in relation to a pre-dam temperature regime... The effect was greatest immediately downstream from the dam where the annual maximum daily temperature was approximately 5.0°C lower... than the pre-dam condition" (Preece 2002). This study tells us that the greatest effect was downstream. By implication, the upstream effect was less. From this fact, we assume that the upstream decline in temperature was 4°C.

Carolyn Gramling writes on Geotimes website: Three Gorges Dam in China "has a significant effect on the climate... To assess how the region's climate had changed, Liguang Wu, a climatologist at NASA's Goddard Space Flight Centre in Greenbelt, Md., and his team analyzed precipitation rates and land surface temperatures collected by NASA's Tropical Rainfall Measuring Mission and Moderate Resolution Imaging Spectroradiometer. They looked at two periods, from January 1998 to January 2003 and from January 2004 to January 2006. The team found that while the average rainfall over the immediate dam area in Yichang had decreased since the reservoir was filled in 2003. It was raining more elsewhere, particularly in the Sichuan Basin... several hundred kilometres to the northwest...Daytime temperatures also decreased by about

0.7 degrees Celsius in the same region. The data suggest that the reservoir is having a regional, rather than local, effect on climate" (Gramling 2006). This study tells us that decline in temperature is 0.7°C several hundred kilometres from the dam. The decline near the dam would be more. This could be similar to the 4°C decline estimated above based on Australia study.

This decline is due to a large reservoir. The Kotlibhel 1B Reservoir is small hence the author's best estimate is that decline may be 2°C in the immediate vicinity of 4 km and 0.5°C in an area of 50 km.

Lower temperature can have a beneficial impact on crop yields if pre-existing temperatures are high and lowered to an optimum level. On the other hand, they would affect crop yields negatively if pre-existing temperatures are low and are further lowered. The situation in Kotlibhel area is of the latter type. Temperatures are already low and likely to be lowered further leading to reduced yields.

People's Assessment of Decline in Yields

Survey of people confirms a decline in yields subsequent to making of dams.

Table 4.50. What is the impact of dam on the yields of wheat? (Details at Annexure 1)

Sl. No.	*Item*	*Net, HEP-wise Impact*
1	Chilla	Reduced 3/8 = (-) 38%
2	Maneri	Reduced 3/10 = (-) 30%
3	Tehri	(0)
4	Combined	(-) 23%

Table 4.51. What is the impact of dam on the yields of paddy? (Details at Annexure 1)

Sl. No.	*Item*	*Net, HEP-wise Impact*
1	Chilla	Reduced 3/8 = (-) 38%
2	Maneri	Reduced 3/10 = (-) 30%
3	Tehri	(0)
4	Combined	(-) 23%

The people living along dams made previously clearly state that there is a negative impact on yields of the two principal crops—wheat and paddy. This may be due to lower temperatures or more fog. The 'no impact' at Tehri may be due to less time that has elapsed after construction of dam.

Costs

An attempt to assess the impact of Kotlibhel 1B Reservoir on yields is made for two major crops—wheat and paddy.

Wheat requires temperatures between 0°C and 11°C before the flowering period and between 12°C and 26°C during grain formation period (Chaurasia 1991, Kreger 2007). A study by Punjab Remote Sensing Centre and Punjab Agricultural University, Ludhiana tells us that a positive or negative departure in temperature by 1°C from these optimum values "causes reduction in yield by about 0.2 tones per hectares" (Chaurasia 1991).

The EIA of Kotlibhel 1B does not give data of month-wise temperatures. It is mentioned, however, that "There exists a dense fog from mid December to mid February. Temperature as low as -2.5°C has been recorded during this season" (HNBU 2006b:450). EIA of Kotlibhel 2 further mentions that "temperature as low as -7.5°C has been recorded at Srinagar during winter" (ICFRE: 41). The Author's best estimate, based on studies mentioned above, is that the temperature will decline from the existing 0°C to -2°C. The ideal temperature for wheat in winter is between 0°C and 11°C. The prevailing temperatures are at the margins of the required temperature. A fall in the same is likely to affect wheat yields adversely.

The estimate of decline in crop yields is made on above basis in table below.

Table 4.52. Cost of decline in crop yields due to fall in temperature

Sl. No.	*Item*	*Amount*	*Basis*
1	Wheat production in 4 km area around Kotlibhel Reservoir	Rs 6.3 crore per year	There are 1536 families in directly affected villages (HNBU 2006b:151). The annual income of a family is Rs 51,400 (HNBU 2006b:159). Assume 80% is from agriculture.
2	Reduction crop incomes from Kotlibhel 1B in immediate area	Rs 1.0 crore per year	Present yield of wheat is 125 kg per nail or 2.5 tons per ha. A reduction of 0.4 tons per ha or 16% is expected from decline in temperature of 2°C.
3	Reduction crop incomes from Kotlibhel 1B in extended area	Rs 2.5 crore per year	Assume total income of farmers in 50 km area to be ten times. A reduction of 4% may take place in this.
4	Other losses	Rs 3.5 crore per year	Additional requirement of fuel and clothing, less yields of milk from livestock and kitchen garden etc. are assumed to be equal to loss from crop yields.
5	Total loss	Rs 7.0 crore per year	

Sand

The Issue

The ownership of the river rests with the Forest Department. Local people are entitled to take minor forest produce from the forests for their personal use. These include sand from the riverbed. A large number of local people are engaged in harvesting of sand for local consumption. These users will be deprived of sand and the horse carriers will be deprived of their livelihood. Local people will have to buy sand that is brought from longer distance at higher rates.

People's Assessment of Loss of Sand

People living near older dams in Uttarakhand have confirmed less availability of sand after making of dams.

Table 4.53. The availability of sand from riverbank for construction of houses has increased or decreased? (Details at Annexure 1)

Sl. No.	*Item*	*Net, HEP-wise Impact*
1.	Chilla	Less 2/18 = (-) 11%
2.	Maneri	More 4/13 = (+) 31%
3.	Tehri	Less 28/32 = (-) 88%
4.	Combined	Less = (-) 23%

There is negative impact on availability of sand at Chilla and Tehri. The dam companies say more sand will be available at the spillway due to flushing but this is not happening in reservoir-based HEPs like Tehri.

There is positive impact at Maneri. This appears to be due to the naked stretch of river bed immediately downstream the barrage. Most water is diverted through the tunnel. The barrage is flushed intermittently into the naked river bed. Sand settles here and is easily harvested.

The design of Kotlibhel 1B is similar to Tehri. A 27 km long reservoir will be made. Accordingly it is likely to lead to less availability of sand as has happened at Tehri.

Costs

The cost to local people is estimated below.

Table 4.54. Cost of deprivation of sand due to Kotlibhel 1B

Sl. No.	*Item*	*Amount*	*Basis*
1	Number of donkeys involved in harvesting sand by local people	216 numbers	27 villages, 8 horses in each village
2	Volume of sand harvested by local people	43,416 cum per year	216 horses × 300 days × 0.67 cum per horse per day.
3	Value of sand lost by local people	Rs 3.5 crore per year	Big truck brings 10 cum sand at Rs 8,000 from the plains. The sand lost is thus valued at Rs 800 per cum.
4	Net loss to local people	Rs 2.5 crore per year	The cost of carrying by horses is reduced from the purchase cost: 216 horses × 300 days × Rs 150 per day = Rs 97 lacs.
5	Volume of sand harvested by contractors at Chauras and Chopadia	180,000 cum per year	60 trucks per day × 300 days × 10 cum
6	Monetary value of sand lost by contractors	Rs 6.6 crore per year	Price of sand from plains = Rs 800 per cum. Cost of local collection by 706 trucks is Rs 2,600 for 6 cum or Rs 433 per cum. Additional cost of getting sand from plains = 800 – 433 = 367 per cum × 180,000 cum per year.
7	Total cost of Kotlibhel 1B HEP	Rs 9.1 crore per year	Total of lines 4 and 6

Inadequacy of Research

The EIA of Kotlibhel 1B does not even recognize this loss of income to the local people. The Author asked NHPC about this matter under RTI. The replies obtained are produced at Table 4.55.

Table 4.55. Replies given by NHPC regarding harvesting of sand

Information Requested under RTI Act	*Reply under RTI Act dated 13.7.2007*	*Reply dated 1.10.07 under Appeal under RTI Act*
How much loss will local inhabitants have to bear due to non-availability of sand locally under Kotlibhel 1B Project.	In the reservoir of Kotlibhel 1B there is only one sand quarry near Bagwan which is leased out by the State Govt hence there may not be appreciable loss to local inhabitants.	It is already informed that the sand stone quarry are being given on lease to the local contractors by State Govt. which suffice the need of the locals, however no study has been undertaken with regard to illegal lifting of sand from riverbed and riverside.

The reply given by NHPC is unsatisfactory for the following reasons:

- Local people are legally entitled to harvest forest produce for their personal use. This is not recognized by NHPC.
- Even if such harvesting is illegal, NHPC is not the police guardian of the area. The Hon Supreme Court has confirmed marriages of juveniles on compassionate grounds even though 'illegal'. The job of NHPC was to evaluate the social and environmental impact upon the people and work out compensatory mechanisms. Instead, NHPC is hiding behind façade of illegality to absolve itself from such liability.
- The loss to the State Government from absence of contracts is not accounted for in the project design.

River Rafting

The area between Dev Prayag and Srinagar has a few river rafting camps. These will be closed after creation of the reservoir. NHPC says new opportunities for water sports will be created. People living around three earlier dams have said that there is increase in tourism. This writer must report that he was taken by a friend to the banks of the Chilla Barrage as a tourist outing. Hence, some positive impact is seen on tourism. Local people confirm this as shown at Table 4.56.

This is the present situation when reservoirs have a sense of newness. This beneficial impact on tourism may not persist after creation of cascade of reservoirs removes their exceptionality. Tourists go to exceptional places. Thus, there is not likely to be any increase in tourism from Kotlibhel Reservoirs. In the result, this author estimates a negative impact. The cost to local people from closure of river rafting camps is estimated below. This will not be compensated by creation of new tourism for the abovementioned reasons.

Table 4.56. Has the number of tourists in your area increased or decreased after making of the dam? (Details at Annexure 1)

Sl. No.	*Item*	*Net, HEP-wise Impact*
1.	Chilla	More 10/19 = (+) 53%
2.	Maneri	More 4/13 = (+) 23%
3.	Tehri	More 9/30 = (+) 30%
4.	Combined	(+) 35%

Further people confirm that tourists like Tehri Reservoir.

Table 4.57. In your opinion, do tourists prefer flowing water or reservoir? (Details at Annexure 1)

Sl. No.	*Item*	*Net, HEP-wise Impact*
1.	Chilla	Flowing water 6/14 = (-) 29%
2.	Maneri	Flowing water 2/12 = (-) 17%
3.	Tehri	Reservoir 19/29 = (+) 65%
4.	Combined	(+) 6%

Table 4.58. Cost of closure of river-rafting camps

Sl. No.	*Item*	*Value*	*Basis*
1.	Number of camps	5 numbers	Author's estimate
2.	Loss of income	Rs 8.0 crores per year	5 camps × 100 tourists per week × Rs 4,000 per tourist (net income) × 40 weeks

Bridges

The Issue

Many infrastructures are submerged or otherwise made redundant such as footbridges, roads, water tanks etc. These are not replaced by the HEP. This imposes a social cost upon the people. This loss is confirmed by the people in study of three dams.

Table 4.59. What is the impact of canal or dam on contacts with relatives etc. on the other side? (Details at Annexure 1)

Sl. No.	*Name of HEP*	*Net, HEP-wise Impact*
1.	Chilla	Better 3/20 = (+) 15%
2.	Maneri	Better 4/13 = (+) 31%
3.	Tehri	Worse 24/32 = (-) 75%
4.	Combined	(-) 10%

The barrages at Chilla and Maneri Bhali have led to better contacts. On the other hand, there is strong negative impact at Tehri. Clearly, the impact depends on the nature of HEP. The structure of Kotlibhel HEP is similar to that of Tehri. Hence, the impact will be strongly negative as at Tehri.

Costs

The cost of Kotlibhel 1B due to submergence of bridges is estimated below.

Table 4.60. Cost of submergence of bridges and other infrastructure

Sl. No.	Item	Amount	Basis
1.	Number of foot bridges to be sub-merged	3	At Maletha, Bagwan and Mulya villages
2.	Number of persons using the bridges	219,000 per year	3 Bridges × 200 persons × 365 days
3.	Additional cost imposed upon people	Rs 3.3 crore per year	Assume these persons have to pay additional fare of Rs 50 and opportunity cost of time Rs 100 per visit.

Aesthetic Value of Free Flow of River

The Issue

We have assessed the loss to pilgrims on account of deterioration in quality of waters due to construction of dams in the section on "Quality of Waters". That loss occurs to those coming to the ghats of the Ganga to take bath or to carry waters home. In addition, people may have a value for free-flowing rivers. That is, even though one does not derive direct benefits from bathing or carrying waters, yet one likes free-flowing river just as one likes the sun shining outside the room even though one does not bask in the sunlight. This liking would extend to even those who do not come to the Ganga. For example, this author may be willing to pay some money for maintaining free flow of the Mahanadi even though he has no inclination to take a bath in that river. The position of Ganga is unique in view of its all-India reach in terms of respect and veneration.

Economists have developed the method of 'willingness to pay' to assess monetary value of such intangible benefits. People are asked how much they would be willing to pay for the specified result. This is taken to be the monetary value of the event.

The economic value of three national parks has been assessed by the Planning Commission with this methodology (Mathur 2003). The Commission has worked out the following values for intangible benefits.

Table 4.61. Willingness to pay for maintaining national parks

Intangible benefit	*Annual value*	*Location*
Recreation/ Eco-tourism	Rs 427.04 and Rs 519 per Indian Visitor (two estimates)	Keoladeo National Park, Bharatpur
Eco-tourism	Rs 34.68 per local visitor	Kalakadu Mundanthurai Tiger Reserve, Tamil Nadu
Eco-tourism	Rs 9.5 per local visitor	Periyar Tiger Reserve, Kerala

The average of these values is Rs 172 per visitor. This can be used as one proxy estimate for the value of free-flowing rivers.

The value of free-flowing waters has been assessed in three surveys got done by the author.

Survey of People Living Around Three Dams

People living near dams were asked "How much annual price you are willing to pay for restoring free flow of water in the river?"

Table 4.62. Willingness to pay for free-flowing waters, Rupees per year (Details at Annexure 1)

Sl. No.	*Name of HEP*	*HEP-wise Average*
1.	Chilla, n=12	71
2.	Maneri, n=13	136
3.	Tehri, n=32	20
4.	Average	76

Survey of Pilgrims at Dev Prayag, Rishikesh and Haridwar

Pilgrims at the three places were asked, "How much are you willing to pay to decommission Tehri Dam and restore free flowing waters of Ganga?"

Table 4.63. Willingness to pay for free flowing waters, Rupees per year (Details at Annexure 2)

Sl. No.	*Location*	*Average*	*Median*
1.	Dev Prayag, n=17	2,083	101
2.	Rishikesh, n=18	986	1,000
3.	Haridwar, n=19	1,663	1,000
4.	Average, n=54	1,577	700

The loss to people not coming to these places, however, may be less.

Survey of Pilgrims at Dhari Devi

Pilgrims were asked, "How much are you willing to pay to decommission Tehri Dam and restore free flowing waters of Bhagirathi at Dev Prayag?"

Table 4.64. Willingness to pay for free flowing waters, Rupees per year (Details at Annexure 3)

Sl. No.	*Location*	*Average*	*Median*
1.	Visitors, n=26	529	100
2.	Local residents, n=6	255	225

The significance of this question lies in that this willingness to pay this amount is for removing the Tehri Dam and restoring free-flowing waters at Dev Prayag—both of which are about 50 km away.

Combined Estimate

We have four estimates for willingness to pay for free-flowing waters.

Table 4.65. Estimates for willingness to pay for free-flowing waters

Sl. No.	*Survey*	*Value*	*Applicability*
1	Three National Parks	Rs 172 per visitor	(1) Relates to visitor, not to a distant person; (2) Relates to national parks, not rivers.
2	Three dams in Uttarakhand	Rs 76 per person	People thought the question of restoring free-flow of waters to be meaningless. This is likely to be an underestimate
3	Pilgrims at Dev Prayag, Rishikesh and Haridwar	Rs 1,577 per pilgrim	Relates to pilgrims—whose willingness to pay is likely to be more than non-pilgrims.
4	Pilgrims at Dhari Devi	Rs 529 per pilgrim	Amount is given by people far away. However, respondents are religiously inclined.

Table 4.66. Monetary value of loss of free-flowing waters

Sl. No.	*Item*	*Amount*	*Basis*
1.	Willingness to pay for free-flowing waters of the Ganga by pilgrims	Rs 1176 crores per year	Rs 588 per pilgrim × 2 crore pilgrims per year (Author's estimate)
2.	Willingness to pay for free-flowing waters of the Ganga by non-pilgrim residents of the country	Rs 3306 crores per year	Rs 58 per resident × 57 crore adult population
3.	Total Willingness to pay for free-flowing waters of the Ganga	Rs 4482 crores per year	Total of lines 1-2
4.	Share of Kotlibhel 1B in Willingness to pay for free-flowing waters of the Ganga	Rs 60.5 crores per year	Kotlibhel 1B will obstruct free flow in 27 Km distance. Total flow of Bhagirathi, Alaknanda and other tributaries may be about 2,000 km from Badrinath to Gangasagar. Value at Line 3 is imputed in ratio of 27:2000.

Average of the above four estimates is Rs 588 per person. This author feels this is correct value for the pilgrims who come to the religious centres along the Ganga. The willingness to pay for non-pilgrims may be taken as one-tenth of this estimate. We have tried to calculate the value of free-flowing waters that will be lost from Kotlibhel 1B on the basis of these estimates.

The wise reader is welcome to make alternate assumptions and arrive at a different value. The humble submission of the author is that totally ignoring such high loss of value is inexcusable.

Miscellaneous Costs

Kotlibhel 1B will impose many other costs upon the local people. A brief estimate of these is given in this chapter.

Immersion of Ashes

The local people cremate their dead along the flowing waters of the Alaknanda. They will have to carry the dead bodies to Byasi—55 km away—where alone they will get access to flowing waters. They will incur additional costs in the same.

Table 4.67. Comments of people on deprivation of free-flowing waters for immersion of ashes (Details at Annexure 1)

Sl. No.	*Name of HEP*	*Number of Respondents*	*Comment*
1.	Chilla	1/19	Previously we used to cremate along the river where barrage stands presently. Now we take the dead body to Rishikesh.
2.	Maneri	1/13	Previously we cremated along the river where barrage stands today. There is much difficulty now.
3.	Tehri	4/30	One person said they take dead body to Dharasu. Three persons said that, financial position permitting, they take the dead body for cremation to Zero Point.

During survey of people living around three dams, a number of people expressed anguish at being deprived of free flowing waters to immerse the ashes of their dead.

People of Uttarakhand have the practice of Lingwas. After cremation, they take a stone from the river back home as representative of the departed soul. This ling is worshipped every year at specified times. People will not be able to take the Ling from a reservoir since it is not from free-flowing waters. One monk told this author that substitute of Lingwas is recitation of Bhagwat Purana, which entails an expenditure of Rs 50,000. The costs to the departed soul are immense if It does not get moksha and has to take rebirth because his body was cremated along a reservoir and Lingwas not done properly.

Table 4.68. Cost to local people from denial of free-flowing waters for immersion of ashes

Sl. No.	*Item*	*Amount*	*Basis*
1.	Population affected	4,92,400 persons	People living along the rim of Kotlibhel reservoir = 4924. Assume number of persons residing in 50 km range to be 100 times
2.	Number of deaths	3,742	Crude death rate is 7.6 MOF 2006, Table 1.1)
3.	Number of dead bodies brought to Alaknanda for creation	1,871	Say 50%.
4.	Total cost of Kotlibhel 1B HEP	Rs 1.9 crore per year	Additional cost of each cremation at Byasi is estimated at Rs 10,000. This includes cost of transport and loss of opportunity value of time lost.

Relocation of Temples

HEPs relocate temples removing them from submergence area and remaking them above the reservoir. Logic as well as experience tells us that the power of the temple is not recreated at the new location.

Monks at Dhari Devi told this author that the rock on which the Dhari Devi temple is located has been charged by hundreds of years of penance and worship. The new temple, even if erected on the same spot, will nevertheless drown the present rock that is charged. The new temple will not have the same power as at present.

They have quoted from the Shiv Purana, Chapter 15: "The worship done within one's own home gives ordinary benefits. Worship done on the banks of a water body gives ten times the benefit. A place near tulsi, bel and pipal trees gives ten times the benefit of water body. Similarly, progressively ten times higher benefit is obtained from temple, teertha, river bank, banks of seven Gangas, seas shore and hill top." This indicates that the place is of great importance. The impact of change of place of the temple is not accounted in EIAs.

Pilgrims at Dhari Devi were asked: If the temple is remade at this same spot on pillars, will the spiritual effect increase or decrease? The answers are tabulated below.

Table 4.69. Impact of relocation of Temple of Dhari Devi (Details at Annexure 3)

Question	*Number of Respondents*	*Small increase*	*Large increase*	*Small decrease*	*Large decrease*	*Net decrease, percent*
Visitors	47	4	9	20	7	-30%
Local	13	1	1	4	6	-62%
Total	60	5	10	24	13	-37%

Conclusion is that pilgrims feel relocation of the temple will reduce the spiritual effect. This negative effect is more strongly felt by local people.

An example of such negative impact is seen at Saccheshwar Temple at Tehri. The original temple was a small dark one but full of vibrations and pilgrims. The new temple has a magnificent building but has few visitors. Enumerator Naresh Chandra Puri sat through the day only to find one solitary visitor! The priest Shri Giriji of the temple lamented: "Every day the offerings made in the old temple were Rs 100-200 plus people used to offer flour, oil, fruit, etc. We used to distribute these among the poor after taking amounts required for the upkeep of our families. Every day 50-100 persons came to take bath in the river and then sat in the temple. Now, in the new temple at Boradi, only 8-10 persons come in a day. People come only on special occasions like Shivratri. If the weather is bad then they do not come even on such days. Offerings are only Rs 5-10 per day. We have to spend from our pockets to burn oil in the lamp" (Details at Annexure 4).

A quick survey was done at Durga Temple at Tehri. Six worshippers were interviewed. In response to the question "Rebuilding here has led to increase or decrease in the spiritual power of the temple?" all six said that the power had much decreased. Three estimated the decrease at 75%, two at 50% and one did not quantify the same.

This author's plea is that EIAs make a grave error in not examining these emotional and spiritual costs that are imposed on the society. This author is afraid of trying to make a monetary estimate of the loss. How much money is one willing to either get moksha or to be deprived of it?

Fishing

The local people will be deprived of the conventional fishing that they undertake presently. However, the reservoir may provide for new species of fish to be cultivated. The final impact is not known.

Another issue here is whether the dam- or forest authorities will give out contracts to big companies for cultivating fish in the reservoir or leave it for local people to exploit. This will have equity implications.

The Kotlibhel 1B HEP requires that the area between Maletha and Srinagar be declared as a Protected Area in order to provide protection to the otter. This clearly imposes a cost upon local people who will be deprived of fishing in the area.

Table 4.70. Cost to local people from declaration of protected area for preservation of -Coated Otter

Sl. No.	*Item*	*Amount*	*Basis*
1.	Rim distance to be declared Protected	10 km	5+5 km on each side of the reservoir.
2.	Number of people affected	60 persons	10 per village located at a distance of 3 km. That is, 30 on each side.
3.	Daily catch	Rs 6,000 per day	Author's best estimate is catch of Rs 100 per day.
4.	Total cost of Kotlibhel 1B HEP	Rs 18 lacs per year	Rs 6,000 per day × 300 days

The costs to the people on account of immersion of ashes, reduced power of temples, deprivation of fishing and other miscellaneous costs is taken at Rs 5 crores per year.

Multiplying Factor of Cascade Effect

The Government is anxious to 'harvest' every meter of the river's gradient for the production of hydropower. HEPs are being made bumper-to-bumper on many rivers. Such a cascade potentially has a larger environmental effect than the sum of the parts. The effects 'build up'—i.e. they add to the effects downstream and upstream.

Intuitively, the author feels that there should be an optimum number of HEPs that a river can bear. Space is left between two beds in a dormitory, between two flowerbeds in a garden and between two fields in a village. Therefore, there must also be some free space between two HEPs.

Experience in other countries indicates that excessive embanking of rivers has led to harmful consequences. The German environment minister commented after severe flooding of Rhine in 1994: "We've paved over too many meadows and straightened too many rivers." Many embankments are now being removed. Similar restoration of the rivers is being undertaken in Loire Grandeur, France; Napa, California, United States; Kissimmee, Florida, United States and Drava, Austria (IRN 2007). It seems that cascade of HEP reservoirs will also have similar effects.

The Author had asked MOWR the following question under RTI: "What is MOWR's assessment of carrying capacity of Alaknanda and Bhagirathi Rivers on the number dams that are sustainable?" MOWR's reply (dated 20.8.2007) stated: "All the proposed HEP on Alaknanda and Bhagirathi Rivers except Tehri HEP are Run-off river schemes. No specific study has been carried as per available information."

The National Environment Appellate Authority has held in the case of Pala Maneri that "The Authority feels the need for advance cumulative study of series of different dams coming on any river so as to assess the optimum capacity of the water resource" (NEAA 2007).

The importance of the cumulative study is highlighted by the case of River Teesta in Sikkim. The total generating capacity of the River and its tributaries is assessed as 5,600 MW. However, the carry capacity is assessed at only 2,000 MW based on cumulative study (Jishnu 2008). The capacity of the River is reduced from 5,600 MW on stand-alone basis to 2,000 MW on cumulative basis because the costs are multiplied in a cascade of dams. Similarly, the costs of KB1B will be multiplied in conjunction with the cascade of dams being made on the entire 270 km stretch from Badrinath to Kaudiyala.

A reduction of carrying capacity of river is estimated from 5,600 MW to 2,000 MW due to making of a cascade of dams at Teesta. Conversely, we may assume that the costs will be

enhanced in the same ratio—from 2,000 to 5,600—or by 180 percent from stand-alone to a cascade of dam. Thus, this writer feel justified in enhancing the costs by 50 percent due to the cascade effect. Not all costs are enhanced due to cascade effect, however. For example, the cost of sediment will be less due to cascade of dams. The sand trapped in one reservoir will not be trapped again.

We give below our estimate of cascade effect of various costs enumerated above. All costs are assumed to increase or decrease by 50% because the author has no better estimate.

Table 4.71. Cascade effect of costs of Kotlibhel 1B (Rs crore/year)

Sl No	*Item*	*Cost as estimated above*	*Impact of cascade—increase or decrease in cost*	*Increase in cost by 50%*	*Decrease in cost by 50%*
1.	Sediment	98.0	Decrease	-	49.0
2.	Quality of water	233.0	Increase	111.5	-
3.	Methane emissions	31.4	Increase	15.8	-
4.	Forests	61.1	Increase	30.6	-
5.	Earthquakes	8.4	Increase	4.2	-
6.	Landslides	30.7	Increase	15.3	-
7.	Malaria and health	21.2	Increase	10.6	-
8.	Biodiversity	11.7	Increase	5.8	-
9.	Otters	20.0	Increase	10.0	-
10.	Road accidents	7.2	No impact	-	-
11.	Decline in temperatures	7.0	Increase	3.5	-
12.	Sand	9.1	Decrease	-	4.5
13.	River Rafting	8.0	No impact	-	-
14.	Bridges	3.3	No impact	1.6	-
15.	Aesthetic value of free-flowing water	60.5	Increase	30.2	-
16.	Loss of soul and miscellaneous costs	5.0	Increase	2.5	-
	Total	-	-	(+) 241.6	(-) 53.5

The net impact of cascade effect is (+) Rs 188.1 crores per year.

A Brief Explanation of Excluded Costs

The Author has not included some benefits and costs in the above calculation. The reason for excluding these, are given in this section.

Social Trauma and Woman's Burden

Displacement due to HEPs affects not only those displaced but also those left behind by splitting their society. Many studies have detailed the loss of self-identity of the displaced, trauma and alienation of all concerned (WCD 2000a:99).

On the other hand, a large number of people from hill- and tribal areas see displacement as a God-sent opportunity that enables them to escape from the low incomes and drudgery of the rural hill areas. Dr B R Ambedkar labelled villages as 'Ghettos'. Youth among tribals have attacked programs to preserve tribal cultures saying that it is a strategy to keep them locked into backwardness.

The Author has personal experience of acquisition of land in Badli Village of Delhi. It is estimated that about one-half of the displaced persons started new occupations and have vastly improved their life. The other one-half has fallen on hard ways. Such trauma is, sometimes, part of the growth process like the labour pains.

The same argument applies to woman's burden. It is observed that families that get huge monies from land compensation often indulge in drinking and wife beating. This cost is real. However, on the other hand, other women have improved their lives much. These benefits and costs defy quantification hence are not accounted in this study.

Valuation of Land

The level of compensation for acquired land is a political process hence costs for under- or overvaluation is not incorporated in this study.

Water Birds

The impact on birds is not known. It is possible that new

species of water birds may find habitat in the reservoirs. Whether this will actually take place is not known.

Increased Rains

Increased evapo-transpiration from HEP reservoirs should, logically speaking, lead to higher precipitation. However, the location of increased precipitation is highly uncertain.

Mike Bettwy of Goddard Space Flight Centre tells about the impact of the Three Gorges Dam being built by China (Bettwy 2007): "The satellite data and computer modelling clearly indicate that the... dam's construction has increased precipitation in the region between the Daba and Qinling mountains...(It) also *reduced rainfall in the region immediately surrounding Three Gorges Dam* after the dam's water level abruptly rose in June 2003."

We have here evidence that rainfall patterns may change in unexpected ways hence this issue is ignored.

Animal Ingress

It is possible that wild animals may ingress more frequently in cultivable lands and cause damage. The area of Kotlibhel 1B has wild pigs that often wreck havoc. This may increase the habitat of wild animals is reduced. On the other hand, some wild animals may be wiped out or relocate resulting in less ingress.

Radiation Losses

The electricity transmission lines will cause some damages to the people due to radiation. However, this is likely to take place also in alternative sources of energy hence it is not considered an additional social cost that must be added to that of hydropower.

Global Warming and Reduces Inflow of Water

Studies indicate that HEPs routinely overestimate the amount of water available, and underestimate the capital cost of dams (WCD 2000a:39). However, this cost is internal to the HEP—in this case NHPC. Hence, there is no 'social cost' involved in this. This also applies to potentially lower flows of water due to melting of glaciers and global warming.

5

ECONOMIC ASSESSMENT OF HYDROPOWER : CASE STUDY OF KOTLIBHEL 1B

Kotlibhel 1B is a Loss Proposition

The benefits and costs estimated in earlier chapters are summarized below:

Table 5.1. Benefits and costs of Kotlibhel 1B (All figures in Rs crore/year)

Sl. No.	*Item*	*Benefit*	*Cost*
1	Benefits from generation of power	103.8	–
2	12% Free power to State	50.2	–
3	Employment	1.5	–
4	Sediment	–	98.0
5	Quality of water	–	233.0
6	Methane emissions	–	31.4
7	Forests	–	61.1
8	Earthquakes	–	8.4
9	Landslides	–	30.7
10	Malaria and health	–	21.2
11	Biodiversity	–	11.7
12	Otters	–	20.0
13	Road accidents	–	7.2
14	Decline in temperatures	–	7.0
15	Sand	–	9.1
16	River Rafting	–	8.0
17	Bridges	–	3.3
18	Aesthetic value of free-flowing water	–	60.5
19	Loss of soul and miscellaneous costs	–	5.0
20	Cascade effect	–	188.1
	Total benefit and cost of Kotlibhel 1B HEP	155.5	798.7

The above table tells us that Kotlibhel 1B project is a loss proposition for the country. The net loss to the country is Rs 643.2 crores per year.

Admittedly these estimates are dependent on many assumptions made by the author. The reader is welcome to make alternative assumptions and arrive at his own assessment of benefits and costs. The author's basic objection is that all the costs enumerated above are totally ignored in Environment Impact Assessment of the Kotlibhel 1B project. There is a deliberate attempt to misrepresent the project as beneficial while actually it is a loss proposition.

Distribution of Benefits and Costs

The puzzle before us is this: Why are such projects made when costs are larger than benefits. This mystery is unravelled when we examine the distribution of benefits and costs between different stakeholders. This author's assessment is that such projects are imposed upon the people of the country by the employees of NHPC and Government of Uttarakhand, who indeed stand to gain.

The share of salaries and wages in the total turnover of NHPC are much higher than private hydropower companies. This is clear from comparison of Balance Sheet of NHPC and Jaiprakash Hydropower.

Salaries and wages constitute 12.5 percent of NHPC's turnover against 1.8 percent for Jaiprakash Hydropower (Table 5.2). On pro-rata basis, a sale of Rs 312.4 crores projected from Kotlibhel 1B will provide for salaries of Rs 39.1 crores for the employees of NHPC (NHPC 2005:1.6). This figure should not be confused with the benefits from additional employment generated in Kotlibhel 1B, which take into account only employees at the field level. This is the gain to all employees of the company, including head office, CMD office, etc.

Table 5.2. Salaries and wages, 2006-07

Sl. No.	*Item*	*Jaiprakash Hydropower (Rediff 2007)*	*NHPC (2007)*
1.	Total sales	Rs 335.8 crore	Rs 1882.9 crore
2.	Salaries and wages (amount)	Rs 5.9 crore	Rs 236.0 crore
3.	Salaries and wages (percent)	1.8%	12.5%

The share of employees of Government of Uttarakhand in the free power to be supplied by NHPC from Kotlibhel is similarly assessed. The Author has been able to access three studies in this regard as given at Table 5.3.

Table 5.3. Share of salaries in State Government Expenditures

Sl. No.	*State (Year)*	*Salary*	*Pension*	*Study Link*
1.	Kerala (2004-05)	31%	15%	Kerala Public Expenditure Review Committee, First Report, May 2006 (Kerala 2006)
2.	Tamil Nadu (2000-01)	39%	13%	White Paper on Tamil Nadu Government's Finances (TN 2007)
3.	All India (1999-2001)	32.1%	NA	MOF (2003)
	Average	34.0%	14%	

Based on these studies we may assume that 48% of the revenues of the Government of Uttarakhand will be spent towards Salaries and Pensions of the government employees. Thus, out of the Rs 50.2 crore received by Government of Uttarakhand, the State Government employees may get an additional Rs 24.1 crores and the people may get Rs 26.1 crores.

Now we can assess the distribution of benefits and costs from Kotlibhel 1B.

Table 5.4. Distribution of Benefits (–) and Costs (+)

Chapter No.	*Item*	*Total*	*Employees of NHPC and Government of Uttarakhand*	*People of India*
1.	Benefits from generation of power	(+) 103.8	-	(+) 103.8
2.	12% Free power to State	(+) 50.2	(+) 24.1	(+) 26.1
3.	Employment	(+) 1.5	-	(+) 1.5
4.	Costs	(-) 798.7	-	(-) 798.7
	Total	(-) 643.2	(+) 24.1	(-) 667.3
5.	Memo: Benefits to employees of NHPC in generation of electricity	-	(+) 39.1	

The above chart gives us an indication of the gainers and losers.

Gainers: NHPC and State Government Employees to the tune of Rs 63.2 crores.

Losers: People of the country to the tune of Rs 667.3 crores.

Kotlibhel 1B HEP is a loss proposition for the nation. Yet it is being implemented because it imposes hidden costs on the people and provides direct benefits to employees of NHPC and Government of Uttarakhand. The CEA is accessory to this damage by making false over-forecasts of energy required. The Planning Commission is accessory to this damage by portraying hydropower as clean and ignoring better alternative of managing peak load by dual pricing. MOEF is accessory to this damage by dilibrately 'ignoring various environmental impacts and costs that are imposed on the country.

6

REPLY TO HYDROPOWER EXPERTS

Two hydropower experts have very kindly commented on an earlier version of this book. Replies to most points raised by them have already been given in the main body of this report. Here we briefly reproduce their comments and this author's replies in a concise manner so that the issues are visible plain and clear to well-meaning supporters of hydropower.

Necessity of Higher Income

Comment by hydropower experts: Your argument that hydropower is iniquitous is flawed. The income distribution mechanism may be improved provided there is 'income' and the income keeps pace with population growth. If there is no income (hypothetically) or if there is actually a reduction in income, nothing would be available for distribution, equitably or inequitably. Hence, HEPs are justified as a source of income growth.

This writer's reply: This is not my argument. I am not against income. The point here is that HEPs are not adding to income to be distributed at all. They are, in my calculation, reducing total income. However, this is done in a way that there is gain for the HEP-and-Government bureaucracies even though the total pie is smaller. Therefore, there is loss of Rs 667.3 crores to the people and gain of Rs 63.2 crores for HEP bureaucracy. Now that is not a model of growth. It is a model of anti-growth.

Secondly, every model of economic growth cannot be justified on the grounds of 'enlarging the pie'. The final objective of growth is people's welfare. So we have to examine the net impact of HEPs on people's welfare from two sources: (1) The indirect positive impact from large pie; (2) The direct negative impact from HEPs. HEPs can possibly be justified after such study only.

Future Demand Scenario of Power

Comment: Projected profits from proposed projects have taken future demand/supply scenario; hence, calculations based on current average price of power are not the best way to challenge such a projection.

This is correct. However, a project is sanctioned on present costs and benefits. Therefore, it should stand scrutiny on present price scenario. Further, if it is based on projected escalation of prices then such basis must be disclosed. Otherwise, any project can be shown to be profitable by assuming increase in price of sale.

Comment: Alternative sources of energy are certainly important but can not bridge the gap in India's energy demand which by 2015-16 could be around 2,00,000 MW. From where to bridge the yawning gap? Why not from large hydropower and why not from nuclear power?

I have shown elsewhere in this book that future demand for power is likely to be much less than projected by CEA. Hence, the need to 'bridge the gap' is non-existent.

Comment: Household consumption of electricity is shown by the Author as 'consumerism' rather than a catalyst of economic growth. This is turning the whole sequence on its head. For example, a tailor could work only during daylight prior to electricity supply, but with electricity supply he stretches his working hours for enhanced productivity per day and thus contributes to growth. He has the "choice" of working hours. Empowerment is having "voice and choice." With electricity supply, people get "choice." No empowerment sustains without economic self-reliance and growth.

We must distinguish between two types of consumption of power—productive and non-productive. It is justified to sell the family silver for setting up a factory or a shop but not for a sumptuous meal in a 5-star restaurant even though the 5-star meal has its own positive value. Therefore, there is no denial of need for more power for consumption. However, that has to be placed at a lower priority.

It is necessary to establish dual pricing regime—separate rates for 'consumption' and 'production'—for this argument to hold. In absence of such regime, this becomes an argument for enhancing ostentatious consumption by the rich in the guise of providing electricity for the poor tailor.

Comment: The demand of Electricity is going to increase in the coming years as ours is a developing country, which requires electricity at the early stages of industrialisation.

Not true. I have shown GDP and electricity have decoupled. It is needed more for consumption by rich.

Hydropower is Cheap and Economic

Comment: Hydropower is not uneconomic. There is no variable cost viz. fuel hence it is beneficial in long run.

Hydropower has low variable cost for the producer but high variable cost for the society—loss of quality of water, loss of sediment, increase in malaria, etc. The real cost of hydropower is much higher than internalized by projects through variable costs.

Comment: Levelised tariff for 35/40 years will come around Rs 1. Tariff structure at initial years is high necessarily because of the interest on capital, repayment of which is for 10-12 years. Thus the long-term tariff structure becomes very less.

NHPC has given a levelised cost of Rs 2.37 for Kotlibhel 1B. We have shown that the gains to the country at this cost of production are less than the environmental and economic costs imposed on the society.

Comment : In the current trading scenario, the average price of power during peak hours hovers around Rs 5 to Rs 6, which is ultimately a burden upon the consumers.

Indeed, the benefit to people from power generated during peak hours is more than during non-peak hours. However, presently SEBs are buying power at Rs 5 to Rs 6 and selling it to consumers at Rs 2 or so. This prevents correct assessment of benefits of power. People are consuming large amount of power during peak hours because it is supplied to them at Rs 2 per unit. The present shortage of peak power is, therefore, exaggerated.

It should be possible for the government to make different peak and non-peak tariff rates for the consumers. I have shown this will be a win-win proposition for producers and well as consumers. Consumption during peak hours will decline very much. Your assumption that benefit from peak power is greater than Rs 5 or Rs 6 does not hold because the consumer is not necessarily willing to pay this price. A child may be happy buying an ice cream at Rs 1. It cannot be concluded from this that demand for ice cream is large and it should be produced even if the cost is Rs 10. Similarly, more generation of peak-power cannot be justified due to present demand which is under-priced.

Comment: You cannot evaluate free power to the State at sale rate. Instead, benefit should be calculated for purchase of the same. For instance, Himachal Pradesh used to buy power @ Rs 6.5 per unit in winter prior to 12% free power arrangements being fully operationalized. The benefit to the State has to be reckoned by opportunity cost of the free power.

I agree to the extent that both sale rate (as I have done) and purchase rate (as the Commentator has done) are not defensible. The simple method is to assess the marginal product. Calculation of this is tricky, however. The reason is that consumers are provided power at a lower than production cost. If, say, peak load power was priced at Rs 4, the demand will be less, and SEBs will have to pay less for buying the same. Therefore, we cannot take the present purchase price as the marginal product of power.

It is necessary to make study of price elasticity of peak consumption of power. Such a study will tell us how much power will be demanded at a particular price. Then we can compare whether hydropower can supply at that price. Such a study is a precondition for making HEPs.

Decoupling of Power and Economic Growth

Comment: The suggested 'decoupling of economic growth and electricity consumption' does not hold against power generation. Even if decoupled, economic growth generates demand for energy/power.

True. We do need more power even after decoupling. The question is how much? On what objective will we assess this? My suggestion is to assess this on the objective of people's welfare. The benefits from additional power should be evaluated against the costs of additional power. I have shown in this study that hydropower is a loss-proposition on this objective.

Comment: The study by Sajal Ghosh titled "Electricity consumption and economic growth in India" actually argues for a case of electricity conservation and not for foregoing electricity generation.

Sajal Ghosh says "Electricity conservation policies can be initiated without deteriorating economic side effects." The implication is that reduced availability of electricity—due to either energy conservation measures or reduced generation—will not have a negative effect on economic growth.

Comment: Swapping electricity supply from industry to services to capitalize on growth in service sector will cause migration of industries, full impacts of which on GDP are presently unfathomable. It requires deeper studies before jumping to any conclusion.

My argument is not that we must close all industries. My argument is that given energy-extensity of services sector, one alternative for us is to switch from industry to services in our growth strategy. Every country must adopt such development strategy that suits its resource endowments. The forecasts made by CEA overlook the increasing share of services sector and are, therefore, bad. We should produce only so much electricity as required for our essential industries.

Value of Cultural Exchange

Comment: Project induced immigration of staff, labour and other service providers has been painted as a serious threat. While some negative impacts can not be denied, benefits like cultural exchanges, trade opportunities, infrastructure facilities like roads, hospitals etc. can not be brushed aside.

I have not painted project-induced migration as a serious threat. I have only said that benefit from employment during construction is setoff against potential losses from AIDS etc. I have no objection if both benefits and costs can be more thoroughly quantified. I did not have access to data to be able to do so.

My assessment is that few trade opportunities are generated from hydropower projects. Hydropower projects have little organic link with the local economy. They do not buy items like sugarcane from local people that would lead to development of vertical linkages. There is some benefit due to infrastructure. However, this too is nullified by the loss of infrastructure such as rope bridges. In absence of data, I have chosen to ignore them.

Environmental Costs of Thermal and Nuclear Power

Comment: The Author as erred by ignoring sustainability and environmental benefits of HEPs. Environmental costs of thermal and nuclear power are well too known to deserve repetition here. People favouring coal based thermal power tend to overlook the impact of mines, which are located far away from power generating units. These mines were established prior to promulgation of FCA 1980; hence, they neither pay for Compensatory Afforestation nor NPV etc.

I agree that FCA should be made applicable retrospectively. However, that does not make a case for hydropower since many hydropower plants were also established earlier.

A comparison of the total costs of hydro-, thermal- and nuclear power should certainly be made. R&R is basically a political problem of sharing of the pie. This I have bypassed in hydro and would do the same for thermal.

The other cost is of carbon emissions. The perplexing matter is that these are taken into account in costing of thermal plants; but ignored in hydropower projects. My case is that true environmental costs of hydro should be assessed.

Comment: The overall environment gets benefited as hydropower projects are renewable in nature. The SOx, NOx and other GHG emission are reduced.

Thermal plants, I believe, factor in the GHG, NOx and SOx emissions. However, HEPs externalize them and pass them to the society.

We must see the impacts on quality of water, sediment, biodiversity, etc. also. We cannot support hydro simply because GHG emissions are less than thermal. A holistic assessment is required. That is what I have done for hydro.

Furthermore, hydro plants are not truly renewable. The United States is finding their life to be only about 50-100 years. That is not 'renewable.'

Water and Irrigation

Comment: Projects generally have a water control system, which is an important element in multipurpose utilisation of water resources and can reduce potential flood damage where storage facilities are involved. The retained floodwater can better be directed to agricultural production, river level regulation, improved navigation, fish and wildlife protection, recreation, multipurpose use and better control of wastewater.

I agree that storage dams like Narmada and Tehri provide this additional benefit of irrigation, drinking water, etc. That is not relevant for ROR Hydropower projects like Kotlibhel. The costs of storage dams are equally massive and they have to be assessed separately.

ROR Hydro Projects have Less R&R Problems

Comment: Hydro projects are normally built on Run of River system and its development has led to minimum rehabilitation and resettlement and environmental problems. The grievances of the villagers are duly addressed.

Sorry, where is the evidence that environmental problems are minimum? Or, that R&R grievance are addressed? Villagers are not even told of the negative impacts such as mosquitoes, lower temperature, lower yields, loss of sediment, decline in water quality, etc.

Local area Development

Comment: Hydropower helps in promoting local industries in remote areas. The cultural heritage of the local area is saved as the local people are able to undertake cultural activities in addition to their routine life. It can be better understood with an example. The District of Uttarkashi is famous for making items like carpets etc. With continuous availability of electricity, they will be able to produce these items 10 times than what they are producing right now. This will increase the financial earnings of the local people. This will also lead to generation of business acumen among the local populace.

This assumes that there will be incremental production from incremental availability of electricity. There is no evidence that this is happening. Sripad Dharmadhikari has done a study of Bhakra. He concludes that the projected benefits for local people have not materialised.

Further, these benefits have to be quantified. How much electricity do weavers need? This cannot be presented as a self-evident case for unending hydropower generation at any cost.

Comment: Hydro projects contribute in solving the low voltage problem in the remote hilly areas and help in reducing the losses in transmission and distribution. Project also help in providing stable electricity supply at remote areas where such facility by other source shall be much costlier and unreliable.

This has nothing to do with hydropower. It is a cross-cutting issue that relates to all supply of power. In any event, we must examine what is the benefit to local people from high voltage and what is the loss to them due to deprivation of good quality water. My assessment is that losses are much greater as shown in this study.

Comment: Hydropower projects lead to generation of employment in the local area and uplifting the economic conditions of the local population. The projects create indirect employment opportunities to unskilled workers for several years, which otherwise would not happen in the absence of the project. In addition, the projects create direct permanent employment to local persons for operation of the project.

These are imaginary benefits. No evidence is available of employment effect. This appears to be hypothetical. Number of jobs in HEPs is small and mostly got by outsiders. The commentator has himself said that the benefit of hydropower is that variable costs are less. Salaries and wages are part of variable costs. Wherefrom will employment be created, then?

A study of employment pattern of NHPC shows that hardly 5 percent of the employees of Kotlibhel are local people.

Comment: Project developers mobilise investment to the region to the extent of hundreds of million rupees which otherwise is not possible. This is a huge investment in the local area that leads to the sustainable development.

Not every investment is growth. The British invested in railways and impoverished the country. Similar is the case with hydropower.

This investment does not lead to sustainable development. As shown in this study, there are huge costs that are imposed on local people.

Comment: Hydropower projects are often made in an area which is backward and poor. Majority of the population depend upon marginal cultivation in the terraced fields or work as labourers in the nearby urban centres. The area is sparsely populated. Agriculture is the source of living for about 80% residents. The inhabitants of the area have their primitive tradition and culture. The literacy rate is low at 30%. The standard of living is low. The burden of work on local populace will be reduced as their villages will be connected to the mainstream.

Agreed that standard of living is low and conditions are hard. However, they become worse with HEPs—more malaria and landslides, less yields and social contacts. What is truly the disease is being presented as the medicine. The alleged benefits to local people from higher income are wholly unsubstantiated.

Comment: After commissioning of the project, local people can develop small industry in the area with the better power availability. These industries can be selected on the basis of raw material available in that place such as wool, wood and herbs etc. People can develop green houses and breeding farms for sheep, rabbits etc.

This can be done even without HEPs. It has no bearing on the issue at hand. The requirement of power for greenhouses, for example, is nil.

Comment: This will result in infrastructure development, which ultimately leads to the rural development and prevent migration of rural poor to cities.

This is entirely hypothetical. There is some improvement in infrastructure in smaller HEPs but evidence from reservoir-based HEPs like Tehri is negative even on infrastructure. Three bridges will be submerged in Kotlibhel 1B and will not be replaced.

Sediment

Comment: Putting a cost on 'loss of sediment' shows complete lack of understanding of silt flow in a cascade of HEPs. Only seasonal distribution of silt changes and not the total amount of silt load. ROR HEPs with diminutive 'reservoir' do not hold water or sediment over long period. The sediments have to be flushed, which only changes the seasonal distribution of sediment in a river. The annual silt loads remains unchanged.

True, sediment is not permanently arrested in barrage-and-tunnel type HEP. However, it is deposited in reservoir type HEP like Kotlibhel which has a 27 Km long reservoir. EIA of Srinagar HEP admits that the reservoir will be wholly silted within 10 years.

Even on Barrage-and-tunnel HEPs, I think there will be some effect. If we take cream out of milk and then refortify the milk with it repeatedly, after a few operations the milk will loose its natural quality. The separation and flushing of silt from barrage is a similar operation. I have read that silt will be flushed once in 15 days from Kotlibhel Reservoir. Will the river carry it? I would like to see HEPs undertaking a study on this. In any case, the impact can only be negative. The fact is that hydropower projects are gnawing at the land of the country by depriving our coasts of sediment inflow.

Natural lake versus Hydropower Reservoir

Comment: If a river is dammed by a natural landslide, it becomes acceptable; but if dammed artificially it becomes objectionable. A series of rapids and cataracts in the course of a river is nothing but geological obstructions developed over time by the river. However, maintaining certain minimum environmental downstream discharge (as is the case in Himachal, where maintaining 15% d/s discharge is mandatory) is a healthy compromise between 'development' and 'conservation'. Again, in HP some rivers and streams have been set aside for aquatic fauna and conservation needs. D/S discharge near Chamba town is kept higher than normative 15%. Thus, holiness of a river can be maintained with local adjustments and compromises.

Indeed, the jungles of Ganges Basin were burnt by Lord Krishna and Arjuna for inhabitation. We now pay laurels to the sustainable agriculture built in that basin. On the other hand, people of the Indus valley cut the forests for baking bricks. That led to denudation of the landscape, floods and ultimate collapse of that civilization.

Man has every right to interfere with nature. Man has the right to make HEPs and to dam the river. However, man being the highest living being, has to do this in a way that leads to overall development. We have to examine whether the damming leads to 'development' as in Khandava burning; or denudation as in the Indus Valley.

When development becomes oppressive for the masses and other creatures—they rebel and cause the decline of a civilization. Therefore, my plea is for making an overall assessment. I have tried to show in this study that Kotlibhel fails on such a touchstone.

The suggested compromise is arbitrary and smacks of convenience and is unscientific. The simple method of determining optimum balance between 'discharged' and 'dammed' would be to look at the incremental benefit of each 1% damming. At 100% discharge a 1% damming may lead to x benefit and y loss. At 99% discharge the benefit will be x- while loss will be y+. This should be done progressively till x=y. My plea is that this study should be done. I am not convinced that the optimum is at 15% minimum discharge. It is possible that optimum may be at 90% discharge.

Comment: It is an established trend that water usable by tourists (in a lake) fetches better tourism value than non-usable running water. Compare Nainital with Karna Prayag;

had it not been for religious reasons, no tourist would visit and spend time and money at Karna Prayag.

My study of three HEPs shows some increase in tourism. However, this benefit has to be seen in totality. Let us think whether the tourist will be attracted to watch the HEP reservoirs after a cascade of dams is built from Badrinath to Kaudiyala. Tourists like the unusual. Presently they like reservoirs because river is usual and reservoir is unusual. After cascade of dams is built it is likely to become converse. Tourists may flock to the few kilometres of flow that remains.

Comment: Development of hydropower leads to development of tourism (natural as well as religious). These are a source of income for the local people.

There is some positive evidence on this as things stand today. However, the benefits are small compared to costs. Moreover, this benefit will vanish when a cascade of dams will be made. Then tourists will pay to see the flowing river.

Methane Emissions

Comment: Reliance has been placed on debatable research finding of dubious origin regarding methane emission from HEP reservoirs.

Once again, if the data available to me is of debatable nature, then NHPC should provide its own studies. It is not acceptable to deplore the available study as debatable and not to provide alternative estimates. People living near three working HEPs (Chilla, Tehri and Maneri) are unanimous that water looses its freshness. Two out of 65 respondents have explicitly reported foul smell coming from downstream water. Hence, the finding is not unreal.

Comment: WCD guidelines on carbon credits already discount these impacts by compliance to prescribed power density formula.

My point is that this has not been implemented in Kotlibhel 1B. The EIA does not mention GHG emissions.

Comment: If renewable project like this will not come up then there will be addition of the non-renewable projects, which will contribute to the GHG emissions.

The reality is opposite of what you are saying. HEPs are passing unaccounted GHG emissions to the society while thermal is factoring it in.

Comment: It is accepted that Hydropower will lead to reduced emissions.

Table 6.1. The weighted average emission factor, simple operating margin (OM), build margin (BM) and combined margin (CM) of all Indian regional grids for FY 2005-06 (inter-regional and cross-border electricity transfers included), in tCO2/MWh

Region	*Average*	*Simple OM*	*BM*	*CM*
North	0.72	0.99	0.60	0.80
East	1.05	1.13	0.97	1.05
South	0.74	1.01	0.71	0.86
West	0.88	0.99	0.63	0.81
North-East	0.33	0.70	0.15	0.42
India	0.81	1.02	0.68	0.85

For 300 MW Power Plant, if the design Energy is 18000 MUs, then the Annual net Generation from the Project = 18000 GWh = 18000000 MWh.

Combined Margin for the Northern region = 0.80.

Projected Emission Reduction = 0.80*18000000 = 14400000 tCO2 per year

You have assumed zero emission from HEP. That is not the case. The difference should be calculated between hydro and thermal emissions. If HEP emissions were 2.1 kg/Kwh, as stated in one study quoted by me, then we would be adding 1.3 kg/Kwh emissions by embracing hydropower. Such stand-alone calculations assuming reductions in emissions equal to thermal emissions are fallacious.

Comment: Methane emission takes place only in the reservoir based project and it does not take place in run of river project.

The distinction between reservoir and ROR is well taken. ROR projects have low volume of reservoir but high inflow of organic matter. The final result is not known. GHG emissions may be substantial as seen from the foul smell coming from a small flower vase. Further, there are other environmental costs like erosion of coastlands, increased landslides due to weakened hills during tunnelling, etc. Tunnel-type ROR projects deprive the river water of micro-chemicals. Absence of GHG emissions is not adequate grounds to support barrage-and-tunnel type ROR HEPs. A holistic assessment of their environmental impact has to be made.

Comment: Global warming is taking place anyways due to various other factors like burning of fossil fuels etc. Why should you single out hydropower as the culprit?

This author has no intention of demonizing hydropower. Other sources of methane emissions have to be likewise tackled. That should not lead us to ignore methane contributions from hydro reservoirs just as others' speaking a lie does not mean we should do the same.

Regeneration of Forests

Comment: The forests that are affected due to the project implementation get replanted in the nearby areas as per MOEF guidelines. The re-plantation leads to the similar climatic condition and the flora and fauna are saved.

The field survey does not establish this. There is little evidence of CAT leading to regeneration of forests. The correct way to regenerate forests is not re-plantation but giving fuel subsidy to local people to make it profitable for them not to cut the forests. Unfortunately, this approach puts money in hands of the local people instead of the hydropower-and-forest bureaucracies. Hence planting is done by forest officials only to be grazed by local people.

Comment: Hydropower reduces deforestation caused by the villagers to meet their daily fuel requirements.

This has nothing to do with hydropower. Local people will cut forests for fuel if alternate arrangements are not made—hydropower or no hydropower.

Health

Comment: The alleged threat of malaria is not founded on facts. Malaria is caused by protozoa, most common being plasmodium falciparum which are carried by female anopheles mosquito. This species of mosquito is ecologically distributed in tropical regions and not in cool temperate zones where RoR type HEPs are constructed.

Factually, not true. There is increased incidence of Malaria around Bhakra. Mosquitoes are seen even in Maneri at a much higher altitude. I am told that a study by Military Hospital, Roorkee has found 32 strains of malaria in the hill areas. Hydropower projects may have contributed to this.

Biodiversity and Global Warming

Comment: If we replace coal/gas or fossil fuel based thermal power with hydropower, we will help reduce global warming and consequent threat to biodiversity and ecotourism.

Global warming is only one cause of loss of biodiversity. Here the issue is loss of biodiversity from submergence of forests. That is an additional cost on society.

Indeed, HEPs contribution to global warming may be less. First, let us establish this. Then let us make a holistic appraisal of the total impact on biodiversity and ecotourism. I concede that lesser GHG emissions could be an argument in favour of HEPs. However, this is not a conclusive argument. It has to be examined along with other environmental aspects mentioned in this study.

Comment: EIA lists flora and fauna. The threatened species are either saved or conserved through a dedicated plan. Fish migration whenever found/reposted is facilitated or restored. Survival issues of Otters, if not found elsewhere, could be a cause of concern, provided their relocation or ex-situ conservation is not feasible.

The track record of HEPs on saving species is poor. EIAs routinely understate the existing level of biodiversity as shown in case studies mentioned in this book. It would be good for hydropower companies to present a case study of such restorations.

The Kotlibhel 1B project has not even studied the nature of Smooth-coated Otter and simply made a façade of resettling that endangered animal. Otters are found elsewhere. My fear is that everywhere they are being made extinct because they are found elsewhere. In the result, they may become extinct. NHPC has not done any study on this. Otters have become extinct around Tehri already.

Road Accidents

Comment: Road accidents can be interpreted both ways.

In the study of three HEPs, it comes out clear that there has been a huge increase in accidents.

Decline in Temperature

Comment: Purported reduction in temperature is yet to be conclusively proven. In addition, offsetting or trading-off with global warming may change it from a 'cost' to a 'benefit'.

There is sufficient proof of decline in temperature. Once again, HEPs want the opponents to 'conclusively' prove what they should have done in the first place. First HEPs do not do their duty. When objection is raised, they say the objector has not provided proof. It is HEPs duty to gather such proofs. As I have shown in my study, NHPC has admitted to make these statements without any study. This is not fair play.

I do not know whether localized decline in temperatures from HEP Reservoirs will lead to 'global cooling'. Has the Indira Gandhi Canal led to cooling of the Thar Desert? This is possible but needs study. If so, let us account for this. I have no objection. But such arguments cannot be made as 'self-evident without study'.

Bridges

Comment: submergence of bridges leading to adverse

impacts etc. is all based on unsubstantiated and doubtful assumptions.

The commentator is making prophetic statements without study. The study of three dams made by this writer indicates there is some positive benefit of HEP barrages but this is more than cancelled by the harm from HEP reservoirs.

Immersion of Ashes

Comment: As far as immersion of ashes is concerned, it can be addressed by maintaining certain minimum downstream discharge.

Not done in practice. In Tapovan Vishnugad, people have to call upon the dam authorities to make some discharge so that they can immerse the ashes. The track record of HEPs on maintaining minimum flows is poor.

All Power and Development is Iniquitous

Comment: The statement 'hydropower is iniquitous' is misleading. All power tends to be iniquitous. Why isolate hydropower for this treatment?

If all power is iniquitous then let us make a beginning by dismantling hydropower. The fact that everyone tells a lie is not a good basis of telling lies.

Opposition to HEPs not Justified

Comment: Opposing HEP per se is not justified. Better would be to seek negotiations with an open mind.

Agreed. There is no opposition to HEP per se. I am serious about this. I may mention I am on repeated record defending both Tehri and Sardar Sarovar. My argument was that if these projects are beneficial for the nation then local loss should be compensated—it cannot become a case against the project. I am now reconsidering my position because I find that costs are huge and these particular HEPs are not in national interest. I understand from NBA-related activists that such a study of earlier dams was, unfortunately, not done. Therefore, there is no difference between the commentator's position and mine. The difference, if any, arises from the nuts and bolts of calculations of costs and benefits.

On Power Bureaucracy

Comment: Criticizing HEPs on grounds of promoting government bureaucracy is flawed. The liabilities of the government on account of salaries are permanent, whether there are HEPs or not. Hence, their correlation with hydropower by the author is not logical.

This is only partly true. While present liabilities may be 'permanent', these are enhanced by easy availability of revenue—from hydropower. More inflow of free money provides more opportunities for making appointments and leakage from contracts. Higher income enables more increase in salaries and benefits of government servants. Therefore, the connection is not illogical.

I was trying to fathom why such HEPs are made. I found that the only beneficiaries were state government employees and NHPC bureaucracy.

7

MAIN CONCLUSIONS

The main conclusions drawn by the author are as follows:

1. The demand for power as projected by CEA is excessive. The country does not need the projected levels of electricity. We may have a glut of power in times to come. However, we would have destroyed our rivers permanently by that time.
2. Dual pricing of peak- and non-peak power will be a win-win proposition for both producers and consumers of power. This will remove the need for harnessing our rivers for generation of peak power.
3. The costs of generating hydropower are huge but these are ignored in EIAs. This misleads the country about the true costs of hydropower.
4. The Kotlibhel 1B project is a loss proposition for the country. It is nevertheless being implemented by NHPC and the Government of Uttarakhand because it provides benefits to these bureaucracies even though the project imposes huge costs on the people—far in excess of the benefits.
5. The future of India in world will be at the spiritual level. Mother Ganga has a special role in this. We should not sacrifice our spiritual role for lowly material benefits.

ANNEXURE-1
Survey of Hydropower Dams and Chilla, Maneri and Tehri

I had initially planned to write only "Costs and Benefits of Kotlibhel 1B". I sent the draft write-up to many friends and officials. One response was that the costs assessed by the author were illusory and unreal.

I had a genuine desire to understand the impacts of hydropower because earlier I have been a supported of these projects. I felt the need for a field investigation. Four surveys were got done with the help of Naresh Chandra Puri of Village Lakshmoli, Dt Tehri. The objective was to ascertain whether the costs enumerated in this book were indeed real and seen in the older hydropower projects. Results of the four surveys are presented in these Annexures.

Objectives of Study

The Garhwal region of Uttarakhand has three HEPs in operation:

- Chilla in District Haridwar. This is a barrage-and-canal based HEP. Water is diverted into an open canal at Rishikesh. Power is generated from this water at Chilla. This HEP has been in operation for about 20 years.
- Maneri: This is a tunnel-based HEP. Water is diverted into a Tunnel at Maneri. Power is generated from this water downstream. This HEP has been in operation for about 20 years. The full name is Maneri Bhali I but is mentioned in this report as Maneri for short.

- Tehri: This is a large storage-based HEP. Water is stored in a large open reservoir. Power is generated at Tehri. This HEP has been in operation for about 4 years.

The impacts of these HEPs are assessed in this study by a survey of the local people.

Methodology

A questionnaire was made to ask respondents about impact of dam on various aspects. Enumerator Naresh Chandra Puri went to each of the three HEPs during November-December 2007. No sampling was done. Assistance of any local person was not sought lest the mediator influence the results. He went to the villages located near the projects and asked people he met spontaneously about the impacts.

Respondents were specifically sought in various locations of HEPs:

- Upstream (All three HEPs)
- Near small reservoir at diversion barrage (Chilla and Maneri).
- Near Large Reservoir (Tehri)
- Around canal (Chilla)
- Around tunnel (Maneri)
- Downstream (All three HEPs)

The results are collated separately for these categories to give an idea of how HEPs impact people at these locations differently. The Uttarakhand Government has decided not to make any more big storage-based HEPs of the type of Tehri. The implicit message is that this type of large reservoir-based

HEP is harmful but smaller canal-, reservoir- or tunnel based HEPs are not harmful. The results have been collated as above to assess the impact of smaller canal- or tunnel based HEPs on the people. The number of respondents in different locations of the three HEPs is given below:

Table A-1.1 : Number of Respondents

Sl. No.	*Item*	*Upstream*	*Small Reservoir (Barrage)*	*Large Reservoir (Tehri)*	*Along Canal*	*Along Tunnel*	*Down-stream*	*Total*
1.	Chilla	3	4	NA	8	NA	5	20
2.	Maneri	3	3	NA	NA	4	3	13
3.	Tehri	9	NA	20	NA	NA	3	32
	Total	15	7	20	8	4	11	65

The study was financed from personal resources of the writer.

The results have been enumerated as follows:

- Respondents answering 'no knowledge' are removed from both denominator and numerator.
- Responses are given as (Numbers responding to the question with a particular answer) divided by (Total number of respondents responding to that question). These are not converted into percentage because often the sample size is small—as few as 3 numbers. The reader should know the small size of sample hence numbers are given.
- Sometimes one respondent has replied positively to two possibilities. His response is added to both responses with the result that in a few case the sum of numerators is greater than denominator.

- The responses are added up and converted into net percentage on the Rightmost Column to give the total impact of the particular HEP.

- This writer's assessment of the responses is given in the bottom line of table. Small positive or negative impacts are given marks of (+) 1 or (-) 1. Like wise medium and strong impacts are give marks of (±) 2, and 3 respectively. These assessments can be crosschecked easily by the reader by looking at the break-up in the table.

- The Rightmost Column is averaged in the last row to give a bird's eye view of impact on local people.

- The Bottom Line of all tables is summarized at the end of this Annexure at Tables A-1.33 and A-1.34 to give a bird's eye view of impacts of HEPs on people located upstream, downstream etc. This gives us an idea of the differential impact of large- and small dams.

The purpose of this study is to bring to public knowledge the kind of impacts that are taking place along old HEPs so that new HEPs can be required to take these impacts into account in designing the projects.

Sediment

Table A-1.2 : Is there more or less sediment in the water downstream of dam?

Sl No	*Item*	*Upstream*	*Small Reservoir (Barrage)*	*Large Reservoir (Tehri)*	*Along Canal*	*Along Tunnel*	*Downstream*	*Net, HEP-wise Impact*
1.	Chilla	No information	No information	NA	No change 2/4 Reduced ¼ Increased 1/4	NA	No change 4/5 Reduced sediment 1/5	Reduced 1/9 = (-) 11%
2.	Maneri	No information	No information	NA	NA	Reduced ¼ No change 3/4	No information	Reduced ¼ = (-) 25%
3.	Tehri	Increased sediment 2/3 Less sediment 1/3	NA	No information	NA	NA	Less (Colour has deteriorated) 2/3 No change 1/3	Reduced 1/6 = (-) 17%
4.	Combined, Author's Assessment	(0) No clear verdict	(0) No information	(0) No information	(0) No clear verdict	(-)1 Less sediment	(-)2 Less sediment	(-) 18%

Conclusion: There is clear evidence of less segiment among downstream respondents. This is expected because sediment loss will be visible downstream only.

Quality of Water

Table A-1.3 : What is the change in level of water in the river in the last 20-30 years during winters? (Water is more in summers, anyways).

Sl. No.	*Item*	*Upstream*	*Small Reservoir (Barrage)*	*Large Reservoir (Tehri)*	*Along Canal*	*Along Tunnel*	*Downstream*	*Net, HEP-wise Impact*
1.	Chilla	Reduced 2/2	Unchanged ¾ Increased ¼ (1)	NA	Unchanged 6/8 Reduced 2/8	NA	Unchanged 2/5 Reduced 3/5	Reduced 6/19 = (-) 32%
2.	Maneri	Unchanged 3/3	Unchanged 3/3	NA	NA	Reduced ¾ No change 1/4	Reduced 2/3 No Change 1/3	Reduced 5/13 = (-) 38%
3.	Tehri	Reduced 2/9 No change 7/9	NA	Reduced 8/20 No Change 12/20	NA	NA	Reduced 2/3 No change 1/3	Reduced 12/32 = (-) 38%
4.	Combined, Author's Assessment	(-)2 Reduced	(+)1 Increase	(0) No change	(-)1 Reduced	(-)2 Reduced	(-)3 Large Reduction	(-) 36%

(1) Shri Raj Kumar, employee of Chilla Dam, Gauge Reader says that water has increased in the recent 3-4 years. However, this may be prejudiced because he is working for the dam company. Reduction of water is confirmed widely.

Table A-1.4 : Do you ever worship on the banks of Ganga? What is the difference in Pooja before- and after making of dam?

Sl. No.	*Item*	*Upstream*	*Small Reservoir (Barrage)*	*Large Reservoir (Tehri)*	*Along Canal*	*Along Tunnel*	*Downstream*	*Net, HEP-wise Impact*
1.	Chilla	Reduced Pooja 2/3 No change 1/3	No change ¾ Less Pooja ¼ (1)	NA	Reduced 1/8 (2) No change 7/8	NA	No change 3/5 Reduced 1/5 Increased 1/5	Reduced 4/20 = (-) 20%
2.	Maneri	No change 3/3.	No change 1/3 Less 1/3 (3) More 1/3 (4)	NA	NA	No change ¾ Less worship ¼ (5)	No change 1/3 Less worship 2/3 (6)	Reduced 3/13 = (-) 23%
3.	Tehri	No change 5/9 Less Pooja 4/9	NA	Less Pooja 19/20 No change 1/20	NA	NA	Less Pooja 2/3 No change 1/3	Reduced 25/32 = (-) 78%
4.	Combined, Author's Assessment	(-)2 Less Pooja	(-)1 Less Pooja	(-)3 Less Pooja	(0) No change	(-)1 Less Pooja	(-)2 Less Pooja	(-) 40%

(1) Chilla, Reservoir (Roob Devi, Bombai Factory Stadium, Rishikesh): Age 50. She lives about 250 meters from the reservoir since her marriage. She says: "I worship every day. Previously I had to go across stone to the river. Now it is convenient with the water coming upward."

(2) Chilla, Canal (Gomati Devi, Village Khadri Khadak Map): We worship of Ganga occasionally. There is less Pooja nowadays. Enumerator Naresh Puri explains: Due to less water, there is less worship of Ganga.

(3) Maneri, Reservoir (Buddhi Lal, Maneri): We do Pooja on festivals. Previously there was more rush. Now there is less.

(4) Maneri, Reservoir (Bajrang Singh Rana, Village Jamak on the head of the barrage): We do Pooja on festival days. It has increased. Enumerator Naresh Puri explains: 85 people died in this village during 1991 earthquake. Since then appears to be more worship.

(5) Maneri, Tunnel (Prem Singh Mahar, Village Netal): We do worship on festival days. There is less Pooja now.

(6) Maneri, Downstream (Dev Singh Gosain, Village Tiloth): We do worship every day. There is less Pooja now. (Chiranji Prasad Joshi, Village Gyansu): He was sitting on strike against Maneri Dam demanding safety wall before water is filled in dam. He said: We do worship every day. Continually water is being polluted. There is less Pooja done now.

Conclusion: Making of dams hits at the people's worshipful attitude to rivers.

Table A.1.5 : Was the water of river fit for drinking previously? What is the condition now?

Sl. No.	*Item*	*Upstream*	*Small Reservoir (Barrage)*	*Large Reservoir (Tehri)*	*Along Canal*	*Along Tunnel*	*Downstream*	*Net, HEP-wise Impact*
1.	Chilla	No change 1/3 Reduced 2/3	No change 2/4 Reduced 2/4	NA	No change 2/8 Reduced 6/8	NA	No change 5/5	Reduced 10/20 = (-) 50%
2.	Maneri	No change 3/3	No change 1/3 Reduced 2/3	NA	NA	No change 4/4	No change 2/3 Reduced 1/3	Reduced 3/13 = (-) 23%
3.	Tehri	No change 4/9 Reduced 5/9 (3)	NA	Reduced 20/20	NA	NA	Reduced 3/3 (4)	Reduced 28/32 = (-) 88%
4.	Combined, Author's Assessment	(-)2	(-)2	(-)3	(-)3	(0)	(-)2	(-) 54%

(1) In Maneri there is provision of overflow, which carries dead matter across the dam.

(2) Tehri: There is sharp decline in water quality. Enumerator Naresh Puri reported that mild foul smell is felt at Chilyanisaur. At the point of entry of water into the reservoir many dead bodies are held up and the area stinks very much. It is difficult to stand there. Dam Company has reportedly given some money to the health department to spray insecticides. The dead matter is moving slowly as the level of water in reservoir is reduced but it still stays at the tail of the reservoir. According to Enumerator Naresh Puri the dead matter will move back upwards along the tail end when water starts rising in the monsoons.

(3) Tehri, Upstream: Village Nagni Chhoti and Tilyada: The villages are on the tail end of the reservoir. The foul smell of the reservoir affects people upstream.

(4) Tehri, Downstream, Village Dharamghat, Chopra: These people did not use river water much for drinking previously since springs and piped water is available.

Conclusion: There is a strong negative impact on the quality of water. People are almost disgusted. Foul smell comes. Dead bodies are held up. Pooja has reduced.

Table A.1.6 : Has the dam affected the water sources of the village, wells in particular?

Sl No	Item	Upstream	Small Reservoir (Barrage)	Large Reservoir (Tehri)	Along Canal	Along Tunnel	Downstream	Net, HEP-wise Impact
1.	Chilla	Reduced 1/3 No impact 2/3	Increased ¼ No impact 3/4	NA	Increased 2/8 Reduced 2/8 No impact 4/8	NA	No impact 4/4	(0)
2.	Maneri	No impact 3/3	Reduced 2/3(1)	NA	NA	Reduced 3/4 No impact ¼	Reduced 3/3	Reduced 8/13 = (-) 62%
3.	Tehri	No impact 9/9	NA	No impact 14/14	NA	NA	No impact2/3 Reduced 1/3(2)	Reduced 1/26 = (-) 4%
4.	Combined, Author's Assessment	(0) No impact	(0) No clear verdict	(0) No impact	(0) No impact	(-)3 Water dried	(-)3 Water dried	(-) 22%

(1) Maneri, Village Jamak. Village is located along the reservoir. The tunnel passes at short distance. The water from wells has seeped into tunnels.

(2) Tehri, Downstream, Village Dharamghat. The village is located at some height from the riverbed. Level may be similar to that of Tehri Reservoir. Distance from Tehri Dam is 8 km. Hence, the recharge effect appears to be less.

Conclusion: Tunnels can lead to dried wells and springs.

Methane Emissions

Table A-1.7 : What is the change in smell of water downstream?

Sl. No.	Item	Upstream	Small Reservoir (Barrage)	Large Reservoir (Tehri)	Along Canal	Along Tunnel	Downstream	Net, HEP-wise Impact
1.	Chilla	No change 1/3 Poorer quality 2/3	No change 2/4 Poorer quality 2/4	NA	Less freshness 5/8 Bad smell comes 1/8 No change 2/8	NA	Less freshness 1/5 No change 4/5	Less freshness 11/20 = (-) 55%
2.	Maneri	No change 3/3	No change 3/3	NA	NA	Less freshness ¼ No change 3/4	Less freshness 1/3 No change 2/3	Less freshness 2/13 = (-) 15%
3.	Tehri	Less freshness 4/9 No change 5/9	NA	Less freshness 17/20 No change 1/20 Bad smell 1/20 Water stinks 1/20	NA	NA	Colour deteriorated 2/3 No change 1/3	Less freshness 25/32 = (-) 78%
4.	Combined, Author's Assessment	(-)2 Less freshness	(0) No change	(-)3 Bad smell and less freshness	(-)3 Bad smell and less freshness	(-)1 Less freshness	(-)1 Less freshness	(-) 58%

A large number of respondents complained of less freshness in water. At least two respondents explicitly mentioned that they found foul smell in the water. One respondent at Chilla made this complaint indicating that deterioration of quality of water takes place in smaller HEPs also.

Conclusion: There is indication of methane emissions.

Forest

Table A-1.8 : What is the impact of dam on grazing and fuel wood?

Sl. No.	*Item*	*Upstream*	*Small Reservoir (Barrage)*	*Large Reservoir (Tehri)*	*Along Canal*	*Along Tunnel*	*Downstream*	*Net, HEP-wise Impact*
1.	Chilla	No change 1/1	No change 2/3 Reduced 1/3	NA	No change 7/8 Reduced 1/8	NA	No change 4/5 Reduced 1/5	Reduced 3/17 = (-) 18%
2.	Maneri	No change 3/3	No change 3/3	NA	NA	No change 4/4	Reduced 2/2	Reduced 2/12 = (-) 17%
3.	Tehri	Reduced 3/9 No change 6/9.	NA	Reduced 18/19. No change 1/19.	NA	NA	No change 3/3	Reduced 21/31= (-) 68%
4.	Combined, Author's Assessment	(-)1 Reduced	(-)1 Reduced	(-)1 Reduced	(-)1 Reduced	(0) No impact	(-)2 Reduced	(-) 34%

Conclusion: Some reduction is due to population pressure. Nevertheless, negative impact is clearly seen.

Table A-1.9 : Has grass, grazing and fuel wood increased or decreased?

Sl. No.	*Item*	*Upstream*	*Small Reservoir (Barrage)*	*Large Reservoir (Tehri)*	*Along Canal*	*Along Tunnel*	*Downstream*	*Net, HEP-wise Impact*
1.	Chilla	No change 1/1	Increased 1/3 No change 2/3	NA	Much reduced 2/8 Reduced 3/8 No change 3/8	NA	No information 5/5	Reduced 4/17 = (-) 24%
2.	Maneri	No change 3/3	No change 3/3	NA	NA	No change 4/4	Increased ½ Reduced ½	No change
3.	Tehri	Reduced 3/9 Increased 1/9 No change 5/9	NA	Reduced 14/20 No change 6/20	NA	NA	Reduced 1/3 No change 2/3	Reduced 17/32 = (-) 53%
4.	Combined, Author's Assessment	(-)1 Reduced	(+)1 Increased	(-)2 Reduced	(-)3 Reduced	(0) No impact	(-)1 Reduced	(-) 26%

Conclusion: There is decline in availability of these items to local people.

Earthquake

Table A-1.10 : The probability of earthquake has increased or reduced due to construction of the dam?

Sl. No.	*Item*	*Upstream*	*Small Reservoir (Barrage)*	*Large Reservoir (Tehri)*	*Along Canal*	*Along Tunnel*	*Downstream*	*Net, HEP-wise Impact*
1.	Chilla	No impact 2/3 Increased 1/3	No impact 4/4	NA	No impact 7/7	NA	No impact 5/5	Increased 1/19 = (-) 5%
2.	Maneri	No impact 3/3	(See 'Along Tunnel')	NA	NA	Increased 3/7(1) No impact 4/7	No impact 2/3 Increased 1/3	Increased 4/13 = (-) 31%
3.	Tehri	No impact 9/9	NA	No impact 20/20	NA	NA	No impact 3/3	(0)
4.	Combined, Author's Assessment	(-)1 Increased	(0) No impact	(0) No impact	(0) No impact	(-)3 Increased	(-)1 Increased	(-) 12%

(1) Maneri, Barrage, Village Jamak. Eighty-five persons died due to collapse of houses in village near reservoir. The geology had become unstable leading to huge loss. The village shakes as in earthquake whenever blasting is undertaken in the tunnel. This impact is truly of the tunnel.

Landslides

Table A-1.11 : Have houses in the village developed cracks or damage due to sinking of earth, landslides, etc. after construction of dam?

Sl. No.	Item	Upstream	Small Reservoir (Barrage)	Large Reservoir (Tehri)	Along Canal	Along Tunnel	Downstream	Net, HEP-wise Impact
1.	Chilla	No 2/2	No 4/4	NA	No 8/8	NA	No 5/5	(0)
2.	Maneri	No 2/2	Yes 1/1(1)	NA	NA	Yes 3/7(2) No 4/7(3)	No 1/3 Yes 2/3	Yes 6/13 = (-) 46%
3.	Tehri	No 5/9 Yes, in fields 4/9	NA	No 9/20 Yes 3/20 Yes, in fields only 8/20	NA	NA	No 3/3	Yes 15/32 = (-) 47%
4.	Combined, Author's Assessment	(-)1 yes, in fields	(-)1 yes	(-)2 Yes, in houses and fields	(0) No impact	(-)3 Yes	(-)2 Yes	(-) 31%

(1) Maneri, Upstream. One respondent said that cracks had developed near the reservoir. His response is shifted to 'Small Reservoir' section.

(2) Maneri, Village Jamak. These respondents are classified in 'Small Reservoir'. However, the village is close to tunnel hence impact of tunnel is told here.

(3) Village Siror and Netal. These villages are down the tunnel near the dry riverbed. They are not much impacted by tunnel, which lies on higher elevation than the village.

Conclusion: People's assessment is that chances of earthquake have increased. Impact on landslides is strongly negative. It is leading to cracks in houses

Malaria and Health

Table A-1.12 : Are mosquitoes and insects seen near the reservoir? When? How many?

Sl. No.	*Item*	*Upstream*	*Small Reservoir (Barrage)*	*Large Reservoir (Tehri)*	*Along Canal*	*Along Tunnel*	*Downstream*	*Net, HEP-wise Impact*
1.	Chilla	Not seen ½ Increased mosquitoes at all times 1/2	Not seen in reservoir 2/4 Seen 2/4	NA	Not seen 6/8 Seen at all times 2/8	NA	Not seen 4/5 Seen at all times 1/5	Increase 6/19 = (-) 32%
2.	Maneri	No 3/3	No 3/3	NA	NA	No 4/4	No 2/2	(0)
3.	Tehri	No 4/9 Yes, mosquitoes seen 3/9 Yes, insects seen 3/9	NA	No 3/20 Yes 16/20 Few seen 1/20	NA	NA	No 3/3	Increase = 23/32 (-) 72%
4.	Combined, Author's Assessment	(-)2 More mosquitoes	(0) No impact	(-)3 More mosquitoes	(-)1 More mosquitoes	(0) No impact	(-)1 More mosquitoes	(-) 35%

Table A-1.13 : What is the change in people's health before and after construction of dam?

Sl. No.	*Item*	*Upstream*	*Small Reservoir (Barrage)*	*Large Reservoir (Tehri)*	*Along Canal*	*Along Tunnel*	*Downstream*	*Net, HEP-wise Impact*
1.	Chilla	No impact 2/2	No impact 4/4	NA	No impact 8/8	NA	No impact 5/5	(0)
2.	Maneri	No impact 3/3	No impact 3/3	NA	NA	No impact 4/4	No impact 2/3 Negative impact 1/3(1)	Negative 1/13 = (-) 8%
3.	Tehri	No impact 8/9 Negative impact 1/9	NA	No impact 19/20 Negative impact 1/20	NA	NA	No impact 3/3	Negative 2/32 = (-) 6%
4.	Combined, Author's Assessment	(-)1 Negative impact	(0) No impact	(-)1 Negative impact	(0) No impact	(0) No impact	(-)1 Negative impact	(-) 5%

(1) Maneri, Downstream (Chiranji Prasad Joshi, Village Gyansu): Temperature has much fallen. Climate is changing and not keeping to the old rhythm.

Table A-1.14 : Does the Dam Company spray insecticides for killing mosquitoes?

Sl. No.	*Item*	*Upstream*	*Small Reservoir (Barrage)*	*Large Reservoir (Tehri)*	*Along Canal*	*Along Tunnel*	*Downstream*	*Net, HEP-wise Impact*
1.	Chilla	No spray 2/2	No spray 2/4 Spraying done 2/2	NA	Previously yes, now no 2/8 No spraying done 6/8	NA	No spraying done 5/5	Not done 15/19 = (-) 79%
2.	Maneri	Never 3/3	Never 3/3	NA	NA	Never ¾ Yes 1/4	Never 3/3	Not Done = 12/13 = (-) 92%
3.	Tehri	No 9/9	NA	No 19/20 Previously yes 1/20(1)	NA	NA	No 3/3	Not done 32/32 = (-) 100
4.	Combined, Author's Assessment	(-)3 Not done	(-)2 Not done	(-)3 Not done	(-)3 Not done	(-)2 Not done	(-)3 Not done	(-) 90%

(1) Tehri, Reservoir, Village Asena: Stone quarry for Tehri Dam was located here. Insecticides were distributed at that time only.

Conclusion: There is clear evidence that more mosquitoes are seen on small reservoirs made by barrage and on large reservoirs like Tehri. This is sufficient to cause increase in incidence of Malaria. Dam companies have not sprayed insecticides. There is negative impact on health of local people.

Biodiversity

Table A-1.15 : Did any trees, plants, butterfly, insects, animals, birds or fish exist previously that have now become extinct?

Sl. No.	*Item*	*Upstream*	*Small Reservoir (Barrage)*	*Large Reservoir (Tehri)*	*Along Canal*	*Along Tunnel*	*Downstream*	*Net, HEP-wise Impact*
1.	Chilla	No change ½ Reduced 1/2	No change 4/4	NA	No change 6/8 Trees less 1/8 Fish less 1/8	NA	Less 1/5 No change 4/5	Less 4/19 = (-) 21%
2.	Maneri	(Fish quantity increased 1/3)	Trees are less 1/3. (Fish quantity is more 2/3).	NA	NA	There is less species 2/2 (no details are available)	No change 3/3	Less 3/11 = (-) 38%
3.	Tehri	(Fish quantity increased 2/3)	NA	(Fish quantity increased 4/20)	NA	NA	No change 3	(0)
4.	Combined, Author's Assessment	(0) No change	(-)1 Tree diversity less.	(0) No change	(-)1 Less	(-)1 Less	(-)1 Less	(-) 20%

Some say new species of fish were introduced.

Snakes have increased Near Old Tehri (Sangeeta, Narayan Singh and Narendra Rao, Village Tiwar, Tehri). They have moved up wards near village habitation. Previously they were living below near the riverbed.

No adverse impact on biodiversity is reported from Tehri. One possibility is that the time of 3-4 years is less for such impact to become visible.

Conclusion: There is a small negative impact on biodiversity.

Table A-1.16 : Wild animal population has increased or decreased due to the dam? What is the impact on agriculture?

Sl. No.	Item	Upstream	Small Reservoir (Barrage)	Large Reservoir (Tehri)	Along Canal	Along Tunnel	Downstream	Net, HEP-wise Impact
1.	Chilla	Reduced ½	Increased 2/4	NA	Reduced 2/8 Increased 1/8	NA	Reduced 2/5	Reduced 2/19 = (-) 11%
2.	Maneri	More 1/3	More 1/3	NA	NA	More 2/4. Monkeys more	Less 2/3	Increased 2/13 = (+) 15%
3.	Tehri	Less 3/9 More 1/9	NA	Less 8/20 More 6/20	NA	NA	No change 3/3	Reduced 4/32 (-) 13%
4.	Combined, Author's Assessment	(-)1 Less	(+)2 Increased	(0) No change	(0) No change	(+)1 Monkeys more	(-)2 Less	(-) 3%

Conclusion: There is no clear evidence of impact on wild animals. Positive and negative impacts are reported in nearly equal measure.

Table A-1.17 : Have there been accidents due to falling of villagers, cyclist or bus passengers in reservoir or canal? How many and when died or injured?

Sl. No.	*Item*	*Upstream*	*Small Reservoir (Barrage)*	*Large Reservoir (Tehri)*	*Along Canal*	*Along Tunnel*	*Downstream*	*Net, HEP-wise Impact*
1.	Chilla	No accident 2/2	No accident ¾ Yes 1/4	NA	Yes 7/8 (4) No accident 1/8	NA	No accident 5/5	More accident 8/19 (-) 42%
2.	Maneri	No accident 2/3. Accident 1/3 (1).	Many animals die 1/3	NA	NA	No accident 4/4	Many accidents every year 2/3 (2). No accident 1/3.	More accident 4/13 = (-) 31%
3.	Tehri	No accident 9/9	NA	No accident 19/20 One death 1/20 (3)	NA	NA	No accident 3/3	More accident 1/32 = (-) 3%
4.	Combined, Author's Assessment	(-)1 yes	(-)2 Yes	(-)2 yes	(-)3 Yes	(0) No accident	(-)2 Yes	(-) 25%

Road Accidents

(1) Maneri, Reservoir: Two busses met with accident in past but no death occurred. It is not clear when. This was possibly before filling of dam.

(2) Maneri: Downstream: (Dev Singh Gosain, Village Tiloth): He is employee in dam company. Every year one or two persons die because of sudden increase in water level due to opening of sluice gates. 2-3 persons sitting there agreed. Announcement is made by the department but some people do not hear and are trapped.

(3) Tehri: Reservoir: (Rakesh, Village Badkot): 7-8 months ago, one boy drowned in the reservoir while playing. 4-5 persons sitting there confirmed this. This was also confirmed by Jamotri Devi who has heard about this (Village Khand).

(4) Chilla: Mathura Prasad (village Kaudiya Talla): About 5-6 months ago, two girls fell into the canal from motorcycle and died. They could not be saved. Many accidents have taken place. Sauna Devi (Village Kunao): Accident has taken place 10-12 years ago. Mohan Singh (Village Malla): Two girls fell into canal from motorbike and died. Many accidents take place.

Conclusion: There is a huge negative impact due to road accidents. This is creating a fear phobia and traumatizing local people.

Decline in Temperature

Table A-1.18 : What is the change in temperature, rain and fog after construction of the dam?

Sl. No.	*Item*	*Upstream*	*Small Reservoir (Barrage)*	*Large Reservoir (Tehri)*	*Along Canal*	*Along Tunnel*	*Downstream*	*Net, HEP-wise Impact*
1.	Chilla	Loss, untimely rains 1/3 No change 2/3	More fog 2/4 No change 2/4	NA	More fog 5/8 No change 3/8	NA	More fog, less temperature and rain 1/5 No change 4/5	Negative 9/20 = (-) 45%
2.	Maneri	Temperature is less 1/3 No impact 2/3	Fog increased 2/3 (Temperature less 1/3) No impact 1/3	NA	NA	Less rain 1/4 (More fog 1/4) No impact 3/4	Fog more 2/3 (Rain less 1/3) No impact 1/3	Negative 6/13 = (-) 46%
3.	Tehri	Temperature is less 1/9 Fog is more 3/9 No impact 5/9	NA	Fog is more 3/20 Temperature is less 1/20 No impact 16/20	NA	NA	No impact 3/3	Negative 8/32 = (-) 25%
4.	Combined, Author's Assessment	(-)2 Low temperature, more fog	(-)3 Low temperature, more fog	(-)1 Low temperature, more fog	(-)2 More fog	(-)1 More fog	(-)2 Low temperature, more fog	(-) 39%

Table A-1.19 : What is the impact of reservoir and canal on rains? Rains have increased or reduced?

Sl. No.	*Item*	*Upstream*	*Small Reservoir (Barrage)*	*Large Reservoir (Tehri)*	*Along Canal*	*Along Tunnel*	*Downstream*	*Net, HEP-wise Impact*
1.	Chilla	Rains increased 1/3 No change 2/3	Increased 1/3 No change 3/4	NA	No impact 8/8	NA	No impact 5/5	Increased 2/20 = (+) 10%
2.	Maneri	No impact 3/3	No impact 3/3 More rain 1/3(1)	NA	NA	No impact ¾ More rain 1/4	Less rain 3/3(2)	Reduced 1/13 = (-) 8%
3.	Tehri	No impact 9/9	NA	No impact 20/20	NA	NA	No impact 3/3	(0)
4.	Combined, Author's Assessment	(+)1 Rains increased	(+)2 Rains increased	(0) No impact	(0) No impact	(+)1 Rains increased	(-)1 Rains less	(+) 1%

(1) This response was made on question no 17 but shifted here.

(2) Maneri, Downstream (Chiranji Prasad Joshi, Village Gyansu): Rain is less and at odd times. No rain when there is need.

Conclusion: There is clear negative impact on climate due to increased fog and lower temperatures. There is no impact on rains.

Table A-1.20 : What is the impact of dam on the yields of wheat?

Sl. No.	*Item*	*Upstream*	*Small Reservoir (Barrage)*	*Large Reservoir (Tehri)*	*Along Canal*	*Along Tunnel*	*Downstream*	*Net, HEP-wise Impact*
1.	Chilla	Reduced 1/1	No information	NA	No change 2/4 Reduced 2/4	NA	No change 3/3	Reduced 3/8 = (-) 38%
2.	Maneri	No impact 3/3	Less yield 1/3 No impact 1/3 More yield 1/3	NA	NA	Less yield 2/3 No impact 1/3	Less yield 1/1	Reduced 3/10 = (-) 30%
3.	Tehri	No impact 5/5	NA	No impact 16/16	NA	NA	No impact 3/3	(0)
4.	Combined, Author's Assessment	(-)1 reduced	(-)1 reduced	(0) no impact	(-)2 reduced	(-)2 reduced	(-)1 reduced	(-) 23%

Table A-1.21 : What is the impact of dam on the yields of paddy?

Sl. No.	Item	Upstream	Small Reservoir (Barrage)	Large Reservoir (Tehri)	Along Canal	Along Tunnel	Downstream	Net, HEP-wise Impact
1.	Chilla	Reduced 1/1	No information	NA	Reduced 2/4 No change 2/4	NA	No change 3/3	Reduced 3/8 = (-) 38%
2.	Maneri	No impact 3/3	Less yield 1/3 No impact 2/3	NA	NA	Less yield 1/3 No impact 2/3	Less yield 1/1	Reduced 3/10 = (-) 30%
3.	Tehri	No impact 5/5	NA	No impact 9/9	NA	NA	No impact 3/3	(0)
4.	Combined, Author's Assessment	(-)1 reduced	(-)1 reduced	(0) no impact	(-)2 reduced	(-)2 reduced	(-)2 reduced	(-) 23%

Conclusion: There is clear negative impact on yields of the two principal crops—wheat and paddy. This may be due to lower temperatures or more fog. The 'no impact' at Tehri may be due to less time that has elapsed after construction of dam.

Sand

Table A-1.22 : The availability of sand from riverbank for construction of houses has increased or decreased?

Sl. No.	*Item*	*Upstream*	*Small Reservoir (Barrage)*	*Large Reservoir (Tehri)*	*Along Canal*	*Along Tunnel*	*Downstream*	*Net, HEP-wise Impact*
1.	Chilla	Reduced ½ No change 1/2	Reduced ¼ Increased 2/4 No change 1/4	NA	Reduced 1/8 No change 7/8	NA	Reduced 2/4 Increased 1/4 No change 1/4	Less 2/18 = (-) 11%
2.	Maneri	More 2/3 No impact 1/3	More 1/3 Less 2/3	NA	NA	More ¾ Less ¼	More 2/3 Less 1/3	More 4/13 = (+) 31%
3.	Tehri	Less 5/9 No impact 4/9	NA	Less 20/20	NA	NA	Less 3/3(2)	Less 28/32 = (-) 88%
4.	Combined, Author's Assessment	(0) No clear verdict	(0) No clear verdict	(-)3 Less sand and stone	(-) 1 Small reduction	(+)1 More	(0) No clear verdict	(-) 23%

(1) The riverbed dries out during non-peaking hours and enables easy lifting of stones.

(2) Stones can be easily taken out from the dry bed of the river.

Conclusion: There is negative impact on availability of sand at Chilla and Tehri. The negative impact at downstream Tehri is especially notable. The dam companies say more sand will be available at the spillway due to flushing but this is not happening in reservoir-based HEPs like Tehri. There is positive impact at Maneri. This may be due to regular flushing along with dry spells for collection of sand. Stones can be collected easily because water in riverbed is less during non-peak hours, which exposes the stones for lifting.

River Rafting

Table A-1.23 : Has the number of tourists in your area increased or decreased after making of the dam?

Sl. No.	*Item*	*Upstream*	*Small Reservoir (Barrage)*	*Large Reservoir (Tehri)*	*Along Canal*	*Along Tunnel*	*Downstream*	*Net, HEP-wise Impact*
1.	Chilla	Increased 2/3 No change 1/3	Increased 4/4	NA	Increased 3/7 Reduced 2/7 Do not come to village 2/7	NA	Increased 3/5 No change 2/5	More 10/19 = (+) 53%
2.	Maneri	No change 3/3. No one comes to the village.	Increased 1/3	NA	NA	Increased 2/4	Increased 2/3 Decreased 1/3	More 4/13 = (+) 23%
3.	Tehri	Increased 4/9	NA	Increased 7/18	NA	NA	Decreased 2/3	More 9/30 = (+) 30%
4.	Combined, Author's Assessment	(+)2 Increased	(+)3 Increased	(+)2 Increased	(0) No impact	(+)2 Increased	(+)2 Increased	(+) 35%

Conclusion: There is positive impact on number of tourists. People are reported to come to see the reservoir. This writer must report that he was taken by a friend to the banks of the Chilla Barrage as a tourist outing. Hence, some positive impact is seen on tourism. However, the next question seems to indicate that tourists also prefer flowing water except for a large reservoir like Tehri dam.

Table A-1.24 : In your opinion, do tourists prefer flowing water or reservoir-canal?

Sl. No.	*Item*	*Upstream*	*Small Reservoir (Barrage)*	*Large Reservoir (Tehri)*	*Along Canal*	*Along Tunnel*	*Downstream*	*Net, HEP-wise Impact*
1.	Chilla	Flowing water 2/2	Flowing water 1/3 Reservoir 2/3	NA	Canal 1/6 Flowing water 4/6 Reservoir 1/6	NA	Flowing water 2/3 Reservoir 1/3	Flowing water 6/14 = (-) 29%
2.	Maneri	Reservoir 3/3	Flowing water 1/3 Reservoir 2/3	NA	NA	Flowing water 3/3	Flowing water 3/3	Flowing water 2/12 = (-) 17%
3.	Tehri	Reservoir 5/9 Flowing water 4/9	NA	Reservoir 16/17 Flowing water 1/17	NA	NA	Reservoir 3/3	Reservoir 19/29 = (+) 65%
4.	Combined, Author's Assessment	(0) No clear verdict	(0) No clear verdict	(+)2 Reservoir	(-)1 Flowing water	(-)3 Flowing water	(0) No clear verdict	(+) 6%

Conclusion: Tourists also prefer flowing water except for strong contrary evidence from large reservoir of Tehri. The final result is near zero.

Bridges

Table A-1.25 : What is the impact of canal or dam on contacts with relatives etc. on the other side? Contact with other side has become easy or more difficult.

Sl. No.	*Name of HEP*	*Upstream*	*Small Reservoir (Barrage)*	*Large Reservoir (Tehri)*	*Along Canal*	*Along Tunnel*	*Downstream*	*Net, HEP-wise Impact*
1.	Chilla	Worse 1/3 No change 2/3	Better 2/4 No change 2/4	NA	Better 5/8 Worse 3/8	NA	No change 5/5	Better 3/20 = (+) 15%
2.	Maneri	Better 1/3 No impact 2/3	Worse 1/3 Better 1/3 No impact 1/3	NA	NA	Better ¾ No impact ¼	Better 1/3 Worse 1/3 No change 1/3	Better 4/13 = (+) 31%
3.	Tehri	Better 1/9 Worse 6/9 No impact 2/9	NA	Better 1/20 Worse 17/20 No impact 2/20	NA	NA	Worse 3/3	Worse 24/32 = (-) 75%
4.	Combined, Author's Assessment	(-)2 Worse	(+)2 Better	(-)3 Worse	(0) No clear verdict	(+)2 Better	(-)2 Worse	(-) 10%

Conclusion: The barrages at Chilla and Maneri have improved contacts. There is strong negative impact of reservoir at Tehri.

Table A-1.26 : Have you got facilities like education, gas connection, hospital, transport, etc. from the Dam Company?

Sl. No.	*Name of HEP*	*Upstream*	*Small Reservoir (Barrage)*	*Large Reservoir (Tehri)*	*Along Canal*	*Along Tunnel*	*Downstream*	*Net, HEP-wise Impact*
1.	Chilla	No change 3/3	No change 3/4 Better, bridge over barrage 1/4	NA	No change 6/8 School and temple ¼ Gas and transport ¼	NA	No change 5/5	Better 3/20 (+) 15%
2.	Maneri	No change 2/3 Facilities provided 1/3	No change 3/3	NA	NA	No change 3/4 Hospital ¼	No change 3/3	Better 2/13 = (+) 15%
3.	Tehri	No change 6/9 Better roads 3/9	NA	No change 18/20 Roads 1/20 All facilities 1/20	NA	NA	No change 3/3	Better 5/32 = (+) 16%
4.	Combined, Author's Assessment	(+)1 Some facilities obtained	(+) 1 Positive impact of .bridge.	(+)1 Some facilities obtained	(+)1 Some facilities obtained	(+)1 Some facilities obtained	(0) no impact	(+) 15%

Conclusion: There is improvement in facilities such as roads and hospitals.

Aesthetic Value of free Flow of River

Table A-1.27 : Do you like flowing river or reservoir or canal? Why? What is the difference?

Sl. No.	*Item*	*Upstream*	*Small Reservoir (Barrage)*	*Large Reservoir (Tehri)*	*Along Canal*	*Along Tunnel*	*Downstream*	*Net, HEP-wise Impact*
1.	Chilla	Flowing water 3/3	Flowing water 3/3	NA	Flowing water 6/8 No difference 2/8	NA	Flowing water 4/5 No difference 1/5	Free flowing water 16/19 = (-) 84%
2.	Maneri	Flowing water 3/3	Flowing water ¾ Reservoir 1/4	NA	NA	Flowing water ¾ No preference 1/4	Flowing water 3/3	Free flowing water 12/14 = (-) 79%
3.	Tehri	Flowing water 9/9	NA	Flowing water 20/20	NA	NA	Flowing water 2/3 Both OK 1/3	Free flowing water 31/32 = (-) 97%
4.	Combined, Author's Assessment	(-)3 Like flowing water	(-)2 Like flowing water	(-)3 Like flowing water	(-)3 Like flowing water	(-)3 Like flowing water	(-)3 Like flowing water	(-) 87%

Reasons for preferring flowing water are that water is no longer fit for drinking. Foul smell comes from water.

Conclusion: There is a strong negative impact of HEPs on the aesthetic value of the local people who very strongly like flowing water.

Willingness to Pay for Flowing Water

Table A-1.28 : How much annual price you are willing to pay for restoring free flow of water in the river?

Sl. No.	*Name of HEP*	*Upstream*	*Small Reservoir (Barrage)*	*Large Reservoir (Tehri)*	*Along Canal*	*Along Tunnel*	*Downstream*	*Net, HEP-wise Impact*
1.	Chilla, n=12	25	0	NA	5	NA	255	71
2.	Maneri, n=13	30	383	NA	NA	112	17	136
3.	Tehri, n=32	2	NA	57	NA	NA	0	20
4.	Combined, Author's Assessment, Rupees per person	19	191	57	5	112	91	76

Table A-1.29 : How many are willing to pay? (Number of respondents)

Sl. No.	*Name of HEP*	*Upstream*	*Small Reservoir (Barrage)*	*Large Reservoir (Tehri)*	*Along Canal*	*Along Tunnel*	*Downstream*	*Net, HEP-wise Impact*
1.	Chilla	½	0/2	NA	2/4	NA	2/4	5/12 = 42%
2.	Maneri	2/3	3/3	NA	NA	2/4	1/3	8/13 = 62%
3.	Tehri	2/9	NA	4/20	NA	NA	0/3	6/32 = 19%
4.	Combined, Author's Assessment, Percent	36	60	20	50	50	30	41%

Enumerator Naresh Puri: People believe that the Tehri dam will not be decommissioned. They are inclined to pay but say unwilling to so because it is an irrelevant question.

Shri Buddhi Lal, Village Maneri (Maneri) says: "Dam is good. It is in national interest. But it affects local people adversely."

Only one person out of total 51 surveyed spoke clearly in favour of dams. He is an electronic engineer named Brahmachari staying in Nitala Village (Maneri). He likes the dam. He says water has not been obstructed—only its direction is changed. He has studied Gita. He quoted Hindu texts saying that the mountains will one day be flattened.

Conclusion: People strongly like free flow of river and 41% are willing to pay for the same.

Table A-1.30 : Where was the cremation of dead done previously? Where is it done now?

Sl No	*Name of HEP*	*Upstream*	*Small Reservoir (Barrage)*	*Large Reservoir (Tehri)*	*Along Canal*	*Along Tunnel*	*Downstream*	*Net, HEP-wise Impact*
1.	Chilla	No change. 2/2	Previously here, now Rishikesh 1/4 No change ¾	NA	No change 8/8	NA	No change 5/5	Negative 1/19 = (-) 5%
2.	Maneri	No change 3/3	No change 3/3 (On reservoir 1/3)	NA	NA	No change 4/4	No change 2/3 More difficulty now 1/3(1)	Negative 1/13 = (-) 8%
3.	Tehri	No change 8/9 Now go to Dharasu 1/9(2)	NA	No change 15/18 (Now on reservoir) On zero point if capacity permits 3/18	NA	NA	No change 3/3	Negative 4/30 = (-) 13%
4.	Combined, Author's Assessment	(-)1 Go elsewhere	(-)1 Go elsewhere	(-)2 Go elsewhere	(0) No impact	(0) No impact	(-)1 Go elsewhere	(-) 9%

Immersion of ashes

(1) Maneri, Downstream (Chiranji Prasad Joshi, Gyansu): Previously the dead were cremated along the Ganga from Gomukh to Ganga Sagar. Now difficulty is being faced in cremation.

(2) Tehri, Upstream (Brij Mohan, Village Nagni Chhoti): "Previously we used to cremate on the traditional ghat. Now we go to Dharasu." There is about 4 km free flow of river water here.

Conclusion: People very much prefer to cremate their dead near flowing waters. Many may not be able to afford this hence have reconciled to doing this near reservoirs.

Fish

People are afraid to tell they are fishing because it is illegal.

At Tehri 7 respondents said that a few persons did business of fish earlier. Now they do not do this.

Conclusion: There is loss of fishing.

Relief and Rehabilitation

Table A-1.31 : Has any one from your family or village got employment from the Dam Company? Please give name, age, salary and designation.

Sl. No.	*Name of HEP*	*Upstream*	*Small Reservoir (Barrage)*	*Large Reservoir (Tehri)*	*Along Canal*	*Along Tunnel*	*Downstream*	*Net, HEP-wise Impact*
1.	Chilla	No job 3/3	No job ¾	NA	No 4/8	NA	No job 5/5	(-) 50%
			Yes 1/4		Yes 4/8			
2.	Maneri	Yes 2/3	Yes 2/3	NA	NA	Yes ¾	Yes 1/3	(-) 23%
		No 1/3	No 1/3			No 1/4	No 2/3	
3.	Tehri	Yes 1/9	NA	Yes 5/20	NA	NA	No 3/3	(-) 63%
		No 8/9		No 15/20				
4.	Combined, Author's Assessment	(+)2 Yes	(+)2 Yes	(+)2 Yes	(+)2 Yes	(+)2 Yes	(+)1 Yes	(-) 45%

Conclusion: Some people have benefited by getting jobs. The record of Maneri is especially positive.

Table A-1.32 : The compensation received from Dam Company has led to improvement or deterioration in the life of the recipients. Please give examples with names.

Sl. No.	*Name of HEP*	*Upstream*	*Small Reservoir (Barrage)*	*Large Reservoir (Tehri)*	*Along Canal*	*Along Tunnel*	*Downstream*	*Net, HEP-wise Impact*
1.	Chilla	Deterioration 1/1	No information 4/4	NA	No impact. Land obtained for land 1/2 Improved 1/2	NA	(No information 5/5)	(0)
2.	Maneri	Improved 1/1	Deterioration 1/1	NA	NA	Improved 1/1	No impact 2/2	(+) 20%
3.	Tehri	No impact 1/1	NA	Deterioration 9/11 No impact 2/11	NA	NA	(No information 3/3)	(-) 69%
4.	Combined, Author's Assessment	(0) No clear verdict	(-)2 Deterioration	(-)2 Deterioration	(+)1 Improved	(+)1 Improved	(0) No information	(-) 16%

Conclusion: There is no clear verdict. There is some improvement and some deterioration. On the whole, the result is negative due to strong deterioration at Tehri.

Comparison of Impacts by Location

We give below the overall impact at different locations. These figures have been taken from the bottom line of the above tables. The different issues are not comparable and results cannot be added. Hence the location-wise impact is assessed by the author and these are given below.

Table A-1.33 : Overall Impact by Location (Author's Assessment on Scale of ±3)

Table No.	*Issue*	*Impact*	*Total*	*Upstream*	*Small Reservoir (Barrage)*	*Large Reservoir (Tehri)*	*Along Canal*	*Along Tunnel*	*Downstream*
2.	Methane Emissions	Impact on smell of water downstream	(-)10	(-)2	(0)	(-)3	(-)3	(-)1	(-)1
3.	Biodiversity	Loss of species of trees, plants, butterfly, insects, animals, birds or fish?	(-)4	(0)	(-)1	(0)	(-)1	(-)1	(-)1
4.	Biodiversity	Wild animal population	(0)	(-)1	(+)2	(0)	(0)	(+)1	(-)2
5.	Eco-tourism	Do you like flowing river, reservoir or canal?	(-)17	(-)3	(-)2	(-)3	(-)3	(-)3	(-)3
6.	Eco-tourism	Number of tourists	(+)11	(+)2	(+)3	(+)2	(0)	(+)2	(+)2

7.	Eco-tourism	Tourists prefer flowing water or reservoir-canal?	(-)2	(0)	(0)	(+)2	(-)1	(-)3	(0)
8.	Forest	Impact of dam on grazing and fuel wood	(-)6	(-)1	(-)1	(-)1	(-)1	(0)	(-)2
9.	Forest	Impact on grass, grazing and fuel wood	(-)6	(-)1	(+)1	(-)2	(-)3	(0)	(-)1
10.	Sediment	Impact on sediment downstream	(-)3	(0)	(0)	(0)	(0)	(-)1	(-)2
11.	Road Accidents	Road accidents due to dam	(-)10	(-)1	(-)2	(-)2	(-)3	(0)	(-)2
12.	Water	Change in level of water in the river in the last 20-30 years during winters?	(-)7	(-)2	(+)1	(0)	(-)1	(-)2	(-)3
13.	Water	Impact on worship on the river	(-)9	(-)2	(-)1	(-)3	(0)	(-)1	(-)2
14.	Water	Water fit for drinking?	(-)14	(-)2	(-)2	(-)3	(-)3	(-)2	(-)2
15.	Evaporation and Seepage	Impact on water in wells and other sources	(-)6	(0)	(0)	(0)	(0)	(-)3	(-)3

16.	Earthquake	Probability of earthquake	(-)5	(-)1	(0)	(0)	(0)	(-)3	(-)1
17.	Earthquake	Landslides and cracks in houses	(-)9	(-)1	(-)1	(-)2	(0)	(-)3	(-)2
18.	Health	Impact on people's health	(-)3	(-)1	(0)	(-)1	(0)	(0)	(-)1
19.	Health	Mosquitoes along reservoir	(-)7	(-)2	(0)	(-)3	(-)1	(0)	(-)1
20.	Health	Spray done by dam company for control of mosquitoes?	(-)16	(-)3	(-)2	(-)3	(-)3	(-)2	(-)3
21.	Climate	Impact on climate	(-)11	(-)2	(-)3	(-)1	(-)2	(-)1	(-)2
22.	Climate	Impact of reservoir on rains	(+)3	(+)1	(+)2	(0)	(0)	(+)1	(-)1
23.	Crops	Impact on yield of wheat	(-)7	(-)1	(-)1	(0)	(-)2	(-)2	(-)1
24.	Crops	Impact on yield of paddy	(-)8	(-)1	(-)1	(0)	(-)2	(-)2	(-)2
25.	Sand	Availability of sand and stone from river bank	(-)2	(0)	(0)	(-)3	(0)	(+)1	(0)
26.	Bridges	Impact on social contacts	(-)3	(-)2	(+)2	(-)3	(0)	(+)2	(-)2

26.	Bridges	Impact on social contacts	(-)3	(-)2	(+)2	(-)3	(0)	(+)2	(-)2
27.	Immersion of ashes	Impact on immersion of ashes of dead	(-)5	(-)1	(-)1	(-)2	(0)	(0)	(-)1
28.	R&R	Jobs obtained in R&R package	(+)11	(+)2	(+)2	(+)2	(+)2	(+)2	(+)1
29.	R&R	Infrastructure Facilities from Dam company	(+)5	(+)1	(+)1.	(+)1	(+)1	(+)1	(0)
30.	R&R	Impact of land compensation	(-)2	(0)	(-)2	(-)2	(+)1	(+)1	(0)
	Total Impact		(-)140	(-)24	(-)6	(-)29	(-)24	(-)19	(-)38

The location-wise conclusions are as follows:

- The total impact on local people is highly negative.
- The impact is least on people living near the barrage. This is because the negative impacts are less while they benefit from provision of facilities like bridge to cross the river. However, even here the impact is marginally negative.
- Impact is most severe on downstream people and those along big reservoirs like Tehri. Similar negative impact will take place at Kotlibhel and Srinagar HEPs.
- People living along canal and tunnel are also much adversely affected.

It is not correct to assume that ROR dams do not have negative impacts like large dams.

Comparison of impacts by HEP

The Net, HEP-wise results are given in table below. These have been taken from the last column of the tables above.

Table A-1.34. Net, HEP-wise Impact on Local People (Percent of respondents)

Table No.	*Issue*	*Impact*	*Chilla (Canal)*	*Maneri (Tunnel)*	*Tehri (Large Reservoir)*	*Total (3 HEPs)*
2.	Methane Emissions	Impact on smell of water downstream	(-) 61	(-) 15	(-) 78	(-) 51
3.	Biodiversity	Loss of species of trees, plants, butterfly, insects, animals, birds or fish?	(-) 21	(-) 38	(0)	(-) 20
4.	Biodiversity	Wild animal population	(-) 11	(+) 15	(-) 13	(-) 3
5.	Eco-tourism	Do you like flowing river more or reservoir or canal?	(-) 84	(-) 79	(-) 97	(-) 87
6.	Eco-tourism	Number of tourists increased or decreased?	(+) 53	(+) 23	(+) 30	(+) 35
7.	Eco-tourism	Tourists prefer flowing water or reservoir-canal?	(-) 29	(-) 17	(+) 65	(+) 6
8.	Forest	Impact of dam on grazing and fuel wood	(-) 18	(-) 17	(-) 72	(-) 36
9.	Forest	Impact on grass, grazing and fuel wood	(-) 41	(0)	(-) 53	(-) 31
10.	Sediment	Impact on sediment downstream	(-) 11	(-) 25	(-) 17	(-) 18

11.	Road Accidents	Road accidents due to dam	(-) 42	(-) 31	(-) 3	(-) 25
12.	Water	Change in level of water in the river in the last 0-0 years during winters?	(-) 29	(-) 38	(-) 38	(-) 35
13.	Water	Impact on worship on the river	(-) 20	(-) 23	(-) 78	(-) 40
14.	Water	Water fit for drinking?	(-) 50	(-) 23	(-) 88	(-) 54
15.	Evaporation and Seepage	Impact on water in wells and other sources	(0)	(-) 62	(-) 4	(-) 22
16.	Earthquake	Probability of earthquake	(-) 5	(-) 31	(0)	(-) 12
17.	Earthquake	Landslides and cracks in houses	(0)	(-) 46	(-) 47	(-) 31
18.	Health	Impact on people's health	(0)	(-) 8	(-) 6	(-) 25
19.	Health	Mosquitoes along reservoir	(-) 32	(0)	(-) 72	(-) 35
20.	Health	Spray done by dam company for control of mosquitoes?	(-) 79	(-) 8	(0)	(-) 29
21.	Climate	Impact on climate	(-) 45	(-) 46	(-) 26	(-) 39
22.	Climate	Impact of reservoir on rains	(+) 10	(-) 8	(0)	(+) 1
23.	Crops	Impact on yield of wheat	(-) 38	(-) 30	(0)	(-) 23
24.	Crops	Impact on yield of paddy	(-) 38	(-) 30	(0)	(-) 23
25.	Sand	Availability of sand and stone from river bank	(-) 11	(+) 31	(-) 88	(-) 23
26.	Bridges	Impact on social contacts	(+) 15	(+) 31	(-) 75	(-) 10

27.	Immersion of ashes	Impact on immersion of ashes of dead	(-) 5	(-) 8	(-) 13	(-) 9
28.	R&R	Jobs obtained in R&R package	(-) 50	(-) 23	(-) 63	(-) 45
29.	R&R	Infrastructure Facilities from Dam company	(+) 15	(+) 15	(+) 16	(+) 15
30.	R&R	Impact of land compensation	(0)	(+) 20	(-) 69	(-) 16
	Total Impact		(-) 22	(-) 16	(-) 31	(-) 24

Conclusions from above table are as follows:

- The total impact on local people is negative in all three dams. The negative impact is greatest at Tehri. However, negative impacts of Chilla and Maneri are not much behind. Thus, we should not be under the impression that smaller dams have positive impacts on local people. Huge negative impacts may be expected on local people due to Kotlibhel and Srinagar dams since the basic structure of reservoir is similar to that of Tehri.
- The positive impacts are on tourism and infrastructure like roads and hospitals.
- The negative impacts are very pervasive and extend to all facets of life. Especially severe negative impacts occur due to Loss of aesthetic and drinking value of flowing water, Air quality, Deprivation of forest produce, Landslides, Mosquitoes and ill-health and Deterioration of climate.
- About 40 percent people are willing to pay money to decommission the dams and to restore the free flow of water. The average price people are willing to pay is about Rs 76 per person per year to restore free flow of river.

ANNEXURE-2
Survey of Pilgrims at Dev Prayag, Rishikesh and Haridwar

Objectives of Study

The cascade of Hydroelectric Projects (HEPs) on River Ganga and its tributaries is going to affect the flow of water at Dev Prayag, Rishikesh, Haridwar and downstream at Prayag, Kashi and Ganga Sagar. The HEP Companies claim that damming the flow of water will provide benefits from generation of power to the people and will *not* reduce the spiritual power of these religious places. The water flowing into Dev Prayag from Bhagirathi is already affected by the Tehri Dam. Tehri Hydropower Development Corporation (THDC), which has built the Tehri Dam, insists that there is no deterioration of quality of water downstream from Tehri Dam. This study is made to assess the impact of Tehri dam on the impact of taking bath at Dev Prayag, Rishikesh and Haridwar as assessed by pilgrims.

The underlying assumption is that if Tehri Dam has affected the quality of waters at these pilgrim centres, then the proposed new HEPs will have a similar effect.

This proposition can be challenged since the proposed HEPs are Run-of-River (ROR) in that they do not store water in one season to be discharged in another season as done in Tehri. However, the study of ROR Dams at Chilla and Maneri given in the previous section indicates that the quality of water deteriorates in ROR dams as well. Thus, we conclude that the proposed ROR dams will also have a negative impact. Since we do not have a study of impact of cascade, we take Tehri as a proxy.

Methodology

The objective of the study is to assess whether and to what extent the construction of Tehri dam has affected the spiritual power of River Ganga. A questionnaire was made to ask respondents about impact of dam on various aspects of worship. Enumerator Naresh Chandra Puri went to these pilgrim centres in December 2007-January 2008 and sought responses from the pilgrims coming to take bath or to collect water for taking home.

No sampling was done. Assistance of any local person was not sought lest the mediator influence the results. The enumerator asked people he met spontaneously at the bathing ghats about the impacts.

The distribution of visitors by home place was as follows:

Table A-2.1 : Distribution of Pilgrims by Home

Sl. No	*Survey Location*	*Total Number of Respondents*	*Uttarakhand*	*Other States*	*Local*
1.	Dev Prayag	55	Dehra Dun (4), Udham Singh Nagar (1), Pauri (2), Tehri (3), Rudra Prayag (1), Unknown (3). Total 11	Gujarat (2), Maharashtra (2), WB (6), Delhi (3), Karnataka (1), Haryana (4), UP (2). Total 20	21
2.	Rishikesh	93	Dehra Dun (8), Tehri (4), Pauri (3), Roorkee (1), Haridwar (2), Udham Singh Nagar (1), Uttarkashi (1), Unknown (1). Total 20	Bihar (2); Chandigarh (3), Delhi (4), Haryana (2), Himachal Pradesh (2), Maharashtra (1), Punjab (2), Rajasthan (2), UP (19), West Bengal (1). Total 38	34
3.	Haridwar	94	Almora (1), Bageshwar (1), Chamoli (1), Dehra Dun (5), Pauri (5), Udham Singh Nagar (1), Uttarkashi (1). Total 15	Bihar (6); Delhi (11), Gujarat (1), Haryana (10), Maharashtra (2), MP (2), Punjab (2), Rajasthan (3), UP (22), West Bengal (1). Total 60.	19
4.	Total	238	46	118	74

The income of respondents was as follows:

Table A-2.2 : Income of Visitors

Sl. No.	*Location*	*Average*	*Median*
1.	Dev Prayag, n=27	15,355	10,000
2.	Rishikesh, n=37	8,166	5,640
3.	Haridwar, n=61	8,473	5,000
4.	Average, n=125	10,665	6,880

Table A-2.3 : Income of Local Persons

Sl. No.	*Location*	*Average*	*Median*
1.	Dev Prayag, n=21	3,042	2,000
2.	Rishikesh, n=21	11,623	6,000
3.	Haridwar, n=15	4,720	3,000
4.	Average, n=57	6,462	3,667

Nature of Benefit Obtained from River Ganga

Table A-2.4 : What is the benefit you have obtained from the blessings of River Ganga? (Percent of Respondents replying in affirmative).

Sl. No.	*Type of Benefit*	*Dev Prayag n=55*	*Rishikesh n=93*	*Haridwar n=94*	*Combined n=242*
1.	Mental Peace	75	71	84	77
2.	Health	25	19	33	26
3.	Business	18	5	19	14
4.	Child	18	9	8	12
5.	Service	5	9	23	12
6.	Success in Examination	11	9	8	9
7.	Others	31	13	17	20

Seventy-seven percent pilgrims obtained mental peace while 26 percent obtained health benefits. The Ganga waters appear to have the power to relax the mind and body of the pilgrim. This gives him mental peace and good health.

Next question was, "How much value do you place on the benefit obtained?" In response to this question a large number of pilgrims replied in terms of 'invaluable', 'lacs' or 'priceless'. These have been mentioned in the last line of table below.

Table A-2.5 : Value of Benefit obtained (As reckoned by those placing monetary value upon the benefit).

Sl. No.	*Type of Benefit*	*Dev Prayag n=11*	*Rishikesh n=6*	*Haridwar n=9*	*Combined n=26*
1.	Average	29,427	59,041	66,177	51,548
2.	Median	1,000	26,500	10,000	12,500
3.	Number responding in priceless, invaluable, etc.	25	23	4	52

The average or median values are based on a small number of respondents, 26. Nearly double this numbers have said that the benefit derived is priceless etc. In view of this, we take the higher average value of Rs 51,548 as the value of benefit derived by pilgrims, and not the lower median value.

Benefit from Generation of Electricity

Pilgrims accepted that there would be much benefit to the nation from generation of electricity from waters of River Ganga.

Table A-2.6 : What is the benefit to the nation from generation of electricity from waters of Ganga? (Number of Pilgrims Responding in Affirmative)

Sl.No.	*Type of Pilgrim*	*Small Increase*	*Big Increase*	*Small Decrease*	*Big Decrease*	*Percent Reporting Increase*
1.	Dev Prayag, n=53	16	34	2	1	95%
2.	Rishikesh n=93	16	72	2	2	95%
3.	Haridwar, n=91	17	71	1	2	97%
4.	Combined, n=237	49	177	5	5	95%

Conclusion: Pilgrims recognize that there is great benefit to the nation from generation of electricity from waters of the Ganga.

Decline in Quality of Water due to Construction of Dams

The question is whether construction of dams also affects the pilgrims? The following question was asked to assess this aspect.

Table A-2.7 : What is the impact of Tehri Dam on flow of waters of Ganga? (Percent Pilgrims Responding in Affirmative)

Sl.No.	*Location*	*Was Better Previously*	*Is Better Now*	*No Difference*	*Net, Percent, Reporting Previously Better*
1.	Dev Prayag, 1 n=41	88	12		76
2.	Rishikesh, n=87	47	15	38	32
3.	Haridwar, n=78	38	26	36	12

Conclusion: The decline in quality of water is less as we move away from Tehri. This is likely because the water gets a chance to regenerate some qualities like Dissolved Oxygen. Further the term 'flow' focuses more on quantity of water than quality. There is more quantity of flow in winters and summers due to construction of Tehri Dam. This positive aspect was probably noted by pilgrims.

Benefit to Pilgrims from Removal of Tehri Dam

There can be an impact on pilgrims due to change in quality of waters due to Tehri Dam. The following question was asked to assess this.

Table A-2.8 : What will be the benefit to the nation if Tehri Dam is removed and pilgrims are able to take bath in free-flowing waters of the Ganga at the Confluence? (Percent Pilgrims Responding in Affirmative)

Sl No	*Location*	*Small Increase*	*Big Increase*	*Small Decrease*	*Big Decrease*	*Net, Percent Reporting Increase*
1.	Dev Prayag, n=34	44	47	6	3	82
2.	Rishikesh, n=78	36	45	11	8	62
3.	Haridwar, n=81	38	32	18	12	40

Conclusion: There is a positive impact on pilgrims if Tehri Dam is removed but the intensity of impact declines as we move downstream.

Pilgrims were further asked to give a percent value to the increase or decrease in the impact. These are tabulated below.

Table A-2.9 : What is the impact of removal of Tehri Dam?

Sl No	*Location*	*Numbers Reporting Increase*	*Percent Increase (By numbers in previous column)*	*Numbers Reporting Decrease*	*Percent Decrease (By numbers in previous column)*
1.	Dev Prayag	31	46.3	3	43.3
2.	Rishikesh	52	46	11	30
3.	Haridwar	42	29.5	17	42.7
4.	Combined	125	40.6	31	38.7

Estimate of Cost of Dam to Pilgrims

We can use these figures to make an estimate of effect of removal of Tehri Dam on pilgrims.

First, the weighted average is calculated:

Weighted Average of impact = (Numbers decrease × Percent decrease) – (Numbers increase × Percent increase)/ (Total number)

= – (125 × 40.6) + (31 × 38.7)/(125 + 31) = – 24.8%

The benefit to pilgrims is increased by 24.8% upon decommissioning of Tehri Dam.

Present benefit per pilgrim is Rs 51,548 (Table A-2.5 above)

Reduction in benefit per pilgrim: 24.8% or Rs 12,784

This figure is used to assess the impact of Tehri Dam on the benefits obtained by pilgrims. The author estimates the number of pilgrims as follows: Dev Prayag 200, Rishikesh

1000, Haridwar 2500, other places before Haridwar 1,300, Total 5,000 per day.

Gain to pilgrims from decommissioning of Tehri Dam: 5,000 pilgrims × 365 days × Rs 12,784 = Rs 2333 crore per year.

Further losses occur to family members who do not make these pilgrimages. Pilgrims take waters to their homes. The power of that water will also be reduced. Further losses occur to local people residing on the banks of Ganga and non-pilgrim travellers in the area.

A similar amount may be assessed for pilgrims downstream from Haridwar at Prayag, Kashi, Ganga Sagar, etc. The total loss to the pilgrims from Tehri may be assessed at double this amount at Rs 4,666 crores per year.

Willingness to Pay for Free Flowing Waters

The above benefit is to pilgrims who are coming to these holy places for spiritual benefits. These benefits occur to the pilgrims personally. Additional aesthetic and spiritual benefits are obtained by people by allowing the waters of the rivers to flow freely.

An accepted methodology in economics to measure such aesthetic benefits is to ask the people what is the amount they are willing to pay for a desired situation. For example, benefits from national parks are assessed in this way by Planning Division of the Planning Commission (Mathur 2003). In order to assess this benefit, visitor pilgrims were asked the following question.

Table A-2.10 : How much are you willing to pay to decommission Tehri Dam and restore free flowing waters of Ganga? (Rupees per year)

Sl.No.	*Location*	*Average*	*Median*
1.	Dev Prayag, n=17	2,083	101
2.	Rishikesh, n=18	986	1,000
3.	Haridwar, n=19	1,663	1,000
4.	Average, n=54	1,577	700

The loss to the pilgrims from deprivation of free flow to the Ganga is assessed, on the lower side, at Rs 700 per person (median value). This is altruistic loss in contradistinction to the loss from bath in Ganga, which is personal. This loss occurs to all people of this country even though they have not come for pilgrimage. However, this figure should not be extrapolated to the whole population because those who have come to take bath are likely to place a higher value on free flowing waters in comparison to those who have not come. We account for this effect in two ways. One, we take the lower median value of Rs 700 instead of the higher average value. Second, we reduce this to one-fifth to account for lower willingness to pay by those who have not come for pilgrimage. The loss of aesthetic, emotional and spiritual benefit to the people of the country is calculated as follows:

57 crore adults × Rs 140 per year = Rs 7,980 crore per year.

Loss of Benefit to Pilgrims from Conversion of River into Reservoir

NHPC has proposed to build a reservoir-based HEP at Kaudiyala. The tail end of this reservoir will extend up to Dev Prayag confluence. It is proposed by NHPC that level of water at Dev Prayag Confluence will be maintained at present average monthly levels (IFGRE: 11). The confluence will become the tail end of Kotlibhel 2 Reservoir but its level will be maintained as at present. The flow of water at the confluence will be affected. This writer has personally observed the flow of water at the Confluence in 1995 when Tehri Dam was not made. The water level varied from day-to-day and also intra-day from morning-to-evening. This 'free' variation will be removed and the confluence will have a fixed level as determined by dam authorities downstream. This is like placing a person in an iron jacket and preventing expansion and contraction of the chest due to breathing. In order to assess the impact of this change from 'free-flowing' to 'regulated reservoir', the pilgrims were asked:

Table A-2.11: Will the impact of the Confluence increase or decrease if the present level of water is maintained but this becomes a tail end of the reservoir?
(Number of Pilgrims Responding in Affirmative)

Sl. No.	*Type of Pilgrim*	*Small Increase*	*Big Increase*	*Small Decrease*	*Big Decrease*	*Net, Percent Reporting Decrease*
1.	Dev Prayag, n=35	23	11	20	46	(-) 32%

The above table tells that in pilgrims' assessment, there will be a decline in impact of the Confluence even if the level of water is maintained as at present.

Benefit from Free-flowing Water Compared to Electricity Generation

In order to assess the pilgrim's view of the relative benefits from generation of electricity and benefits from bath in free-flowing water, they were asked to indicate which was higher.

Table A-2.12 : There is benefit to the country from generation of electricity. However, it may have negative effect on the pilgrim. Which of these do you consider more?
(Percent Responding in Affirmative)

Sl. No.	*Type of Pilgrim*	*There will be more benefit from generation of electricity*	*There will be more benefit from bath by pilgrims in free-flowing waters*	*No difference*	*Percent Net Benefit from free-flowing water (Col 3-Col 2)*
1.	Dev Prayag, n=51	29	49	21	(+) 20%
2.	Rishikesh, n=88	50	25	25	(-) 25%
3.	Haridwar, n=88	65	18	17	(-) 47%
4.	Combined, n=227	48	31	21	(-) 17%

This table places the problem before us squarely. It tells us that downstream pilgrims assess greater benefits from generation of electricity. Pilgrims assess that gains from generation of electricity are greater *in comparison to losses from free flowing waters.* Thus, there exists an overall perception in the country that harnessing potential of rivers for generation of electricity is good.

This table does not cancel the costs mentioned above, however. It only tells us that, in the perception of pilgrims, the gains from generation of electricity are greater than the loss from free flow of waters assessed above.

These gains from generation of electricity can be quantified. Well-developed methods are available for the same. This writer has assessed the benefits from Kotlibhel 1B Project at Rs 154 crores in earlier part of this study.

This author feels that it is incorrect to rely on pilgrims' perception that gains from electricity will be more than loss from waters because economic theory provides clear-cut methods to assess the same. On the other hand, the loss to pilgrims can only be assessed by an interview-based methodology as has been adopted above. Hence this author feels justified in accepting the pilgrim's assessment of loss from deprivation of free-flowing waters; and not accepting the perception that gains from generation of electricity will be more than this figure.

The assessment of losses made by pilgrims relates to their own life and being hence stands on solid rock. Their assessment of benefits from generation of electricity appears to be overplayed and it is incumbent upon leaders to correct this misconception.

ANNEXURE-3
Survey of Pilgrims at Temple of Dhari Devi

Objectives of Study

The cascade of dams being made by Uttarakhand Government is going to affect the flow of water at Dhari Devi temple at Kalia Saur. The HEP Companies claim that damming the flow of water will not reduce the spiritual power of these religious places. This study is made to assess the correctness of this claim and assess the likely impact on these centres of pilgrimage.

Methodology

Dhari Devi temple is located on the banks of Alaknanda River at Kalia Saur about 15 km from Srinagar. The reservoir of Srinagar HEP being made by GVK Alaknanda Hydropower Ltd will extend many kilometres beyond it. The Dhari Devi temple will be submerged. It is proposed to re-erect the temple at the same spot on pillars. The Temple will then stand in midst of the reservoir and connected with a bridge to the road.

The objective of the study is to assess whether and to what extent this will affect the spiritual power of Dhari Devi. Total 60 respondents were surveyed.

A questionnaire was made to ask respondents about impact of dam on various aspects of worship. Naresh Chandra Puri went to Dhari Devi Temple in January 2008 and sought responses from the pilgrims coming to the temple.

No sampling was done. Assistance of any local person was not sought lest the mediator influence the results. The enumerator asked people he met spontaneously about the impacts.

The distribution of respondents by home place was as follows:

1. Nearby districts (38)—Pauri (15), Tehri (11), Chamoli (11), Rudra Prayag (1).
2. Rest of Uttarakhand (5)—Almora (1), Dehra Dun (4)
3. Other states (4)—Delhi (2), UP (2).
4. Local (13)—Pauri (4), Tehri (9)

Income

The income of respondents was as follows:

Table A-3.1 : Income of respondents

Sl. No.	*Level of Income*	*Visitors*	*Local*
1.	Number of Respondents replying	27	9
2.	Average	7,437	2,255
3.	Median	5,000	2,500
4.	Value (Average of 'Average' and Median)	6,218	2,378

Benefit from Dhari Devi

Pilgrims were asked what type of benefit they obtained from worship at Dhari Devi.

Table A-3.2 : What is the benefit you have obtained from the blessings of Dhari Devi? (Number of Respondents replying in affirmative)

Sl No.	*Type of Benefit*	*First Visit*	*Many Visits*	*Local*	*Total Numbers*	*Percentage*
1.	Number of Respondents	11	36	13	60	100
2.	Mental Peace	2	22	10	34	57
3.	Health	2	13	4	19	32
4.	Business	1	7	4	12	20
5.	Child	-	5	1	6	10
6.	Success in Examination	-	9	3	12	20
7.	Service	1	6	1	8	13
8.	Others	5	5	-	10	17

Fifty-seven percent pilgrims obtained mental peace while 32 percent obtained health benefits. Dhari Devi appears to have the power to relax the mind and body of the pilgrim. This gives him mental peace and good health.

Table A-3.3 : How much benefit have you obtained?

Sl No.	*Classification*	*Little*	*Average*	*High*
1.	Visitors	1	20	23
2.	Local	1	6	6

An attempt was made to arrive at the monetary value of the benefit. This is necessary in order to assess the economic loss to the pilgrims from relocation of the temple. Pilgrims were asked "How much value do you place on the benefit obtained?" In response to this question a large number of pilgrims replied in terms of 'invaluable', 'lacs' or 'priceless'. These have been valued at two month's income of the respondent. The underlying idea is that 'invaluable' benefit would at least be equal to two month's income of the pilgrim. This writer feels this is a deep undervaluation. 'Invaluable' would be better valued at a year's income. However, in order to avoid unnecessary arguments it is conservatively valued at two month's income.

Table A-3.4 : Benefits from visit to Dhari Devi

Sl No	*Pilgrims responding in money value income*	*Pilgrims responding in 'Priceless' =two month's*	*Final Value*
Number of Respondents	9	12	
Average	86,784	10,516	
Median	10,000		
Value(Average of 'Average' and Median)	48,392	10,516	29,454

Relocation of the Temple

The proposal to rebuild the temple on pillars will have two types of effects. At a physical and economic level, it will change the appearance of the place and may lead to more- or less tourism. As a spiritual level, it may lead to reduced- or enhanced effect. Separate questions were asked to elicit the pilgrim's response to these two impacts.

Table A-3.5 : If the temple is remade at this same spot on pillars, will the effect on tourism increase or decrease?

Type of Pilgrim	*Number of Respondents*	*Small increase*	*Large increase*	*Small decrease*	*Large decrease*	*Net increase percent*
Visitors	47	11	18	7	4	+38%
Local	13	5	4	3	1	+38%
Total	60	16	22	10	5	+38%

Conclusion: Pilgrims feel relocation of the temple will improve the tourist effect. There is no difference on this among visitors and local worshippers.

Second question was regarding the spiritual impact.

Table A-3.6 : If the temple is remade at this same spot on pillars, will the spiritual effect increase or decrease?

Type of Pilgrim	*Number of Respondents*	*Small increase*	*Large increase*	*Small decrease*	*Large decrease*	*Net increase percent*
Visitors	47	4	9	20	7	–30%
Local	13	1	1	4	6	–62%
Total	60	5	10	24	13	–37%

Conclusion: Pilgrims feel that relocation of the temple will reduce the spiritual effect. This negative effect is more strongly felt by local people.

Pilgrims were next asked to estimate the level of decline in spiritual effect. They were asked to give a percentage value to the change that will occur on spiritual effect upon rebuilding the temple on pillars.

Table A-3.7 : What is the percent change in spiritual effect?

Item	*Increase*	*Decrease*
Number of Respondents	14	29
Median	62	30
Average	60	35
Value (Average of median and 'average')	61	33

Fourteen pilgrims said that spiritual effect of rebuilding the temple on pillars would be positive, while 29 said it would be negative. The weighted average is calculated as follows:

(+ (Value increase – 14) – (Value decrease – 29))/43

(+ (61 – 14) – (33 – 29))/43 = –2.4%

The spiritual loss to pilgrims at Dhari Devi from rebuilding the temple on pillars is calculated as follows:

Present benefit per pilgrim: Rs 29,454 (Table above)

Decrease in benefit per pilgrim: –2.4% or Rs 707.

Number of Pilgrims: Winters 100 per day, Summers 300 per day, Average 200 per day.

Loss to pilgrims from building on pillars: 200 × 365 × 707 = Rs 5.2 crore per year.

The author feels this loss is understated because the average increase is reported at 61% while average decline is reported at 33%. Be that as it may, we take the pilgrim's statement as sacrosanct and proceed on these figures. This, however, needs deeper study.

Loss Due to Extraction of Electricity

Another way of assessing impact of dams on pilgrims was to ask them:

Table A-3.8 : What will be the change in spiritual power of water after extraction of electricity? (Number of Pilgrims Responding in Affirmative)

Sl. No.	*Type of Pilgrim*	*Number of Resp-ondents*	*Small Incre-ase*	*Big Incre-ase*	*Small Decre-ase*	*Big Ddecre-ase*	*Per-cent Respo-nding Decre-ase*
1.	Visitors	39	10	8	17	4	54%
2.	Local	13	2	4	2	5	54%
3.	Total	52	12	12	19	9	54%

Pilgrims were asked to give percentage to the loss. The results are tabulated below.

Table A-3.9 : Extent of loss due to rebuilding the temple on pillars

Item	*Increase*	*Decrease*
Number of Respondents	21	25
Median	30%	40%
Average	35.7%	46.7%
Value (Average of median and 'average')	32.9%	43.4%

21 pilgrims said that effect of free-flowing waters would be positive, while 25 said it would be negative. The weighted average is calculated as follows:

(+ (Value increase × 21) – (Value decrease – 25))/46

(+ (32.9 × 21) – (43.4 × 25))/46 = –8.6%

The spiritual loss to pilgrims at Dhari Devi from rebuilding the temple on pillars is calculated as follows:

Present benefit per pilgrim: Rs 29,454 (Table A-3.4 above)

Decrease in benefit per pilgrim: –8.6% or Rs 2,533.

Number of Pilgrims: Winters 100 per day, Summers 300 per day, Average 200 per day.

Loss to pilgrims from building on pillars: 200 × 365 × 2533 = Rs 18.5 crore per year.

This is higher than the earlier calculation of Rs 5.2 crores per year from rebuilding of the Dhari Devi temple on pillars.

Benefit from Free-flowing Water Compared to Electricity Generation

In order to assess the pilgrim's view of the relative benefits from generation of electricity and benefits from bath in free-flowing water, they were asked to indicate which of these was more.

Table A-3.10 : There is benefit to the country from generation of electricity. However, it may have negative effect on the pilgrim. Which of these do you consider more? (Numbers Responding in Affirmative)

Sl. No.	*Type of Pilgrim*	*Number of Respondents*	*There will be more benefit from generation of electricity*	*There will be more benefit from bath by pilgrims in free-flowing waters*	*No. difference*	*Percent Net Benefit from rebuilding of temple on pillars (Col 2-Col 3, percentage to Col 1)*
	Column No	1	2	3	4	5
1.	Visitors	46	20	14	12	13%
2.	Local	13	8	3	2	38%
3.	Total	59	28	17	14	18.6%

The pilgrims believe that benefits from generation of electricity will be more. The author feels this is not supported by facts. As shown in this book, the economic benefits from generation of power are few. However, this is the people's perception and is accepted with respect.

Willingness to Pay for Free-flowing Water

Pilgrims were asked how much they were willing to pay to maintain free-flowing waters at Dev Prayag.

Table A-3.11 : How much are you willing to pay to decommission Tehri Dam and restore free flowing waters of Bhagirathi at Dev Prayag? (Rupees per year)

Sl. No.	*Item*	*Visitors*	*Local*
1.	Number of Respondents	26	6
2.	Average	Rs 529	Rs 255
3.	Median	Rs 100	Rs 225
4.	Value (Average of 'Average' and median)	Rs 315	Rs 240

We can conclude that pilgrims are willing to pay about Rs 250 per person for maintaining free flow of rivers.

ANNEXURE-4
Survey of Temples of Tehri

Saccheshwar Temple, Tehri

The Saccheshwar Temple was originally located at the confluence of Bhagirathi and Bhilangana Rivers at Tehri. The original temple was small and dark with smoke. Few people could sit inside. According to the priest, Shri Giri, people used to come to take a bath at the confluence and visit the temple also. During summers, people would come to sit and rest there on festivals such as Janmashthami, Navratri, Shivratri and Basant Panchami. The Hanuman Temple was in the same compound hence people came on Tuesdays especially. Daily offerings of flour and pulses were large and sufficient for some to the distributed to the poor. Daily offering in cash was Rs 50 to 100 on an ordinary day and more on special occasions. The temple also got a grant called 'Bandhan' from the State Government for expenses of lamp etc. Many generations of the Priest made their livelihood from that temple.

The new temple is made at Boradi—near bus stand at mid-town. It was opened about 1½ years ago. The new temple is very large—height is about 40 feet. The hall is about 40x30 feet. The temple stands on a large piece of land. The location is about 12 km from the Tehri Reservoir. The link between bath and worship has been totally broken. People no longer come to rest at the temple as they would at the old temple. "People's mentality has changed now," the priest said, "When Navratri comes and goes, nobody knows. Nowadays only, the Shivratri Festival is celebrated. Hanuman temple is made separately hence, there are no special visitors on that day."

The income per day is Rs 4 to 5 only. Enumerator Naresh Chandra Puri reached the temple at 11 am one sunny morning in January 2008. At that time only the priest was present in the temple. Only one woman worshipper came at about 12 noon. Puri stayed there till 5 pm. No other soul came to the temple. The Bandhan has been stopped since last 2-3 years or so. Priest Giri said it would be better if THDC had given a corpus of Rs 5 lacs instead of such a huge temple. His family would have lived off the interest from that deposit. He does not even have the money to buy brooms to sweep the huge compound of the temple.

Laxmi Narayan Temple, Tehri

The old temple was located in Tehri.

This temple has also been made anew. It is about 25 x 25 feet in size, bit smaller than Saccheshwar. This located above the Boradi Stadium.

Naresh Chandra Puri reached the temple at about 9 am. The temple was locked. Wife of the priest told Puri that Panditji has just completed the Pooja and left. “Few people come these days,” she said.

Then Enumerator Puri then went to the home of Secretary of the Temple, Shri Chandan Singh Rana. The Secretary told that all temples—present and new—are managed by a Committee constituted by the State Government and presided presently by Manujendra Shah, scion of the Royal Family of Tehri. Now donation from the Temple Committee has ceased. There is not much income from the temple now. His family manages the temple. He gets pension of about Rs 2700 from which he manages his livelihood.

Enumerator Puri then surveyed eight persons living near the temple.

Table A-4.1. What benefit you have obtained by the grace of the Lord from this temple:

Sl. No.	*Type of Benefit*	*Number Reporting Favourably*
1.	Health	2/8
2.	Service	0/8
3.	Business	1/8
4.	Child	0/8
5.	Examination	0/8
6.	Mental Peace	2/8
7.	Others	0/8

Number of persons who said 'no benefit' was 4/8. (This is not exactly comparable to surveys at Dev Prayag etc. because those surveys were made of pilgrims while this survey is made of people living nearby). However, they said that power of the temple had reduced consequent to relocation.

Table A-4.2. Change in Laxmi Narayan Temple at Tehri

Sl. No.	*Question*	*Small Increase*	*Big Increase*	*Small Reduction*	*Big Reduction*
1.	Number of tourists in the new temple	-	-	1/8	7/8
2.	The power of the new temple	1/6	-	-	5/6

Question: What is the difference in benefit from taking bath in the Reservoir in comparison to taking bath in flowing waters?

Answer: Was better in flowing waters (8/8).

Question: How much are you willing to pay if Tehri Dam is removed and free flow of the River is restored?

Answer: This is impossible (3/8). No comment (5/8). People think this is a nonsensical question.

Temples in Villages on Reservoir Rim

Enumerator Naresh Chandra Puri visited four villages on the rim of the Tehri Reservoir on the Bhilangana side. There was on temple at Dewal. This temple was serving 32 villages. This has been remade at Dewal, above the Reservoir.

Table A-4.3. Impact of relocation on Temples of Villages near Tehri

Sl. No.	*Question*	*Asena*	*Khand*	*Nandgaon*	*Dewal*
1.	Name and Status of respondent	Uday Singh, Pradhan	Rajendra Singh, Member, Kshetra Panchayat	Khushi Ram, Husband of Pradhan	Satya Giri, Punari of Submerged temple of 32 villages
2.	Condition of the forest in last five years has:	No change	Worse	No Change	Worse
3.	Change in people's health	No change	Worse	No change	No change
4.	How much grant obtained for village temple	None	None	None	None

The survey indicates a sharp decline in number of visitors to the temples consequent to relocation.

Table A-4.4. Number of worshippers coming every day at old and new temple

Sl. No.	*Question*	*Uday Singh, Asend*	*Satya Giri, Dewal*
1.	Number of worshippers every day in old temple	100	7
2.	Number of worshippers in new temple	30	3
3.	Daily offering old temple	Rs 100	Rs 20
4.	Daily offering new temple	Rs 30	Rs 5

Relief and Rehabilitation

Table A-4.5. Use of money received as compensation, n=11

Sl. No.	*Use of money*	*Numbers*
1.	House	8
2.	Marriage	3
3.	Motor cycle	-
4.	TV	-
5.	Business	-
6.	Land	2
7.	Others	-

Table A-4.6. Impact of acquisition of land on standard of living, n=11

Improved	*Reduced*	*No Change*
–	6	5

Table A-4.7. Impact on number of livestock, n=11

Sl. No.	*Livestock*	*Increased*	*Reduced*	*No Change*
1.	Buffalo	-	7	3
2.	Cow	-	3	1
3.	Bullock	-	7	2
4.	Goat	-	3	2

Table A-4.8. Impact on health, n=11

Increased	*Reduced*	*No Change*
-	-	6

Table A-4.9. Are you happy with land acquisition? n=11

Yes	*No*	*No Difference*
-	5	6

The survey indicates that people are not happy with compensation though they may not be affected materially.

Notes

1. The River is given the name Ganga after the Confluence of Bhagirathi and Alaknanda at Dev Prayag.
2. The role of agriculture in national income, electricity consumption and employment is all receding hence it has not been given here in interests of simplicity of presentation.
3. The figures given are for share of energy consumption. This does not mean that the total consumption by agriculture and manufacturing will be less. Lower share comes with increased consumption by these sectors.
4. By Meeta Mehra, as per footer in the downloaded article.
5. Mr R C Nakul, CE, CEA has stated in his email communication regarding an earlier version of this study: "Mathematical manipulations of various growth rates in electricity generation and GDP..have not been used as such in demand forecast." This is not disputed. However, it is incumbent upon CEA to explain why the trend forecasts made on basis of GDP growth show a huge variation with the PEUM forecasts.
6.

Sl No	*Sector*	*Share of Electricity Consumption, 2005-6 percent*	*Share of Electricity Consumption, 2011-12 percent*	*Change in Share of Electricity Consumption*	*Share in GDP 1999-00*	*Share in GDP 2005-06*	*Change in Share in GDP in 2006-12 (assume same as in 2000-06)*
	Basis	*CEA estimates, 17th Power Survey*	*Forecast by CEA, 17th Power Survey*	*Col 2 – Col 1*	*Economic Survey 2006-07*	*Economic Survey 2006-07*	*Col 5 – Col 4*
	Column No	*1*	*2*	*3*	*4*	*5*	*6*
1.	Domestic	25.26	29.16	+3.9			
2.	Services (Commercial)	8.25	8.69	+0.4	49.7	54.2	+4.5
3.	Agriculture (Irrigation)	22.87	20.23	-2.6	27.3	21.7	-5.6
4.	Manufacturing (Industry)	35.53	34.50	-1.0	23.0	24.1	+1.1
5.	Others	8.09	7.43	-0.7			
6.	Total	100.0	100.0	0.0	100.0	100.0	0.0

7. The method adopted hax has a margin of error because the mid-year elasticity may not follow a linear trend. The CEA does not give annual figures hence the author is forced to make this best approximation.
8. Forecast of Sectoral rates of growth: The forecast of demand for 2003-04 at 16th Survey is given in Column 1 and actual as per 17th Survey at Column 2. We may assume that CEA has similarly wrongly estimated sectoral demands in 17th Survey. This past tendency of CEA can be extrapolated to the projections made for 2011-12 in 17th Survey. Accordingly, the

Sl.No.	Sector	Share of Electricity Consumption 2003-04 Forecast (16th Survey)	Share of Electricity Consumption 2003-04 Actual (17th Survey)	Under- and over-estimation of demand by CEA	Share of Electricity Consumption 2011-12 per cent (Forcast by CEA)	Share of Actual Electricity Consumption, 2011-12 (CEA Forecast Adjusted for unver- and over-estimation	Actual Consumption 2003-04, CEA	True Forecast of Electricity Consumption 2011-12. (Total 524299 mkwtt for 2003-04 increased @ 4.8% for 2004-07 and @4% for 2007-12. Then distributed as per col. 5	Annual Rate of Growth, Percent
	Source	CEA 16th Survey Page 251	CEA 17th Survey Page 183	Col 2- Col 1	CEA 17th Survey Page 1834	Col 4+ Col 3	CEA 17th Survey Page 183	Ratio as per Col 5	Col 7/Col 6
1.	Domestic	22.62	24.79	2.17	29.16	31.33	129974	230033	7.4
2.	Productive (Commercial+ Irrigation + Industry	71.42	67.38	–4.04	63.42	59.38	353273	435983	2.7
3.	Others	5.96	7.83	1.87	7.43	9.3	41053	68283	6.6
4.	Total	100	100	0	100.01	100.01	524299	734298	4.3

'true' sectoral shares of electricity consumption likely to obtain in 2011-12 are shown in Cols 5. The rate of growth of consumption for sectors is calculated in Col 8.

9. This section draws heavily from suggestions made by Shri Shankar Sharma.
10. CEA has informed the Author that "no list of studies of demand side management" is available with it (RTI Reply dated 3rd March, 2008).

Sl No	*Source / Scenario*	*Coal Dominant Case*	*Forced Hydro*	*Forced Nuclear + Hydro + Gas*	*Forced Nuclear + Hydro + Gas + DSM*	*Savings from DSM*	*Suggested Nuclear + Gas + DSM*	*Percent Change Col 6 to Col 4*
	Column No	*1*	2	3	4	5	6	7
1.	Crude oil	486	485	486	486	-	486	-
2.	Natural gas	104	105	197	174	23	174	-
3.	Coal	1022	953	835	715	120	737	(+) 3.1%
4.	Hydro	13	35	35	35	-	13	(-) 62.9%
5.	Nuclear	76	76	98	98	-	98	-
6.	Renewables	2	2	2	2	-	2	-
7.	Non-Commercial	185	185	185	185	-	185	-
8.	Total	1887	1840	1837	1695	142	1695	-

11. Energy Sources: After Table 3.7 of Integrated Energy Policy Report, planning commission.
12. This is levelised cost of production. Hydropower projects are capital intensive. The burden of interest and depreciation is large in initial years and low in later years. This is equalized or 'levelised' like Equal Monthly Installments on consumer loans. This may be taken as the average cost of production during the life of the project.
13. Peak- and base load shares of power generation from Kotlibhel 1B. The generation of peak- and non-peak power from the project is estimated as follows:

    In monsoons, for 4 months, 4 turbines of 80 MW will be operated continuously. They will produce 6 hours of peak power and 18 hours of non-peak power every day. In remaining eight months, two turbines will be operated for 6 hours every day during peak hours only. The total generation of peak- and non-peak power is estimated as follows:

Item	*Turbine hours*	*Ratio of power*	*Production of power*	*Free power to state, 12%*	*Power available for sale by NHPC*	*Implied Price*
Peak Power (Author's estimate)	(1) Monsoons: 4 months (120 days) x 4 turbines x 6 hours = 2880; (2) Winters and summers: 8 months (240 days) x 2 turbines x 6 hours = 2880; Total 5760 turbine hours	40%	57.1 crore units	6.1 crore units	44.6 crore units	4.00 per unit

Non-peak power (Author's estimate)	Monsoons: 4 months (120 days) x 4 turbines x 18 hours = 8640 turbine hours.	60%	76.1 crore units	9.1 crore units	67.0 unit	2.00 per unit
Total (according to DPR-ES)	14,400 turbine hours	100%	126.8 crore units	15.2 crore units	111.6 crore units	2.80 per unit

14. This author requested Dr Pradeep Kumar to send full copy of the report, in vain. This section is based on analysis of the letter under reference.
15. Some HEPs provide for compensatory afforestation while others provide for payment under CAMPA. We need not go into this issue here. Let us assume that the direct costs calculated under NPV by Kanchan Chopra Committee are approximately the same as incurred under compensatory afforestation as proposed in Kotlibhel 1B. Our purpose is to assess the true costs of hydropower. We, therefore, focus on the costs excluded in NPV calculations and assume them to be equal to those not accounted under compensatory afforestation.
16. This study gives figures in two ways—change in number of patients and change in percent of population affected. Only the latter have been given below. This is done because comparison based on number of patients depends upon the baseline. This baseline data was not available to the author hence that information could not be converted into percentages and therefore had to be ignored.
17. Steven Russell of School of Development Studies, University of East Anglia, Norwich, United Kingdom has estimated on the basis of three studies that the annual direct costs were 2.3 percent and indirect costs were 4.3 percent of household incomes. The total cost is estimated at 6.6 percent of the household income (Russell 2004). Additional costs are incurred by family members and also there is loss of income due to morbidity.
18. A report presented at UNHYDRO conference in Beijing in 2004 says: "The River downstream of Owen Falls had been a breeding area for the black flies which transmit river blindness. Entomologists proposed treatment of the river with DDT during the construction of the dam, to at least protect the construction workforce. Unexpectedly, after several years of repeat treatments, the black fly disappeared permanently. DDT treatment stopped about 1970, but apparently, the change in river regime due to the dam had made the rapids unsuitable for the species of black fly, Simulium damnosum, which transmits the blinding parasite. Other species of black fly with lower velocity requirements did reinfest the river however, but they tend to bite animals, not people. There may be other explanations for the disappearance of River Blindness, but certainly, this seems to be a rare example of a positive health impact from a hydropower project" (Jobin 2004).
19. Points 4 and 5 are not drawn from Abbasi (undated)

REFERENCES

Abbasi (undated), S A, Environmental impact of water resources projects: a general introduction, http://nih.ernet.in/incoh-web/pdffilesofCompletedproi/s.a.abbasi-EIAy*Volume_I_PDF_Version/Chapterl.pdf.

ABCG (undated), Africa Biodiversity Collaborative Group, Conferences Discussing HIV/AIDS and Biodiversity Conservation Linkages, http://www.frameweb.org/ev.php?ID=9018_201&ID2=DO)_TOPIC

Audinet (2002), Pierre, Desk Officer for South Asia and Korea, Office of Non-Member Countries, International Energy Agency, Electricity Prices in India, Energy Prices and Taxes, 2nd Quarter 2002.

Bahuguna (2007), Harsh and D P Dangwal, "A Preliminary Report of the Stability of Slopes Above the Rim of Tehri Reservoir," Geological Survey of India.

Bettwy (2007), Mike, NASA monitors China's Three Gorges Dam, Goddard Space Flight Center, June 13, 2007, http://news.mongabay.com/2007/0613-nasa.html.

Bhargava (1977), Devendra Swarup, *Water Quality in Three Typical Rivers in U.P.—Ganga, Yamuna and Kali,* PhD Thesis, IIT, Kanpur.

Blonyx (undated), Otter Site, http://www.amblonyx.com/index.asp?id=QuickGuide

Boyle (2003), Tim, Lessons for the Future, Conserving Forest Biodiversity, Threats, Solutions and Experiences United Nations Development Programme, Global Environment Facility, November 2003.

Brier (2003), Tim, Lessons For The Future, Conserving Forest Biodiversity, Threats, Solutions and experiences United Nations Development Programme, Global Environment Facility, November 2003.

Brier (2003), Andrew, Reservoir Evaporation Losses, NCEA, Toowoomba, http://www.irrigation.org.au/NWIAAMeeting10Dec03AndrewBrier.doc.

Brown (Undated), Malaria in India,
http://www.brown.edu/Research/EnvStudies- Theses/full9900/creid/malaria_in_india.htm

Business Standard (2007), Report on Carbon Credits, Misplaced by author hence details not available.

Caruso (2008), Guy, Administrator, Energy Information Administration, U.S. Department of Energy, Statement Before The Committee on Energy and Natural Resources, United States Senate, March 4, 2008.

CEA (2000), Central Electricity Authority, *Sixteenth Electric Power Survey of India,* New Delhi, September 2000.

CEA (2007), Central Electricity Authority, *Report on Seventeenth Electric Power Survey of India,* New Delhi, March 2007.

Chaurasia (1991), R., and others, Climatic change and wheat yield in semi ARID region of Punjab-India Punjab Remote Sensing Centre, Ludhiana, ACRS 1991, GISdevelopment.net.

Chopra (2006), Report of the Expert Committee on Net Present Value (Professor Kanchan Chopra Committee), Submitted to the Honourable Supreme Court of India, May, 2006.

CIA (undated), https://www.cia.gov/library/publications/the-world-factbook/print/in.html

Costanza (1997), R. and others, 'The values of the world's ecosystem services and natural capital,' *Nature,* 253-260,1997.

CPCB (2001), Bio-Monitoring of Surface Water Bodies in Certain Problem Areas in The Country-Case Studies, Parivesh, April 2001, http://www.cpcb.nic.in/oldwebsite/app2001bio.htm.

CPCB (2005), Water Quality of Rivers in Ganga Basin-2005, Central Pollution Control Board,
http://www.cpcb.nic.in/oldwebsite/wq-2005/GANGA.htm

CPCB (undated), Assessment and Development Study of River Basin, Central Pollution Control Board, Parivesh, Undated, http://www.cpcb.nic.in/oldwebsite/mar95iv.htm

CPIM (2007), Nuclear Energy and the Electricity Sector: False Promises, http://www.cpim.org/nuclear/folders/08292007_energy_ shortfall.pdf

DAE (undated), Department of Atomic Energy, Introduction, http://www.dae.gov.in/publ/doc10/pg10.htm

Defra (Undated), Floods and Reservoir Safety Integration, Appendix G: Techniques For Estimating Probability of Failure of Dams, Defra Research Contract. URL Not available.

Doya (2008), David Malingha, Sudan seeks to revive Nile power project at Nimule, *The East African,* March, 17 2008.

Dua (2004), Gaurav, National Thermal Power Corporation, 23 Sept, 2004, http://moneypore.com/IpoNtpc23092004.htm

Eberhard (2000), Anton, Electricity Supply and Demand Side Management Options, WCD Thematic Review, Options Issues Series IV. 1, Final Version: November 2000, Prepared for the World Commission on Dams, University of Cape Town, South Africa, http://www.dams.org

Electricity Forum (2007), U.S. Electricity Glut Dims Peaker Plants' Future, New York, URL Not Available

FAO (2005). Corporate Document Repository, FRA 2005-Pilot study for country reporting; India, http://www.fao.org/docrep/007/ae354e/AE354E30.htm

FAO (2007), Pakistan, FAO's Information System on Water and Agriculture, http://www.fao.org/nr/water/aquastat/countries/pakistan/index.stm.

Forster (2003), Master plan for development of trekking routes in Uttaranchal, Prepared for the Department of Tourism, Government of Uttaranchal, By Pannell Keir Forster Consultants Pvt. Ltd., New Delhi, October 2003.

Gaur (1993), Vinok K, Editor, *Earthquake Hazard and Large Dams in the Himalaya,* INTACH, New Delhi, 1993.

Genesis (1992), Global Biodiversity Strategy, A Policy-maker's Guide 1992, Genesis of Eden Diversity Encyclopedia, http://www.dhushara.com/book/globio/globb/gbs.htm

Ghosh (undated), Sajal, Sustainable Energy Policies for Clean Air In India, Background Paper Prepared for The Atlantic Council of USA, Confederation of Indian Industry, New Delhi, http://www.weea.org/Occasional%20Papers/Documents/india.pdf

Ghosh (2007), Sajal, Electricity consumption and economic growth in India, Indira Gandhi Institute of Development Research, Mumbai, http://cat.inist.fr/?aModele=afficheN&cpsidt=l 3417474

GOO (2007), Government of Orissa, Revenue & Disaster Management Department, No. GE(GL) S-30/07 34969/R&DM., 31.08.2007, http://www.orissa.gov.in/revenue/circular/settlement_of_govt-land/34969Dt.31.08.07.htm

Goodbred (2005), Steven, Stony Brook University and Yoshiki Saito, Holocene evolution of deltas, Coastal and Urban Geology Research Group, Asian Delta Project, Geological Survey of Japan/AIST, http://unit.aist.go. jp/igg/rg/cug-rg/ADP/ADP_E/a_about_en.html

Goodbred (2005), Girish and P. Seralathan, Rapid erosion of the coast of Sagar island, West Bengal - India, Department of Marine Geology and Geophysics, Cochin University of Science and Technology, Cochin. Abstract.

Gopinath (2005), Girish and P. Seralathan, Rapid erosion of the coast of Sagar island, West Bengal - India, Department of Marine Geology and Geophysics, Cochin University of Science and Technology, Cochin. Abstract.

Gramling (2006), Carolyn, China's massive dam alters weather, Geotimes, http://www.geotimes.org/sept06/NN_Dam.html

Gupta (1986), Harsh and Kusala Rajendran, "Large Artificial Water Reservoirs in the vicinity of the Himalayan foothills and Reservoir-Induced Seismicity," *Bulletin of the Seismological Society of America,* Vol. 76, No 1, February 1986.

Gupta (2005), Harsh, and others, An earthquake of M5 may occur at Koyna, National Geophysical Research Institute, Hyderabad 500 007, India, http://www.ias.ac.in/currsci/sepl02005/747.pdt

Hartje (1999), Prof. Dr. Volkmar, and Dr. Klaus Horstmann, Dams and development co-operation, Experiences and perspectives in German bilateral development co-operation with selected topics, Discussion Paper for the World Commission on Dams, December 1999, http://www.landschatlsoekonomie.tu-berlin.de/fileadmin/a0731/uploads/pub likationen/edocuments/1999_KfW_WCD.pdf.

Hebert (2007), Paul, Biodiversity Institute of Ontario; Jim Kundell, "River" In *Encyclopedia of Earth,* Eds. Cutler J. Cleveland (Washington, D.C.: Environmental Information Coalition, National Council for Science and the Environment), Published in the Encyclopedia of Earth June 5, 2007, Retrieved January 27,2008, http://www.eoearth.org/article/River.

HNBU (2006a), HNB Garhwal University, *Comprehensive Impact Assessment and Environment Management Plan for the Kotlibhel Hydroelectric Project (Stage 1A),* Srinagar.

HNBU (2006b), *Comprehensive Impact Assessment for the Kotlibhel Hydroelectric Project (Stage IB),* Srinagar.

HNBU (2006c), *Environment Management Plan for the Kotlibhel Hydroelectric Project (Stage IB),*

ICFRE (undated), Indian Council of Forestry Research and Education, *EIA and EMP of Kotlibhel 2,* Dehradun (Original title page is missing and date not given in the photocopy available with the author).

IRN (2006), International Rivers Network, Fizzy Science: Loosening the Hydro Industry's Grip on Reservoir Greenhouse Gas Emissions Research, November 1, 2006, http://www.irn.org/programs/greenhouse/index.php?id=061101 fizzy_intro.html

IRN (2007), International Rivers Network, *Before the Deluge.*

Isavasya, Upanishad, Gita Press, Samvat 2059.

Jain (2001), L C, *Dam Vs Drinking Water: Exploring the Narmada Judgment,* Parisar, Pune, 2001

Jain (undated), Sharad K, Cumulative Impact of Dams and Diversions, National Institute of Hydrology, Roorkee, India, http://www.gwsp.org/downloads/dayl_dams/05_JAIN.pdf

JICO (2005), Japan International Cooperation Agency, http://www.jica.go.jp/english/evaluatior/program/thematic/pdf/2005_09_03.pdf

Jishnu (2008), Latha, "Business cascades over ecology in Sikkim," *Business Standard,* January 7, 2008.

JNNURM (2006), City Development Plan, Guwahati, July 2006, http://innurm.nic.in/toolkit/CDP_Guwahati.pdf.

Jobin (2004), William, Director, Blue Nile Associates, Prediction of Health Hazards in Tropical Reservoirs and Evaluation of Low-Cost Methods For Disease Prevention, UNHYDRO 2004 Beijing.

Joshi (2006a), V K, Ganga Plains: World's Largest Flood Plains, http:/Avww.boloji.com/environment/77.htm

Joshi (2006b), V K, Uttaranchal Developing on Shaky Ground, http.7/www.boloii.com/environment/62.htm

Keiser (2004), Jennifer and others, "Effects of Large Dams on the Burden of Malaria on a Global and Regional Scale," Swiss Tropical Institute, Basel, Switzerland.

Kerala (2006), *Public Expenditure Review Committee,* First Report, May 2006, http://www.kerala.gov.in/dept_finance/perc_lrep.pdf

Kreger (2007), Chris, Wheat: Temperature, Maintained by ETE Team, Last updated October 29, 2007.

Kumar (2007), Pradeep, "Water Quality Studies for Tehri Project," Letter No IITR/CED/Env-PK/THDC Project/757 dated July 04,2007 addressed to THDC.

Latin Focus (2008), Argentina-Economic Briefing, Economic Recovery Proceeding Favourably but Energy *'Concerns Mount, March* 11,2008.

Letschert (2007), Virginie E., Michael A. McNeil, Coping with Residential Electricity Demand in India's Future - How Much Can Efficiency Achieve? Ernest Orlando Lawrence Berkeley National Laboratory, Environmental Energy Technologies Division, July 2007, http://eetd.lbl.gov/ea/ies/iespubs/63199.pdt

Maria (2003), A, The Costs of Water Pollution in India, CERNA, Ecole Nationale Superieure des Mines de Paris, http://www.cerna.ensmp.fr/cerna_globalisation/Documents/maria-delhi.pdf

Mathur (2003), Archana S And Arvinder S Sachdeva, Towards An Economic Approach to Sustainable Forest Development, Perspective Planning Division, Planning Commission, Government of India, November 2003, Working Paper Series, Paper No. 2/2003-PC

Mathur (undated), Vinod B., and Asha Rajvanshi, Integrating Biodiversity into Environmental Impact Assessment, A National Case Study from India, Prepared under Biodiversity Planning Support Programme of UNDP,UNEP & GEF.

McCully (1998), Patrick, *Silenced Rivers: The Ecology and Politics of Large Dams,* Orient Longman, Hyderabad, 1998.

Meisen (2006), Peter, President, Global Energy Network Institute, Overview of Renewable Energy Potential of India, October 2006, http:/www.geni.org/globalenergv/library/energytrends/curren-tusage/renewable/Renewable-Energv-Potential-for-India.pdf.

MOF (2003), *Economic Survey 2002-2003,* Review of Developments, Ministry of Finance, Government of India.

MOF (2006), *Economic Survey 2005-06,* Ministry of Finance, New Delhi, 2006.

Mukherjee (2007), Dipankar, Heady Times Or Crazy Times? *People's Democracy,* Vol. XXXI No. 23 June 10,2007, http://www.cpim.org/pd/2007/0610/06102007_dipankar.htm

NBA (2005), National Biodiversity Authority, Chennai, *Annual Report 2004-2005,* www.nbaindia.org

NBSAP (undated), Introduction To NBSAP And To The National Plan, http://www.sdnp.nic.in/nbsap/nbsapplan/chapterl.html

NEAA (2007), National Environment Appellate Authority, Order in Appeal No 5/2006, April 16.

NEERI (2004), Self Purification Capacity of River Bhagirathi: Impact of Tehri Dam, *Annual Report 2003-04.*

Nema (undated), A.K., Nuclear Generation Cost in India, NPCIL study on the 'Long Term Cost Effectiveness of Nuclear Energy' in India, http://www.npcil.nic.in/nupower_voll3_l/nugenn.htm

Newswire (2006), Indian Power Sector-Existing Scenario Vs Future, *Newswire Today,* New Delhi, India, 08/25/2006, http://www.newswiretoday.com/news/7962/

NHPC (2005), National Hydroelectric Power Corporation, *Kotlibhe Hydroelectric Project Stage-IB (Uttaranchal), Detailed Project Report—Executive Summary,* Faridabad.

NHPC (2007), Audited Financial Results As Per Listing Agreement For Bonds Between National Hydroelectric Power Corporation Limited And The National Stock Exchange Of India Limited For The Half Year And Year Ended 31st March, 2007, http://www.nhpcindia.com/English/Scripts/Financial.aspx?Vid=24

Nielsen (2004), D,C., Halvorson, A.D., Vigil, M.F., Byme, P.P. 2004. Predicting winter wheat yield from temperature and rainfall. Agronomy Abstracts. Presented at the 2004 ASA-CSSA-SSSA International Annual Meeting. Oct. 31-Nov. 4,2004. Seattle, WA.

NPC (1995), National Productivity Council, *Physio-chemical & Bacteriological Analysis of Water Samples at Hydroelectric Power Stations of NHPC,* New Delhi.

NTPC (2004), Vidyut Vyapar Nigam Limited, Proforma for submission of information for the Quarter (Jan 2004 to March 2004), Form -HI, http://nwn.co.in/form III III.html

Panda (2004), Mahendra, and A. Mohapatra, Malaria Control - An Over View in India, *J. Hum. Ecol.,* 15(2), 2004.

Paul (1987), A.K., and Bandyopadhyay, M.K.. Morphology of Sagar Island, a part of Ganga delta, *J. Geol. Soc. India.* 29(1); 1987;412-423, http:/www.mangroveindia.org/resOurl.php?query= LAUNAEA&p=OFL

Pearce (2001), David W., The Economic Value of Forest Ecosystems, University College of London, *Ecosystem Health,* Vol 7, No 4, December 2001.

Pearsall (2002), Paul, Gary E. Schwartz and Linda G. Russek, Organ Transplants and Cellular Memories. *Nexus Magazine,* Volume 12, Number 3 (April-May 2005), www.nexusmagazine.com.

Planning Commission (2006), *Integrated Energy Policy,* New Delhi, August 2006.

Planning Commission (2007), Report of The Steering Committee on the Environment and Forests Sector for The Eleventh Five Year Plan (2007-2012), Government of India, Planning Commission, New Delhi, March, 2007.

Prajadelhi (undated), Praja's Objections to Delhi Transco's ARR Petition for FY 2005-06, http://praiadelhi.org/docs/Praia's%20Obiections%20to%20DTL% 20ARR%202005-06.pdf

Prakash (1997), Anil, Farakka Barrage: Cause for Concern, Ganga Mukti Andolan, http://www.ben-center.org/rivers/RiverFarakkaConcem.htm

Prasad (1977), Kashi, *Survival of Coliform Organisms in River Ganga water near Kanpur and Applicability of Water Quality Indices,* MTech Thesis, IIT, Kanpur, 1977.

Preece (2002), Russell M., and Hugh A. Jones, The effect of Keepit Dam on the temperature regime of the Namoi River, Australia, NSW Department of Land and Water Conservation, PO *Box* 3720, Parramatta, NSW 2124, Australia, *River Research and Applications,* Volume 18, Issue 4, Published Online: 15 Jul 2002, http.//www3.interscience.wilev.com/cgi-bin/abstract/96516362/ABSTRACT?CRETRY=1&SRETRY=0

Raghavendra (2002), Dr K, Malaria Research Centre, New Delhi, Malaria in India, *ICMR Bulletin,* October 2002.

Ramachandra (undated), T. V., and R. Rajinikanth, Economic Valuation of Wetlands, Energy & Wetlands Research Group, Center for Ecological Sciences, Indian Institute of Science, Bangalore, http://ces.iisc.ernet.in/energy

Ramana (undated), M. V., Antonette D'Sa, Amulya K. N. Reddy, Economics of Nuclear Power from Heavy Water Reactors, http://iei-asia.org/IEI-CISED-IndNukeVsOtherCosts.pdf

Ramanathan (2007), Gayatri, Without 123, we'll have to scale *down',Mint,* Sunday, October 21,2007, http://www.livemmt.com/2007/10/14235819/8216Without-123-we82171.html.

Rao (undated), K. Nageswara, Coastal Forms and Processes of the Godavari Delta, India, http://www.megadelta.ecnu.edu.cn/main/upload/Kakanaiextended.pdf.

Rediff (2007), Jai Prakash Hydro-Power Ltd., http://money.rediff.eom/money/jsp/p_l.jsp?companyCode=15130060

ROPS (undated), Lutra Perspicillata, River Otter Preservation Society, http://www.riverotter.net/lutra_per.html

Russell (2004), Steven, School of Development Studies, University of East Anglia, Norwich, United Kingdom, The Economic Burden of Illness for Households in Developing Countries: A Review of Studies Focusing on Malaria, Tuberculosis, and Human Immunodeficiency Virus/Acquired Immunodeficiency Syndrome, *Am. J. Trap. Med. Hyg.,* 71 (2 Supplement), 2004.

Ryan (undated), Peter, The Spiritual Discipline of Pilgrimage, URL Not Available.

Schmitt (1999), Penny, Turbine venting improves water quality, October 1999 Engineer Update, http://www.hq.usace.army.mil/cepa/pubs/oct99/story7.htm

Sharma (2006), R C, Restoration of aquatic habitat and fish passage degraded *by* widening of Indian Highway 58 in Garhwal Himalaya, hi *Proceedings of the 2005 International Conference on Ecology and Transportation,* Eds. frwin CL, Garrett P, McDermott KP. Center for Transportation and the Environment, North Carolina State University, Raleigh, NC: pp. 40-51, http ://repositories. cdlib.org/jmie/Toadeco/Sharma2005a/

·Shenoy (2006), Kausalya and Varma, Surendra and Devi Prasad, KV, Factors determining habitat choice of the smooth-coated otter, Lutra perspicillata in a South Indian river system. *Current Science* 91 (5):pp. 637-643, http://eprints.iisc.ernet.in/archive/00008831 /

Singh (1998), Abhay Kumar and Syed I. Hasnain, Major ion chemistry and weathering control in a high altitude basin: Alaknanda River, Garhwal Himalaya, India, Himalyan Glacier Project, School of Environmental Sciences, Jawaharlal Nehru University, *Journal—des Sciences Hydrologiques,* 43(6) December 1998.

Singh (2002), Shekhar and Pranab Banerji, *Large Dams in India: Environmental, Social and Economic Impacts,* Indian Institute of Public Administration, New Delhi.

Smith (1759), Adam, *Theory of Moral Sentiments* in K William Kapp and Lore L Kapp, Editors, *History of Economic Thought: A Book of Readings,* Barnes & Noble, New York, 1949.

Smith (2003), Rebecca, Surplus of Electricity Supplies May Persist At Least Until 2005, *The Wall Street Journal*, Http:/ /Stoft.Com/Metapage/Lib/Wsi-2Q03-02-Generation-Glut-Risk.pdf

Somanathan (2006), E, and R Ravindranath, Measuring the Marginal Value of Water and Elasticity of Demand for Water in Agriculture, *Economic and Political Weekly,* June 30, 2006.

Sudhi (1998), K S, Maritime states to get 12 cr to prevent coastal erosion, The, June 15, 1998, http://www.ecoindia.com/ adban.jpg

Talwani (1997), Pradeep, on the Nature of Reservoir-induced Seismicity, *Pure appl. geophys.* 150 (1997), http:// scsn.seis.sc.edu/Publications/pageoph97l/pageoph971 .pdf

TERI (undated), Demand Forecasting for Electricity, by Meeta Mehra as per footer.

TheFreeDictionary (2008), River, http://legal-dictionary. therreedictionary.com/river

TN (2007), White Paper on Tamil Nadu Government's Finances, Government of Tamil Nadu, http://www.tn.gov.in/budget/ archives/white5-l.htm

Toynbee (1939), Arnold J, *A Study of History,* Abridged by D C Somervell, Dell Publishing Co, New York, 1974.

UIA (undated-a), Union of International Associations, Ensuring sustainable use of biological resources, http:// www.diversitas.org/db/x.php?dbcode=st&go=e&id=12018640

UIA (undated-b), Union of International Associations, Conserving global biodiversity, http://www.diversitas.org/db/x.php?dbcode=st&go=e&id=12006470

University of California (undated), Davis, Chapter XX: Middle East Water, http://www.geology.ucdavis.edu/~cowen/~GEL115/115CHXXMideastwater.html

Upadhyaya (2007), Himanshu, Compensation Payments, How much for that forest? Civil Society Information Exchange Pvt. Ltd, 06 March 2007, http ://www. indiatogether.org/2007/mar/env-forestnpv.htm

Verma (2000), Madhu, "Economic Valuation of Forests of Himachal Pradesh", mimeo, Indian Institute of Forest Management, Bhopal, 2000, quoted in Archana S Mathur and Arvinder S Sachdeva, Towards an Economic Approach to Sustainable Forest Development, Perspective Planning Division, Planning Commission, Government of India, November 2003, Working Paper Series, Paper No. 2/2003-PC.

WAPCOS (2001), Water and Power Consultancy Services (I) Ltd, *Shrinagar Hydroelectric Project, Uttaranchal: Environment Impact Assessment and Resettlement and Rehabilitation Plan,* Gurgaon.

Wasson (2003), R. J., A sediment budget for the Ganga-Brahmaputra catchment, Centre for Resource and Environmental Studies, Australian National University, Canberra, ACT 0200, Australia.

Wasson (2006), R.J., Upstream-downstream in the Himalaya, An old debate revisited, Charles Darwin University, http://www.icimod.org/home/uploads/newsletter/nl50/upstream.pdf

Watcher (2007), Bruno De, Electricity prices and economic growth-a weak link, 13.4.2007, Leonardo Energy, http://www.leonardo-energy.org/drupal/node/1888.

WBPCB (2003), Biodiversity Conservation, Proceedings Of The Round Table Discussion, EMCBTAB & ENVIS Programme,

December 11,2003, Kolkata, Department of Environment, West Bengal Pollution Control Board, Kolkata

WCD (2000a), World Commission on Dams, *Dams and Development,* Earthscan, London.

WCD (2000b), Thematic Review, Environmental Issues II.2, Workshop on Dam Reservoirs and Greenhouse Gases, Part III, February 24 & 25, 2000, Hydro-Quebec, Montreal, Final Minutes.

Webdictionary (2008). River, http://www.webdictionary.co.uk/definition.php?querv=river

Wehrfritz (1994), George, "China's Millions on the Move," *Newsweek,* March 7.

Westphal (2003), Sylvia Pag, Ultra-thin 'blankets' cut reservoir evaporation, *New Scientist,* November 2003, NewScientist.com news service, http://www.newscientist.com/article/dn4323.html

Wheelwright (1970), E L and Bruce McFarlane, *The Chinese Road to Socialism,* Monthly Review Press, New York.

WHO (1999), World Health Organization, *Human Health and Dams,* Submission By The World Health Organisation To The World Commission On Dams, Geneva, November 1999

Wikipedia (2007), Akosombo Dam, http://en.wikipedia.org/wiki/Akosombo_Dam

Wikipedia (2008), River, http://en.wikipedia.org/wiki/River

World Bank (2007), *World Development Indicators, 2007,* Washington.

WWF (2007), Threats to the Smooth-coated Otter, WWF, http://www.wwfindia.org/help/affiliate_wwfindia/oappeal/wet/index.cfm

Yan (2000), Xie, and Wang Sung, 1st Workshop on National Biodiversity Strategies and Action Plans in Northeast and Central Asia: Experiences and Lessons, 26-28 April, 2000, Beijing, China, http://www.chinabiodiversitv.com/shengwudyx2/experiences-lessons/experience.htm

Yoo (2005), S.-H., The causal relationship between electricity consumption and economic growth in the ASEAN countries, School of Business and Economics, Hoseo University, Republic of Korea, 7 September JOGS. *Energy Policy,* Volume 34. Issue 18, December 2006, Pages 3573-3582, http ://www. sciencedirect. com/science

Zhou (undated), Fengqi, Economic Development, Energy, And The Environment in The People's Republic of China, http:/ /www.unu.edu/unupress/unupbooks/uul7ee/uul7ee0o.htm

Index

A

Afforestation in Rajasthan, 123

Agricultural Land, 21

AIDS, 144, 192

Alaknanda, 95, 102, 171

At Dev Prayag, 89

Waters, 92, 95

Alang, Ship Breaking center Gujarat, 24

Alexander, 23

All India Electricity Consumption, 50

American Culture, 22

Anti-Malarial Drugs, 135

APL and BPL, 23

Arjun, 29

Arth-Kam-Dharma-Moksha, 107, 108

Asian Development Bank, 144

Assam-Arunachal Border, 149

Aswan High Dam, 77

Afforestation, 75, 123

Aswan High Dam, 136

B

Badri Vishal Temple at Badrinath, 99

Badrinath, 112

Badrinah to Kaudiyala, 13, 95, 179, 199

Bangladesh, 84, 85

Bay of Bengal, 76

Bear Lock Dam of Pennsylvania, 22

Bhagirathi, 72, 95, 97, 102, 255

Bhilanganga Area, 156

Valley, 131

Bhairon Ghat Waters, 98

Bhakra, 194

Biodiversity, 142-144, 202

Biosphere Reserve, 151

BJP, 106

Blue Line Association, 138

BOD (Biological Oxygen Demand), 95

Brahma Kapali Shila, 99

Brazil, 136

British Rulers, 32, 33

British Empire, 31

C

CAGR (Compound Annual Growth Rate), 43, 44

Electricity Consumption, 43

Carbon Emission, 117, 193

Cascade of Dams, 111, 112, 168, 199

Cellular Memory, 102, 103, 104

Central Electricity Authority (CEA), 39-41, 43-48, 51-53, 61, 188, 192

Econometric Study, 50, 51

Forecasting by-, 39

Central

Pollution Control Board (CPCB), 92, 95, 97, 98, 150

Water Commission on Coastal ension, 87

Centre

For Research and Environmental Studies, Australia, 76

Of Earth Science Studies, 125

Champaran Weavers, 18

Chicago, 24

Chilla, 16, 17, 113, 209, 216, 231

And Tehri, 165

Barrage, 168

Canal, 216

Reservoir, 216

Chilla—Maneri Bhali, 169

China, 19, 21, 22, 23, 25, 26

Chinese Road to Socialism (Book), 21

Civilization, 31

Indus Valley, 25, 30

CO2 Emissions, 27

Coal Based Thermal Plants, 60

Coastal Erosion, 77

Cochin University of Science and Technology, 76

Compensation, 33

Conservation Measures, 120

Convention on Biodiversity Conservation, 147

Conventional Weapons, 23

Corbett Tiger Reserve, 156

CPDAC (Coastal Protection and Development Advisory Committee), 78

Creative Minority, 31

Cultural

Exchange, 192

Revolution, 22

D

Dam

Companies, 16, 88, 218

Structure, 63

Dams, 13, 16, 17, 21-24, 57, 76, 77, 168,

Aswan High-, 77

Hoover, 79

Types, 17

Xiaolangzi, 77

Dams of Utarakhand, 33

Cilla, 33

Maneri Bheli, 33

Tehri, 33

Dams on Alaknanda, 14

Decline of, 31

Ancient Greece, 31

Imperial Rome, 31
Kauravas Indraprastha, 31
Princely States of Rajasthan, 31
Ravana's Lanka, 31
Deforestation, 201
Degradation of Forest, 123
Demand Side Management (DSM), 58-60
Deng Xiaoping, 21
Dev Prayag, 16, 17, 31, 69, 89, 90, 95, 108, 109, 111, 112, 153, 168
Dev Prayag Confluence, 102, 262
Developing Countries, 20, 24, 56
Dhari Devi, Benefits from, 266, 267
Dhari Devi Temple, 76, 266
Survey of Pilgrims, 265
To be Submerged, 16
Dharma-Arth-Kama-Moksha, 30
Displaced Persons, 33
Dominant Minority Leaders, 31
Drought Control, 62
Duel Pricing Regime, 189

E

Earthquake, 124, 128, 130, 131
Natural, 126
Uttarkashi, 130
Ecological Destruction, 15
Ecology, 16, 35
Economic Growth, 13, 15, 17, 18, 19, 20, 24, 39, 52, 187, 188, 191
Economy, 16, 18
Ecuador, 136
Egypt Coastline Erosion, 82
Electricity
Consumption, 19, 20, 43
Conservation Policies, 19, 191
Generation, 271
Employment, 73
Energy Conservation, 58
Environment, 22
And Forest, 16
Environmental
Impact Assessment, 147
Impacts, 79
Management, 147
Pollution, 35, 36
Problems, 62
Erosion, 77
European Union, 21

F

Fish
And Wildlife Protection, 193
Migration, 202
Five Year Plan (11th), 120
Flood
Control, 62
Recession, 84

Flooding of Rhine, 179
Foreign Exchange Reserves, 25
Fragile Ecosystem, 120
Farakka Barrage, 85
Free Trade, 24, 26
Freedom Fighters, 32

G

Gandhi, Mahatma, 32
Ganga, 16, 29-32, 35, 36, 38, 77, 85, 92, 95, 97, 103, 104, 106, 108, 109, 170, 172
  Coastline Erosion, 82
  Sagar Island, Erosion, 82
  Spiritual Power of-, 29
  Waters, 97, 98
Ganga-Brahmputra, 77
Gangasagar, 255
Garhwal
  Region of Uttarakhand, 209
  University, 121, 150
Generation of Employment, 69
Generation of Electricity, 258, 263, 264
Geological Survey of Japan, 77
Ghana, 136
Global
  Economic War, 21
  Environmental Facilities, 149
  Markets, 17
  Temperature, 143
  Warming, 59, 85, 182, 202
Godavari
  Coastline Erosion, 82
  Delta Shoreline, 77
GO Uttarakhand, 13
Graphim, 149
Green House Gases (GHG), 35, 36, 63, 113, 114, 117
  Emissions, 59, 114, 116, 117, 193, 199-202
Green Technologies, 24
Growth Rates, 43

H

Habitat Preservation, 147
Haridwar, 16
Harry Purcel Dam (New Jersey), 22
Himachal Pradesh, 39
Himalayan Environment, 118
Himalayan Rivers, 76
HNB University Srinagar, 153
Hoogly, 85
Hydro Plants, 193
Hydroelectric Power, (HEP), 32, 34, 35, 105, 109-118, 120, 121, 124, 130, 133, 139, 140, 143, 144, 146, 147, 169, 175, 178, 181, 187, 188, 191, 193, 195-200, 202-205, 209, 210-212, 255
  At Kaudiyala, 262
  Benefits, 145
  Companies, 255, 265

In Uttarakhand, 80, 132
On Biodiversity, Negative Impact of-, 144, 145
Projects, 97
Reservoir, 80, 84, 85, 91, 112, 142, 199
Hydropower, 58, 61-63, 90, 113
Benefits, 69
Cheap and Economic, 189
Cost of Producing-, 75-81
Dams, 26, 209
Economic Assessment, 183
Case Study of Kotlibhel IB, 183-185
Experts Views, 187-
Experts, 79
Projects, 13, 193, 195, 196, 202

I

IT Roorkee, 99
Immersion of Ashes, 174, 204, 245
Immigration, 192
Impact of
Dams on Dolphins, 156
Hydroelectric Power, 161
Impacts on Flora, 152
India and Zimbabwe, 24
India's
Downfall, 30
Energy Demand, 188
Enslavement, 25
Water Security, 62
Indian
Coastline Erosion, 82
Institute of Public Administration, 124
Institute of Science, 146
Wildlife Protection Act, 149
Indira Gandhi Canal, 203
Indonesia, 10
Indus
Dolphins, 144
Valley, 198
Infrastructure Facilities, 192
Integrated Energy Policy Report, 27
International
Energy Agency, 19
Hydropower Association, 144
Irrigation, 40, 62, 79
IUCN Red Data Book, 149

J

Jawahar Lal University, 97
Jhalkari Devi, 32

K

Kanchan Chopra Committee, 118, 120, 121
Karna Prayag, 91, 198, 199
Kashi, 255
Kaudiyala, 79, 81, 82, 109, 111, 112

Kenya, 56
Khandava
- Burning, 198
- Forests, 29

King Bhagirath, 29
Kotlibhel
- Costs and Benefits, 209
- Hydroelectric Power, 169
- IB, 189
- Case Study, 75-181
- Project, 17, 37, 38, 132, 203
- Reservoir, 168
- IB Project, 63-74

Kuomintang, 23

L

Lake
- Country Conservation Alliance, 56
- Jocassee, 125
- Mead, 125
- Volta, 136

Land Acquisition, 34, 75
Landslides, 130, 131, 132
- Cost of-, 132

Laxmi Bai, 32
Lord
- Krishna, 29
- and Arjun, 198

Loss of Biodiversity, 152
Low Voltage Problem, 195
Lower Subansiri, 148

M

Manchester Textiles Mills, 17
Maneri Bhali, 16, 17, 209, 218
- Reservoir, 105
- Downstream, 216, 231, 245
- Reservoir, 216, 231
- Tunnel, 216

Mao Zedong, 21, 22, 23
Marine Geology and Physics, 76
Master Plan, 121
Mauryan Empire, 25
Meditation, 104
Methane Emissions, 63, 112, 113, 114, 116, 117, 199
Migration, 192
Migratory Fish Species, 149
Ministry of Environment and Forest, 123, 148
- Guidelines, 201
- Finance, 47, 49
- Planning, 58
- Power, 58

Modernization, 26
Montecello Reservoir South Carona, 125
Mother
- Dhari, 31
- Ganga, 31

Myanamar, 19

N

Nainital Lake, 91
Narmada
- And Tehri, 194

Bachao Andolan Case, 34-36

Judgement, 34, 37 38

NASA's Tropical Rainfall Measuring Mission, 161

National

Appellate Authority, 179

Biodiversity Strategy Action Plan (NBSAP), 148

Coastal Protection Project (NCPP), 78

Cyclone Mitigation Project, 78

National Parks, 151, 171

Keoladeo, Bharatpur, 171

Periyar Tiger Reserve, Kerala, 171

Tiger Reserve, Tamil Nadu, 171

National Productivity Council, (NPC), 98

Natural

Gas, 56

Lakes, 91

New Economic Policy, 22

NHPC, 17, 71-73, 75, 79, 98, 114, 140, 167, 168, 182, 189, 195, 199, 203, 262

Bureaucracy, 205

On Alaknanda River, 69

Nityananda Swamy Ashram, 105

NPV (Net Present Value), 118, 122

Calculations, 120

NTPC Vidyut Vyapar, 71

O

Operational Management, 137

Otter (s), 153-159, 202, 203

Conservation, 155

From Kotlibhel Reservoir, 153

Owen Falls, 142

P

Partial End Use Method (PEUM), 40-44

Peak

Electricity Load, 51

Load Pricing, 62

Periyar Tiger Reserve, 156

Pilgrim Centres, 256

Pilgrimage, 27, 91, 92

Pilgrims (at), 109-112, 170, 171, 172, 255, 256, 257, 260, 261

Dev Prayag, 170, 255

Dhari Devi, 170

Haridwar, 170, 255

Rishikesh, 170, 255

Planning Commission, 29, 39, 47-49, 51, 52, 58-63, 69, 113, 118, 120, 171, 261

Integrated Energy Policy, 58

Plant Load Factor (PLF), 58

Pollution, 106

Polymers, Micro Organism, 97
Population Growth, 187
Porus, 23
Potable Water, 86
Power
 Nuclear, 27
Planning, 61
Plants, 58
 Survey, (17th), 40, 41, 44
 Systems, 59
 Thermal and Nuclear, 27
Pricing Policy, 15
Pump Installations, 40
Punjab Remote Sensing Centre, 163

Q

Quality of Water, 170, 218, 259

R

Radioactivity, 97
Rehabilitation, 16
Relief and Rehabilitation, 32, 75
Reservoirs, 17
 Induced Seismicity, (RIS), 126-127
Rim, 276
Resettlement and Rehabilitation, 62
Right to Information Act, 61, 87, 140, 141, 179
Rishikesh, 16, 79, 174
River
 Alaknanda, 13, 92, 95, 97
 Alaknanda and Bhagirathi, 179
 Bhagirithi, 13
 Bhagirathi and Bhilanganga, 273
 Blindness, 136, 142
 Ganga, 27, 29, 76, 99, 255, 257, 259-263
 Gangetic, 76
 Godavari, 82
 Mahanadi, 170
 Nile, 77
Rafting, 168
Rafting Camps, 168
 System, 37
 Teesta Sikkim, 179
 Waitaki, New Zealand, 145
 Yamuna, 97
 Yellow in China, 77
Run-Of-River Type (ROR), 13
(Run of River), Dams, 13, 15-17, 61, 79, 80, 106-108
 Dams at Chilla, 255
 Hydroelectric Power, 88, 113, 131, 197, 201
 Hydroelectric Project, 69, 79, 81, 84, 151, 194, 201
Reservoir, 117
Russia, 21, 23
 And Arab Countries, 23

S

Sagar Island, (West Bengal), 76

Sardar Sarovar Dam, 36, 204
SEBs (State Electricity Boards), 15, 40, 190
Sector,
    Environment and Forest, 120
    Information Technology, 31
Sediment, 75-79, 80, 81, 84, 85, 87, 197
    Cost of-, 81, 88
Seismic Events, 63
Seismicity of Koyna, 125
Shiv Purana, 176
Shivaji, 32
Singapore, 19
Small Scale Industries, 22
Soil Erosion, 35
South East Asian Countries, 19
Spiritual
    Effects, 268, 269
    Quality of Ganga Water, 106
Srinagar, Hydropower Scheme, 81
Standard of Living, 13, 34, 53
Storage Dams, 62
Submerged Forest Land, 118, 121
Submergence of Forests, 124
Sudan, 56
Swayambodhananda, Swamy, 104

T

Tariff
    Infrastructure, 189
    Rates, 190
Tehri, 16, 21, 69, 72, 79, 109, 111, 112, 114, 204, 209, 210, 218
    Dam, 13, 90, 95, 97, 99, 108, 109-111, 255, 259, 260, 261, 262
    Reservoir, 33, 131, 156, 231, 273
Temple
    Dhari Devi, 16, 176, 265
    Durga, Tehri, 177
    Hanuman, 273
    Lakshmi Narayan, 274
    Saccheshwar, 273
Temples of Tehri, 273
    Survey, 273
Tennessee
    Dam, 138
    Valley Authority, 138
TERI (Tata Energy Research Institute), 40
Thailand, 19
Thar Desert, 203
THDC (Tehri Hydro-Development Corp), 255
Thermal
    Plants, 193
    Power Plants, 113
Three Gorges Dam, 21, 22, 23
Tourism, 22, 27, 168

Trade in Herbs, 27

Transcendental Meditation, 104

Trend Forecast, 43, 47

U

UN Development Program, 143, 146, 148

Union of International Association, 142, 146, 147

University of

Arizona, 102

Cape Town, South Africa, 54

Upanishads, Isavasya, 30

Uranium Import, 27

US, 21-23, 27, 37, 55-57, 138

Energy Information Administration, 20

Uttarakhand, 16, 106, 121, 128, 139, 145, 165, 175

Pollution Control Board, 114

Uttarkashi, 194

V

Venezuela, 136

W

Water

Birds, 181

Borne Diseases, 138

Control System, 193

Sports, 168

Wildlife, 149

Institute of India, Dehradun, 153, 154

Protection Act, 1972, 153

Sanctuary, 151

World

Commission of Dams, 54, 113, 114, 128, 144, 145

Guidelines, 199

Planners, 115

Wildlife Fund, 153

Y

Yaeyreta Dam, 57

Yoga of Patanjali, 106